Successful Secondary Schools

Education Policy Perspectives

General Editor: Professor Ivor Goodson, Faculty of Education,
University of Western Ontario, London,
Canada N6G 1G7

Education in general and schools in particular are at the forefront of public debate in most industrialized societies. Only a decade ago, there was a pervasive belief that education 'didn't matter' and that educational reform and expansion as attempted worldwide in the 1960s and 1970s would inevitably produce failure and disillusionment.

Now, however, the work of academics, practitioners and policy-makers in the effective schools movement shows that schools can generate excellence *and* equity if they are run in certain ways. School improvement researchers and practitioners are also showing how schools can be made more effective and efficient.

This series aims to bring to the attention of teachers, administrators, policy-makers and academics the latest research, practice and thinking in these fields. It aims to stimulate academic debate about school effectiveness and improvement, and to provide practitioners with the detailed analysis and description of effective school strategies that they need as societal and legislative pressures on schools grow even stronger. Now more than ever before, educationists need to know about 'good schools' and about 'how to make schools good'. This series aims to provide just that information.

School Organization and Improvement Series

Editor: David Reynolds, University College, Cardiff, UK

Improving the Quality of Schooling
Edited by David Hopkins

The Comprehensive Experiment
David Reynolds and Michael Sullivan with Stephen Murgatroyd

The Self-Managing School
Brian J. Caldwell and Jim M. Spinks

Successful Secondary Schools
Bruce L. Wilson and Thomas B. Corcoran

Whole School Approaches to Special Needs: A Practical Guide for Teachers
Edited by Arlene Ramasut

Education Policy Perspectives

Successful Secondary Schools

Visions of Excellence in American Public Education

Bruce L. Wilson

and Thomas B. Corcoran

The Falmer Press

London • New York • Philadelphia

UK   The Falmer Press, Falmer House, Barcombe, Lewes,
            East Sussex, BN8 5DL

USA   The Falmer Press, Taylor & Francis Inc., 242 Cherry Street,
            Philadelphia, PA 19106-1906

© Bruce L. Wilson and Thomas B. Corcoran 1988

First published 1988

Library of Congress Cataloguing in Publication Data

Wilson, Bruce L.
    Successful secondary schools.

    Bibliography: p.
    Includes index.
    1. High schools—United States—Case studies.
2. School improvement programs—United States—Case studies. 3. High school environment—United States—Case Studies. 4. High Schools—United States—Administration—Case studies. 5. Education—United States—Aims and objectives—Case studies. I. Corcoran, Thomas B. II. Title.
LA222.W48 1987   373.73   88-3920
ISBN 1-85000-200-2
ISBN 1-85000-201-0 (soft)

Jacket design by Caroline Archer

Typeset in 10½/12 California by Chapterhouse, The Cloisters, Formby L37 3PX Printed and bound in Great Britain by Redwood Burn Limited, Trowbridge, Wiltshire.

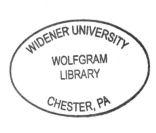

Contents

Preface

In the last ten years the American effective schools movement of researchers, practitioners and policy-makers has acquired an international reputation for the quality and the vision of its writing and its scholarship. Whereas countries like Britain, Australia, Sweden and Norway have only recently begun to search for effective schools in order to learn the lessons from them that may help others, the United States has seen literally hundreds of such studies and attempts.

This book by Bruce Wilson and Thomas Corcoran is one of the most unusual and exciting to appear in this field for a considerable time. It is unusual in that its findings are accessible to teachers and policy-makers, since it is clearly written and is full of actual examples of effective organizational and curricular practice drawn from its sample of 571 public secondary schools recognized by the United States Department of Education as unusually successful. The authors' summary of the academic literature, which is often of course inaccessible because of its language and statistical context, must be something of a model for others to follow.

For academics and policy-makers, also, the book is unusual and exciting. It combines quantitative and qualitative methodologies. It provides a chance to test on a large sample some of the preliminary findings of the school effectiveness literature. It also contains some of the most detailed information yet on the complex interactions of leadership styles, learning environments, staff attributes and school/community relations that are found in achieving schools.

The task for researchers and practitioners now is clearly to ensure that all schools reach the levels of the most effective, yet the authors note that each school is in a unique cultural and historical situation and that it is difficult to change schools in a 'top-down' fashion without undermining the local pride and ownership in which effective schooling develops. These further much needed attempts and programmes to 'make schools good' will clearly come soon and they will clearly be all the better for the fascinating accounts of 'good schools' given by Bruce Wilson and Thomas Corcoran in this book.

David Reynolds

Acknowledgements

Work of this magnitude could not have been completed without the support and cooperation of a wide range of individuals and organizations. Bruce Haslam, Patricia McKee, and Kathy Crossley, who worked for the United States Department of Education, Recognition Program and who implemented the processes which produced the data for this book, were instrumental in encouraging and assisting the authors. They saw the value of sharing examples from these successful secondary schools. The US Department of Education provided financial support allowing the authors to code the data from the 571 schools and establish a computerized database. Research for Better Schools offered institutional support that enabled the authors to carry out the analysis and prepare a manuscript.

A large group of colleagues offered personal and intellectual encouragement during the writing process, including Gretchen Rossman, Dick Corbett, Bill Firestone, Rima Miller, Michele Woods-Houston and Barbara Hansen. Several dedicated coders spent hours reading files from each of the schools and making judgments about the quality of the school programs and practices. The coders were Patricia Bates, Tina Clark, Diane Goldstein, Joan Luckhardt, Mal O'Connor, Mike Palladino, Sally Peterson, and Carolyn Stetson.

Marge Connelly provided expert guidance in preparing computer programs to help analyze data from the schools. Early in the process an informal group of advisers was established to help with conceptualization of the research and review of manuscript drafts. A special debt of gratitude goes to Richard Pesquiera, Joseph Richardson, Dorothy Shipman, Pamela Thomas, Dan Deschamp and Barbara Polling for their thoughtful critiques and suggestions.

A list of people too long to mention individually, the panel of 85 reviewers who made the decisions about which schools to recognize and the 78 site visitors who spent several days in each of the schools and an equal amount of time preparing reports of their site visits, played an invaluable part of this research endeavor. The site visitors made rich contributions to the portraits of the schools.

Without the vision and persistence of those responsible for making these schools so successful: the central office administrators, principals, teachers, support staff, students, parents and community members, there would have been no data. These people spent many hours preparing their nomination forms and willingly gave time to answer questions and be observed by site visitors. An important acknowledgement must be made to their continued efforts to make these schools places where parents are pleased to enroll their children, teachers are pleased to work, and students enjoy learning.

Finally, a special vote of gratitude goes to the authors' families for sacrificing precious time together while the authors were writing one more section or reviewing drafts exchanged between computers. While credit for all the positive features of this book must be shared with all those who helped contribute to it, any errors or omissions rest with the authors.

Introduction

The early years of this decade brought a great deal of criticism of American public education. Test scores were declining, the quality of the teaching force was being questioned, standards of academic performance were being challenged, and norms for student conduct were being criticized. A succession of national reports (Presseisen, 1985) were issued, each documenting the apparent sorry state of public education and each offering recommendations for their improvement. Public secondary schools (high schools, junior schools, and middle schools), in particular, were subjected to harsh criticisms. Yet, there were public secondary schools that were doing a good job, schools that could serve as models of high quality for educators and policy-makers, and provide roadmaps for improvement.

Almost unnoticed during this period of strong public demand for improvement in secondary education, many of these public schools had a long standing tradition of quality while others had made significant gains as a result of persistent struggles against difficult odds. This book documents success stories in American public education by reviewing data from nearly 600 secondary schools which have recently received national recognition for their success. But more than an accounting of individual successes, the contents of this book provide critical analysis of the common features across these successful public secondary schools. It attempts to develop a framework based on their common features which can be refined and modified to guide the improvement of secondary schools operating under diverse conditions.

The central theme emerging from these schools is that significant reforms are being initiated in local communities all across the American continent, that parents, teachers, administrators, students, and civic leaders are working together to create and preserve unusually successful schools. These local successes are documented in the files of the nationally recognized secondary schools. Some of these schools have experienced dramatic turnarounds; for example:

Four years ago this was the worst school in the county. Now there is total unity and we are the best. We are like a family. We have learned to live with each other. The principal has showed us how to have pride, how to work, how to have confidence, how to succeed.

Dixie Hollins High School, St Petersburg, FL. *

The principal is the recipe for administrative leadership that is so often cited in articles. He works hard on a visible presence. He calls kids by name. Students and staff affirm repeatedly his accessibility, his personal kindness, and firmness in applying the rules . . . Besides visibility and a leadership style that cultivates respect and attention, the principal shrewdly structures the school day to gain the most flexibility to match staff with student academic need.

Pioneer High School, Whittier, CA.

From what was once a racial/ethnic battleground comes this testimony of a unique high school. It is a tri-ethnic school that is tri-ethnic in every sense. The classes, particularly honors and AP classes, reflect the ethnicity of the school (25 per cent white; 25 per cent Hispanic; 50 per cent black). This didn't just happen. There was a conscious effort on the part of the administration to make this a reality. The Valedictorian and Salutatorian are black. One of these youngsters was going to drop out three years ago — he is now carrying a 4.0 GPA. The top 12 seniors, academically, again are representative of the ethnicity of the school. If one would want to see the American dream in action, a visit to this high school would be appropriate.

American High School, Hialeah, FL.

These participant accounts describe some of the exciting efforts underway to create successful secondary schools. This book draws upon these accounts and other school data to document the school characteristics commonly associated with success in these nationally recognized schools.

The author's analysis shows the characteristics associated with school success fall into six clusters or themes. Each of these themes describes an essential and dynamic aspect of good secondary schools. Through the discussion of the six themes, the authors document that it is possible to

---

*This example, and those that follow, represent the conditions existing in the schools at the time they were recognized for their unusual success. Given the dynamic nature of schools and the turbulent environments in which they must operate, the authors offer no guarantees that similar conditions still exist, particularly for those schools recognized in the first year for which we had data (1982-83). However, such a caution in no way should detract from the lessons that can be learned from the successes of the schools.

achieve success even under the most unlikely circumstances. The six themes
that they conclude characterize school success are:

- active leadership
- professional work environments
- positive learning environments
- broad community involvement
- continuous school improvement
- service to all students.

The analysis of data from these successful public secondary schools not only
provides many examples of good practice, but, more importantly, demonstrates the enormous potential of American public schooling. The purpose of
this book is to share some of the programs, policies and practices that have
made these schools so successful. The examples should inspire and guide
those seeking to improve their schools.

The data for this analysis derive from documentation of 571 public
secondary schools that were recognized by the United States Department of
Education as unusually successful schools over the course of three years,
1983 to 1985. The selection of these schools reflects the judgments of
educators and community leaders at local, state and national levels. Their
assessments were based on evaluations of a wide range of school performance indicators such as results of achievement tests, attendance statistics, dropout rates, numbers of suspensions and awards to staff and
students. In addition, qualitative aspects of the schools were reviewed
including their goals, staff expectations, climate, the character of instruction, student discipline, and incentives for staff and students. No
attempt was made to reduce the data to quantitative scales nor statistically
analyze the results. Selection of the schools was based on a consensus among
those involved that the schools were centers of excellence and deserved
recognition.

The primary lessons of this book are that the energy, commitment, and
vision of the professionals working in these schools are central to their
success and that their successes can be replicated by others who are willing
to dedicate themselves to a similar pursuit of excellence. In the chapters that
follow accounts of such efforts by local educators are presented. Others
interested in raising the quality of public secondary education would be
well-advised to examine the accomplishments of the staffs in these schools
and to consider how to replicate their efforts.

Chapter 1 reviews the research literature that addresses factors
affecting success in secondary schools. The chapter begins with an overview
of effective schools research, one important basis for school reform. This is
followed by discussions of the limits of that knowledge base and their
implications for practical applications. Particular attention is paid to the
unconditional and universal character of the advice offered to policy-
makers by effective schools advocates. Central to this criticism of the

formula approach to reform is the significance of the local context to school effectiveness and the variation in specific operational conditions associated with success in particular schools. A number of important differences between elementary schools, the level at which most of the research has been conducted, and secondary schools, have simply been ignored. Similarly, those who promulgate simple formulae of effectiveness under-estimate the importance of idiosyncratic aspects of an organization's history and culture to the success of efforts to enhance quality. The third section reviews five studies from the limited literature on the effectiveness of secondary schools and examines the policies and practices found to be associated with school success. The findings from these studies are then juxtaposed with the popular model of school effectiveness outlined in the first section. The final section offers some thoughts on the implications of this research for reform of American public secondary education.

Chapter 2 describes the data on which this book is based. Five hundred seventy one high schools, junior highs and middle schools from across the nation became part of the sample of successful secondary schools from 1983 through 1985 when they received recognition from the United States Department of Education for their efforts to establish and maintain exemplary local programs, policies and practices. The chapter begins with a general discussion of the problems associated with defining criteria for success. It then describes the criteria used in the recognition progam and outlines its procedures. A detailed description of the data available from each school is presented as well as an explanation of how that data was compiled and analyzed for this book.

Chapter 3 contains a statistical profile of the 571 successful secondary schools. Statistics do not adequately communicate the diversity of social contexts in which these schools are located. Nevertheless, by reviewing some common social indicators, the varying contexts in which these successful schools function are generally described. Data are reviewed across three broad categories — demographics, organizational characteristics, and outcomes — and all three sets of indicators reveal a rich diversity among the 571 schools. Comparisons with national data suggest that these schools are generally representative of public schools in America with regard to demo-graphics and are not merely the products of more privileged or high status contexts. This chapter concludes with a comparison of the adequacy of the fit between data available on these schools and the variables contained in the effective schools framework.

The heart of the book is contained in Chapters 4 through 9. These six chapters describe the essential character of success in American public secondary education. Each chapter addresses a theme or central tenet that the authors have found is a common, perhaps essential, dimension of the successful schools. The themes were derived from a careful analysis of the data on the schools. The discussion of each theme begins with a brief review of literature documenting that theme's importance. This is followed by examples of school policies and practices illustrating the variety of ways in which the themes play out in different school settings. What most distinguishes these six themes from some other models of school effectiveness is their focus on people, their talents, their energies, and their relationships. The focus is on the dynamic and human dimensions of school success, rather than static variables.

Chapter 4 addresses the role of leadership. Not surprisingly, effective leadership has been an essential factor in the success of these schools. Almost all parties associated with these schools cited the work of school leaders as critical. It was often the school leaders who provided the vision and encouragement to create or sustain other conditions supporting success. The focus of this chapter is on how the actions of school leaders are linked to the instructional work in their schools. Linkages to instruction through both bureaucratic and cultural devices are illustrated. The bureaucratic linkages include supervision and evaluation, structuring of time for academic tasks, the manipulation of class size and grouping of students, the arrangement of physical space and free time, the use of discretionary resources, and the emphasis placed on knowledge and skills. Cultural linkages focus on the value systems in the schools, the goals and the processes by which they are set, and the use of stories and rituals to help build staff and student commitment and define standards for the schools. This chapter also documents the diversity of successful leadership styles and illustrates how individuals in a variety of roles can take on leadership responsibilities.

Chapter 5 addresses the working conditions in these schools and examines how these conditions interact and serve as positive incentives for maximum effort. Seven essential conditions are described in the literature as having significant impact on the behavior and attitudes of teachers and each one is illustrated by examples from these schools. These conditions include communal work identity, respectful treatment as professionals, participation in decisions, collective responsibility for results, recognition and rewards, professional growth, and physical conditions. The chapter concludes with a discussion of two alternative models for implementing reforms in working conditions in public secondary schools.

Chapter 6 discusses the learning environments in schools and how those environments are used to motivate students. Particular attention is paid to expectations, standards, and rewards. Expectations refer to the attitudes about students' potential for academic achievement. Standards are the written guidelines or staff norms defining minimum levels of performance and behavior for students. Standards are inexorably intertwined with expectations. Rewards are the mechanisms by which school staff acknowledge the positive outcomes of students who are attempting to meet the standards of the school. Examples are offered of schools that set high standards and reward students who strive to meet them. The examples demonstrate that it is not necessary for staff and students to bargain for mediocrity in public secondary education.

Chapter 7 calls attention to the value of positive school-community relations. Staff in these successful secondary schools recognize that their strength grows when there are positive linkages with their local communities. Those schools that flourished had opened themselves up to the community rather then defensively closing themselves off. Given the history of local control and the fact that a significant portion of funding for public schools in the United States derives from local property taxes, it seems only commonsensical that schools would seek strong linkages to their communities. However, the bonds between public secondary schools and their communities have never been particularly strong, the possible exception being community support for athletic teams. These successful secondary schools offer useful examples of how community linkages can be strengthened. By making efficient use of human and fiscal resources in the community, introducing aggressive public relations campaigns, developing community service programs that place students more prominently in the community, and building school identities that are consciously associated with characteristics of the community, these schools have become more lively, interesting places and have expanded opportunities for students. Collaborative links with the community also strengthen the technical aspects of the school, build political support among local constituencies, set positive examples for youth, and shape school cultures that encourage concern about the quality of community life.

Chapter 8 draws upon the school improvement literature and examples from these successful secondary schools to offer suggestions about how efforts to improve schools can succeed. Not all of these schools have had long histories of success. Indeed, some of them were only recently places to which parents avoided sending their children. Even those with long-term reputations for excellence have not been able to rest on their laurels, past history could not always sustain them through difficult times. In other words, these schools are not immune to the problems faced by most other public schools. What does set these schools apart from most other secondary schools are their creative approaches to commom problems. Rather than viewing problems as constraints, these schools view them as opportunities. A focus on continual improvement, regardless of their previous success, is a characteristic central to their continued success.

Chapter 9 focuses on those groups of students served least well by public education, those describes as 'at-risk youth'. What typifies the schools reported in this book is their strong commitment to serve these students and their resourceful efforts to raise the achievement of their at-risk population. This chapter describes particularly successful efforts in eleven schools with large proportions of at-risk youth. Some of the common elements in these efforts include positive attitudes towards the students, willingness to question conventional practices, strong leadership, highly committed staff, high expectations, emphasis on achievement in academics, quality support services, willingness to try new approaches, and public support for a period sufficient to implement new policies. Success has come from a real commitment to these students, and the use of multi-faceted approaches that emphasize student bonding to the school and strong family and community involvement.

The final chapter, Chapter 10 discusses the implications of these success stories for policy-makers. The success of these schools represents an important national resource that can be tapped to improve program and practice in American public education. But the rich diversity of programs, policies and practices utilized in these schools also represent varied responses to unique sets of local conditions. How can such success stories be replicated without undermining the local pride and ownership on which they rest? This is a central question for policy-makers. Specific recommendations are organized around the six themes presented in the earlier chapters.

Chapter 1

Successful Secondary Schools: The Literature*

The American public believes that good schools affect the educational achievement of students who are fortunate enough to attend them. For confirmation of this common wisdom, one need only examine the concern with which parents of school-aged children investigate the quality of local schools when choosing their places of residence. A major factor in family decisions about housing and, therefore, the value of real estate in the United States, is the reputation of the local public schools. Parents believe that the character of the policies, practices, programs, and personnel in public schools affect the achievement and behavior of their students in significant and systematic ways and that these school characteristics vary from community to community. Parents also believe that these qualities can be assessed and they frequently conduct their own assessments of schools when they are choosing a place of residence.

The views of parents are consistent, in this instance, with findings from recent studies of effective schools. These studies, often referred to collectively as the 'effective school research', have demonstrated that good schools, like excellent corporations, have some common characteristics. Furthermore, it appears that some, if not all, of these characteristics can be molded and shaped to improve school effectiveness. The purpose of this chapter is to review and summarize this knowledge about effective schools and to provide a frame of reference for the analysis of characteristics of schools selected for national recognition.

This chapter is organized into four sections. The first section presents a general overview of the findings emerging from the effective schools literature. Section two examines some of the limits of this knowledge base,

*Parts of this chapter originally appeared in a chapter entitled 'Effective Secondary Schools' by Thomas B. Corcoran in *Reaching for Excellence: An Effective Schools Sourcebook*, R.M.J. Kyle (Ed.), Washington, DC: US Government Printing Office, 1985.

1

particularly as it applies to secondary education. Studies of effective secondary schools are summarized in the third section. The final section examines the implications of the literature reviewed in the first three sections for the reform of secondary education.

The Effective Schools Literature

Based largely on studies of elementary schools, the effective schools research has contributed to the development of new theory in education and has become the basis for an ideology adopted by both grassroots and state reform movements seeking school improvement and greater equity in educational attainment. The most popular summary of this research, the so-called 'Five Factor Theory', identifies strong building leadership, clear goals, an orderly school climate, high expectations and standards, and frequent monitoring and assessment of student progress as the essential characteristics of effective schools (Edmonds, 1979). These variables are often referred to as the 'Five Correlates'.

Based on this research, effective schools are believed to differ from schools in general in some systematic and predictable ways. They are described as being more tightly managed. Their curriculum, instructional practices, and tests are more carefully aligned and the work of their staffs more focused upon school goals. They are 'strong' schools, able to make greater demands on their students, and their policies and practices reduce the influence of social environment and peer cultures on student behavior and academic performance. Such schools, it is contended, are able to reduce, if not eliminate, the connection between socio-economic background and academic achievement, hence contributing to greater equity in the distribution of educational attainment. The critical point, however, is that studies of effective schools have found that the internal processes and social environments of schools account for a significant portion of the variation in student achievement. In short, researchers have confirmed the beliefs of parents; there are 'good' schools and they do make a difference for students.

Comprehensive reviews of this research have been prepared by Cohen (1983), MacKenzie (1983), Purkey and Smith (1983), and Clark, Lotto, and Astuto (1984). The school and classroom variables associated with effectiveness have been summarized in many forms and have been widely distributed to educators and to the general public. Almost all American educators are likely to have some familiarity with the findings. The 'summaries' vary from Edmonds' (1979) 'five correlates' to the state of Arizona's (1983) nine page check list containing 95 specific characteristics. Some of the summaries include only findings from studies of effective schools; others combine these with results of other research drawn eclectically from studies of teacher effectiveness, classroom management, instructional leadership, and school climate. The bibliographies accompanying these summaries often contain hundreds of references and new studies continue to appear. A great deal of useful information has been gathered about school effectiveness, but the popular summaries of this knowledge vary in their comprehensiveness and the accuracy of their interpretation.

For the purposes of this discussion, the synthesis prepared by Stewart C. Purkey and Marshall S. Smith (1983) will be treated as the 'state of the art' summary of current knowledge about effective schools. Purkey and

Table 1.1   Dimensions of Effective Schooling*

A.   Organizational – Structural Dimensions
1. School-site management. '. . . the leadership and staff of the school need considerable autonomy in determining the exact means by which they address the problem of increasing academic performance'.
2. Instructional leadership. '. . . leadership is necessary to initiate and maintain the improvement process'.
3. Staff stability. In a successful school, further success is promoted if the staff remains together.
4. Curriculum articulation and organization. '. . . a planned, purposeful program of courses seems to be academically more beneficial than an approach that offers many electives and few requirements'.
5. Schoolwide staff development. '. . . staff development should be schoolwide rather than specific to individual teachers and should be closely related to the instructional program. . . '. Long-term support and reinforcement are required.
6. Parental involvement and support. '. . . parents need to be informed of school goals and student responsibilities, especially with regard to homework'.
7. Schoolwide recognition of academic success. When schools publicly honor academic achievement, students are encouraged to adopt similar norms and values.
8. Maximized learning time. Schools emphasizing academics devote a greater portion of the day to academics, with more active learning and fewer interruptions.
9. District support. Few significant changes can be realized without district support. Guiding and helping is probably the best role for the district office.

B.   Process Dimensions
1. Collaborative planning and collegial relationships. '. . . change attempts are more successful when teachers and administrators work together. Collegiality breaks down barriers, encourages sharing, promotes unity and commonality among the staff'.
2. Sense of community. The feeling of being a part of a supportive community contributes to reduced alienation and increased achievement. Schools can create a sense of community through use of ceremony, symbols, and rituals.
3. Clear goals and high expectations. Schools need to focus on goals they deem most important and continually monitor pupil and classroom progress toward those goals. High expectations for work and achievement also characterize successful schools.
4. Order and discipline. An environment which is quiet, safe, and non-distracting promotes learning. '. . . clear, reasonable rules, fairly and consistently enforced, . . . reduce behavior problems . . . and promote pride and responsibility in the school community'.

* Adapted from Purkey, S. and Smith, M. S. (1983), 'Effective schools: A review' in *The Elementary School Journal*, 83 (4), 427–452.

Smith are quite critical of the studies on conceptual and methodological grounds, but express optimism about the utility of the findings for school improvement. Their summary is presented in Table 1.1. The variables or characteristics listed by Purkey and Smith, taken as a whole, suggest a distinctive type of school culture and, in the view of most of the effective schools researchers, it is this organizational culture that is the key to effectiveness. It is not simply the presence or absence of these characteristics individually that accounts for the effectiveness of a school. The norms, rules, rituals, values, technology, and curriculum combine to create a culture of achievement, a press for excellence. This is the 'ethos' (Rutter, Maughan, Mortimore, Ouston and Smith, 1979) or climate identified in other effective schools studies as being the critical factor in their success. Rutter and his associates (1979) concluded that it was the total *gestalt* of these characteristics, rather than the specific practices, that most contributed to student achievement.

The Limits of the Knowledge Base

The studies of effective schools cited above have been the subject of considerable criticism on conceptual and methodological grounds (Tomlinson, 1980; Purkey and Smith, 1983; Rowan, Bossert and Dwyer, 1983; Cuban, 1984; Sirotnik, 1985; Stedman, 1985). Critics have pointed to the absence of longitudinal designs, the reliance on ambiguous and poorly measured variables, the use of basic skills performance as the sole criterion of effectiveness, the neglect of variation in achievement within schools, the lack of attention to variations in resources, the absence of concrete, operational definitions of key factors believed to be related to effectiveness, the small sample sizes, and other methodological and conceptual problems. These would appear to be telling criticisms but they have had little effect on the popularity or credibility of this research literature.

These same critics have uniformly concluded that the direction of the research is promising. They tend to agree that the research on school effectiveness is important because it has restored optimism about the possibilities of school success, revived feelings of efficacy among educators and served as a valuable template for diagnosis of school problems. Thus, the research, with all of its limitations, is seen as making important contributions to the improvement of schools.

One serious concern about the practical applications of this research is the unconditional character of the advice being offered to policy-makers by effective schools advocates. Popular summaries of the effective schools literature appear to promise a degree of certainty about results that has been lacking in educational research. 'Every child will learn' is a common slogan in this literature. Policy-makers have generally understood that the outcomes of educational actions were uncertain. They have typically based their actions upon concrete examples of successful practice, common sense, professional judgement, public opinion, and other sources of 'ordinary' knowledge. They have made only limited use of findings drawn from social science research. One reason that policy-makers have neglected social science findings or treated them with skepticism is that social scientists seldom have agreed among themselves about the significance of their findings. Social science has generally failed to deliver the scientifically verifiable knowledge that it has promised (Lindblom and Cohen, 1979). Policymaker audiences have been led to expect universally valid propositions in the form of 'action X will generate a gain of Y on a measure of student outcome Z', but such results have seldom been achieved. Social science research typically has produced inconclusive results in which causation has been unclear and generalizations severely limited by the influence of contextual factors on the behavior studied. Now the effective schools studies appear to deliver the promised empirical propositions that social science was supposed to produce, propositions that guarantee results.

Some observers of educational policy-making in the United States, such as Kirst (1983b), Finn (1984), and Sirotnik (1985), have expressed concern about this assumption of certainty. They are dismayed that policy-makers are using the research to justify increased standardization of educational goals and curricula and top-down approaches to school change. They have called for caution in applying the findings, especially as the basis of state mandates or other prescriptive policies. Their warnings have been futile, however, as local and state policy-makers continue to treat the effective schools research as a formula for raising student achievement. Policymakers are ignoring the more complex and subtle issues of school quality raised by the studies. Raising standards for promotion or graduation, changing instructional time allocations, or aligning curricula to tests may be beneficial actions in many schools but such policies may not, in all cases or under all conditions, contribute to the sense of a shared moral order, the press toward excellence, or the high levels of collegiality characteristic of highly successful schools.

Paul Berman (1981), in his review of research on school improvement, concluded that context was the dominant factor in successful change efforts and that researchers should focus on the specific conditions associated with success in particular settings. He called for the formulation of conditional propositions in the form of 'action A will produce result B under conditions C, D, E, and F'. Hallinger and Murphy (1986) have noted that the same problem arises with research on school effectiveness. They point out that schools which are effective with affluent populations employ different criteria of success than schools judged to be effective with low income populations. Moreover, the school policies associated with success are different in the two settings. Variations are found in curricula, time allocations, expectations, school climate, modes of instruction, student and staff roles, and home–school relations.

5

School Effectiveness Studies and High Schools

Perhaps the most important but neglected contextual factor in discussions of school effectiveness is the age range of the students. Reviewers of these studies have questioned the application of the school effectiveness 'theory' to secondary schools (Firestone, 1983; Cohen, 1983; Rutter, 1983). Their skepticism is based on the lack of research data from secondary schools, the reliance of researchers on a narrow range of learning outcomes to determine effectiveness, neglect of the differences in the populations served, and the existence of significant organizational differences between elementary and secondary schools. Results of the few studies that have been conducted in secondary schools, however, have been strikingly similar to the findings from the elementary school studies (MacKenzie, 1983). The same or similar factors appear to be related to effectiveness in both types of schools.

Even if the constructs associated with effectiveness are similar, their meaning in practice may differ across levels of schooling because of differences in the structure and organization. Comparing elementary schools with high schools, Firestone and Herriott (1982) found that high schools had:

- less consensus about goals;
- fewer formal rules (except for non-instructional activities);
- greater teacher autonomy;
- less influence by principals over policy;
- less communication among staff members; and
- more administrator-teacher conflict.

They concluded that high schools were more loosely coupled, less bureaucratic, and less centralized in development of curriculum and policy.

There are other significant organizational differences. High schools tend to be larger institutions in which administrators are faced with greater spans of control. Parents tend to be less involved in high schools than in elementary schools. Teachers are more likely to be content specialists and to be influenced more by their peers in their disciplines than by administrators.

Students in high schools are older and do not accede as automatically to the wishes of adults as elementary students. Order and work demands must be negotiated in secondary schools. This is one reason for the classroom bargaining that has been observed by researchers and criticized by reformers (Cusick, 1983; Sizer, 1984; Powell, Farrar, and Cohen, 1985). Peers become powerful competitors to adult authority. Students are more aware of their interests and may become more critical of the link between these interests and curricular options. Also, their interests are strongly influenced by the social and economic environments in which they live. Secondary students also have more personal freedom, more mobility, and more options. They often hold part-time jobs and the jobs compete with schools for their time and attention. Adolescents have become a major market for consumer goods in the United States and advertisers spend millions to persuade youth that they need their products. The desire for these products generates the need for income and, hence, employment. In addition, major industries such as the fast food business, are founded on the use of adolescent labor. All of these factors compete with the schools for the attention of youth. In sum, motivation to perform school tasks is likely to be problematic among adolescents and to vary more than it does among their younger siblings.

In addition to these organizational differences, there are also differences in educational goals between elementary and secondary schools. Secondary schools, with the possible exception of middle schools, focus on the development of higher-order skills, mastery of content in the disciplines, and vocational preparation. The basic skills are important building blocks underlying the achievement of these goals but they are not usually central to the instructional mission of the high school. Indeed, successful high schools often are able to assume that the basic skills have been mastered by their students prior to enrollment.

These dissimilarities in the two levels of schools influence their organizational policies and practices directly and indirectly and the resulting differences suggest that the research findings on elementary schools be applied to secondary schools only with caution. Even if the core propositions apply, their expressions in practice are likely to be different. The problems associated with elementary school success may be on the verge of being well understood but the task of achieving success at the secondary level remains more complex and illusive. Secondary school effectiveness is more powerfully influenced by an historically defined set of circumstances — economic opportunities, social norms, public policies, and so forth — that are often beyond the control of local school authorities (Firestone, Herriott, and Wilson, 1984; Chubb and Moe, 1986).

There also are critical issues in secondary education that are simply not addressed by the effective schools studies. Among these are questions of resource distribution and adequacy, the impact on students of different curricular paths and tracking, and the influence of school size on culture and program. These are important issues that should be addressed. While there is an extensive literature on each of these topics, there are few studies examining how the variables in each of these areas interact and affect general school success. Clearly the structure of the curriculum, its appeal to adolescents, and its efficacy at promoting their intellectual development are important. But the long continuing debate over the value of vocational education reveals the difficulty of making curricular determinations on the basis of empirical evidence.

There has been a similar debate over tracking. Clearly who gets into which curricular track, who makes these decisions, and what criteria are used are important factors in determining school outcomes. Research has been conducted on these questions for decades but the studies have produced equivocal results (Northwest Regional Educational Laboratory, 1981; Alexander and Cook, 1982; Goodlad, 1983; Oakes, 1985). Reformers see tracking as inequitable and argue against it. Many educators find it a practical necessity given the diversity of student abilities and interests. Research does not provide clear answers to questions concerning how to structure programs to optimize both high individual achievement and aggregate school achievement.

School size also has been identified as a factor that affects student commitment, participation, and attendance (Barker and Gump, 1964; Lindsay, 1982). There may be trade-offs, however, between greater school size and program offerings, whilst smaller size facilitates the personalization of instruction and the development of strong bonds between students and their schools. More careful examination of the relationship between size and quality is needed. Finally, the opportunity structure facing adolescents outside of school and after they graduate influences their motivation, commitment, time allocations, and ability to remain in school (US General Accounting Office, 1982). Youth may choose to work or get pregnant. They may expect to go to college or to be unemployed. These social realities affect secondary school success and must be factored into future research. Studies that examine how successful schools adapt to varying conditions will help both program designers and policy-makers.

In applying the effective schools research to the improvement of secondary education, there is a great risk of over-promising. The research is often presented and accepted by policy-makers as a set of verified and universal propositions that if applied will produce quick results in the form of higher academic achievement. Moreover, it is often claimed that this can be achieved without significantly increasing the costs of education. This is a misrepresentation of the nature of the research and a misunderstanding of the findings. There is a risk that educators who fail to reach the levels of effectiveness prescribed by policy-makers will be branded as incompetent or ineffective. After all, if research had provided the formula for achieving success, then there is no other explanation for failure. There also is the further risk that an important line of inquiry will be discredited by promising more than can be delivered.

Studies of Successful Secondary Schools

In addition to the reform reports, a number of widely-read studies of secondary schools were published in the late 1970s and the early 1980s. Some of these studies have involved the systematic collection of data about the schools; others have drawn upon expert opinion or relied upon techniques of social criticism or journalism. Some have examined the relationships between specific characteristics of the schools and student outcomes; others have not. In a review of twenty-eight such studies, Newman and Behar (1982) concluded:

> Research on schooling typically lacks information powerful enough to support confident causal statements ('Schools of a particular type produce particular learning outcomes'), longitudinal claims ('Between ninth grade and graduation, students learn the following...'; 'Schools with certain features maintain consistently high performance over several years'), or even valid claims of a comparative nature ('Public schools differ from private schools'; 'Minority students may have different learning styles from majority students'. 'Small schools have different effects from large schools'). Based on the projects' designs, we assess their potential for increasing descriptive knowledge in each of these ways. Almost half of the projects are not likely to contribute to a systematic study of cause, historical (longitudinal) change, or comparison, although they will produce general narratives and calls to action.

Research on secondary schools suffers from flaws that limit the utility of the findings. Most of the well-known studies have one or more of the following problems: the absence of longitudinal data, a narrow definition of outcomes, a small sample, the use of either observational or survey methods but not both, and the lack of information on individual student learning outcomes and the school activities that may affect them (Newman, Smith, and Wehlage, 1983). As a result, research on secondary education has not provided generalizations robust enough to guide public policy. This is one of the reasons why the propositions drawn from the effective schools research have been so attractive to policy-makers frustrated by the ineffectiveness of many secondary schools.

Yet there is a limited literature on secondary schools that examines the policies and practices associated with school effectiveness or school success. While imperfect, it is of interest to those faced with the necessity of making decisions. The results of such studies can guide program designs even if they do not always provide the strong empirical propositions needed for good theory or good policy. The requirements for design parameters are less demanding. Propositions need not be universally true; they need merely serve as useful guideposts to critical issues. Good design requires a comprehensive framework and means of generating alternatives for consideration.

It is in this spirit that five studies have been singled out for special review in this chapter. They include a study of basic skills effectiveness in seventeen California high schools conducted by the California Assembly Office of Research (1984), the analysis of public and private schools conducted by Coleman, Hoffer, and Kilgore (1982) using data drawn from the 'High School and Beyond' survey, six case studies of public and private high schools by Lightfoot (1983), four case studies of middle schools by

Lipsitz (1984), and the well-known study of twelve London secondary schools by Rutter, Maughan, Mortimore, Ouston and Smith (1979).

The five studies listed in Table 1.2 met the minimum criteria for consideration: systematic research methods were used in a general study of secondary school effectiveness and specific school policies and practices were related to school success. These criteria resulted in the exclusion of 'studies' such as those by Boyer (1983) and Sizer (1984) because, however useful their recommendations may prove to be, their conclusions are based on impressions and expert opinion, rather than systematic data collection and analysis. Other recent studies of high schools such as those published by Cusick (1983); Goodlad 1983; Powell, Farrar, and Cohen (1985); and Sedlak, Wheeler, Pullin, and Cusick (1986), while useful and provocative, were excluded because they provide so little insight into the elements associated with success. They have focused on describing and explaining typical conditions rather than identifying policies and practices associated with success. Indeed, they paint bleak pictures of the typical public high school, describing poor teaching, demoralized staffs, and inadequate working conditions. Other studies were judged to be too narrow, focusing on a narrow range of outcomes or on classroom success with a select group of students in a particular discipline. (For example, see Anderson, 1970, or McDill, Meyers and Rigsby, 1967.)

The flaws and inadequacies of the selected pieces of research also are apparent even from the limited information presented in Table 1.2. Only two of the studies involved comprehensive studies of secondary school effectiveness (Coleman, Hoffer, and Kilgore, 1982, and Rutter, Maughan, Mortimore, Ouston and Smith, 1979). The other three are more limited by their sample sizes, methods, or scope of inquiry.

Table 1.2   Studies of Successful Secondary Schools

Study	School Type	Sample Size	Method Data	Outcome Data	Longitudinal Design
California Assembly (1984)	HS	17	O	Yes	No
Coleman, Hoffer, and Kilgore (1982)	HS	1345	S	Yes	No
Lightfoot (1983)	HS	6	O	No	No
Lipsitz (1984)	MS	4	O	No	No
Rutter, Maughan, Mortimore, Ouston and Smith (1979)	HS	12	O/S	Yes	Yes

1. HS = high school and MS = middle school.
2. O = observation/case study and S = survey methods.
3. In following tables, studies are referred to by the first author only.

Juxtaposing the five studies to the thirteen dimension model of school effectiveness defined by Purkey and Smith (1983), produces the results displayed in Table 1.3. The figure graphically portrays the variation in conceptual frameworks and findings that is characteristic of the effective schools literature. Five of the thirteen dimensions are supported by only one of the five studies. Conversely, another five dimensions receive support from four or more of the studies. Yet it is not possible to draw the conclusion from this information that the latter set of dimensions deserve more attention by educators than the former. The variation in fit between the model and the findings largely reflects variations in the research designs, that is, the questions examined rather than differences in findings. Questions not asked do not produce negative findings. It also is interesting that the studies provide stronger support for the 'process' variables in the Purkey–Smith paradigm than for the 'organizational-structural' variables. The findings for each of the thirteen dimensions, and the issues they raise, are discussed below.

Table 1.3 Dimensions of Effective Secondary Schooling

	California Assembly	Coleman	Lightfoot	Lipsitz	Rutter
Organization Structural Variables					
1. School-site management	S	—	S	S	—
2. Instructional leadership	X	—	S	X	—
3. Staff stability	—	—	—	—	—
4. Curriculum articulation and organization	S	—	—	—	—
5. Schoolwide staff development	—	—	—	S	—
6. Parental involvement	—	—	—	S	—
7. Schoolwide recognition of academic success	—	S	S	S	S
8. Maximized learning time	—	S	—	—	X
9. District support	X	—	—	—	—
Process Variables					
1. Collaborative planning	S	—	X	X	X
2. Sense of community	S	—	X	X	X
3. Clear goals and high expectations	X	X	X	X	X
4. Order and discipline	—	X	X	S	X

S – indicates some evidence indicating support.
X – indicates a strong finding verifying the importance of a dimension.

School-site Management

The research on effective schools has fostered the belief that school improvement planning should occur at the building level. Advocates of school-site management use the research to support their approach to school organization. Up until the mid-1980s, researchers generally ignored the role that school districts played in promoting school effectivenes (Corcoran, 1987; Cuban, 1984; Schlechty, 1985). If the schools district or central office were considered at all, it was as an obstacle to school effectiveness. It was suggested that successful schools succeeded in spite of their school districts' policies or politics. Edmonds described effective schools as 'mavericks' that had ignored or circumvented district policies and procedures. Indeed, much of the research was conducted in large districts whose central office bureaucracies were often regarded as barriers to excellence by school staff. In short, there was a bias in the studies that favored school autonomy. None of the five studies reviewed here looked at the role of the district, although the California study (1984) did examine the level and character of district support for school improvement. Nevertheless, three of the studies reported findings supporting the notion of enhanced autonomy at the building level.

Lightfoot (1983) noted that the principals and headmasters in the schools she studied had clear authority to coordinate instruction and the power to take action in response to problems. The California study (1984) concluded that it was critical that staff at the high school, typically department chairpersons, have authority over curriculum and that staff play a major role in curriculum design and review. This suggests considerable autonomy from central office staff in this policy area. Lipsitz (1984) described how principals in several of the sites she studied served as buffers against external interference and acted to protect the policies and programs in their schools. The school autonomy described in these accounts was not so much granted as it was taken by strong leaders who protected their visions from the intrusions of a turbulent environment.

The policy issue that faces boards of education is what should be tightly controlled and monitored by the school district and what should be the areas of discretion and flexibility at the building level. Answers to such questions seem to be dependent upon the context. Research findings indicate that school staffs need some discretion to solve everyday problems, develop a sense of ownership, and coordinate activities. However, the district needs mechanisms to ensure that the approved curriculum is implemented and that the curriculum is properly aligned to the tests used to assess progress. If a school is performing poorly, these control mechanisms may initially be more restrictive in order to ensure that clear and common expectations are established and student interests are protected. Clarity and balance are needed in the allocation of responsibilities. School-site management may be good practice but its operational meaning is not clearly defined by the research literature.

Instructional Leadership

Three of the five studies identified instructional leadership as a critical factor for school success but the researchers also found that the forms of successful leadership varied. In the schools studied by Lightfoot (1983) and Lipsitz (1984), principals played critical roles in articulating the school ideology; setting goals; and selecting, motivating, and supporting the staff. The strength and character of leadership in the building is linked to the issue of school autonomy. Principals who lack broad discretionary authority may find it more difficult to build a distinctive school culture or create a strong sense of community. Both Lightfoot and Lipsitz noted that it was important that there be a match between culture of the organization and leadership style.

Research on the roles of principals in successful high schools is sparse. In a recent review of this literature, Firestone and Wilson (1985) suggested that principals attempt to overcome the 'loose-coupling' in their schools by manipulating both bureaucratic and cultural linkages in the organization. The former are the rules, procedures, and authority relations in the organization while the latter are norms, symbols, rituals, and stories that characterize a school. Firestone and Wilson conceded, however, that it was not clear how altering a school's culture affected instructional effectiveness. They noted that is was not unusual to discover that 'turn-around' schools had improved student discipline and developed a more positive climate but it was less common to find significant and permanent changes in levels of student achievement. Principals should be able to influence instruction through decisions on class size and composition, grouping, resource allocations, time allocations, and the use of knowledge and skills of the staff. And they may be able to alter the tone of the learning and teaching environment through the manipulation of organizational culture: by telling stories, creating symbols and ceremonies, communicating norms, and serving as role models (Firestone and Wilson, 1985). Yet the scant evidence available indicates that secondary principals exercise less influence over classroom instruction than their elementary counterparts (Firestone and Herriott, 1982).

Leadership may also be provided by department chairs, teachers, or central office personnel. There have been few studies of the roles such individuals play or how their behavior affects the role of the principal and the overall effectiveness of the organization. One recent study, however, reported that department chairs did not often play leadership roles and that their roles are poorly defined (Hall and Guzman, 1984).

Everyone agrees that visible and active instructional leadership is important to school success but there is no clear pattern to guide principals or others in potential leadership roles. Research provides no precise definition of the principal's role. What is clear is that leadership functions are carried out differently in secondary schools and that successful styles vary with the context. More needs to be known about what type of leadership can create the conditions described by the successful schools literature and under what conditions.

Staff Stability

This issue was not directly examined in any of the studies. In fact, the schools studied by Rutter, *et al.* (1979) experienced high staff turnover. Some turnover may be desirable to bring new ideas and new energy on board and it may be absolutely necessary in cases where questions of competence or commitment arise. Little is known about the overall impact of staff stability on school effectiveness. It may be an effect rather than a cause of success. Whether it is beneficial obviously depends on the quality and commitment of the staff.

Curriculum Articulation and Management

Only the California study examined the management of the curriculum in secondary schools. The authors concluded that careful curriculum management and regular curriculum review were essential to school success. Other studies also have documented the importance of curricular alignment (Stallings, 1984) and the need to bring some order to the curriculum in secondary education (Kirst, 1983a). The case for improving curricular management in high schools and for a more carefully aligned and articulated curriculum seems strong even though the question has not been addressed directly in the few general studies of secondary school effectiveness.

School-wide Staff Development

Evidence that the approach to staff development or the amount of it provided influences school effectiveness is scant (Griffin, 1982). None of the five studies shed any light on this issue. Staff development in secondary schools is seldom conducted on a school-wide basis nor is it typically linked to school-wide goals. Most of it is planned by individual teachers or in departments. But more inter-departmental staff development might help overcome the fragmentation that characterizes secondary schools and contribute to improved curricular integration, more uniform standards, and stronger staff consensus on goals. The critical factors in successful staff development seem to be the frequency and quality of the opportunities for social interaction and dialogue about teaching (Little, 1983).

Increasing or altering staff development activities cannot be justified on the basis of school effectiveness research alone. New approaches are certainly needed and some clues to their design will be found in this literature, for example, placing more stress on staff cooperation, community, collegiality, and collective responsibility. These objectives can be pursued through staff development programs that bring people together and provide opportunities to discuss common instructional problems or successful techniques.

Parental Involvement and Support

None of the studies directly addressed the relationship between parental involvement and effectiveness in secondary schools. Parental involvement in secondary schools is generally lower than in elementary schools. Parental involvement in the form of active participation in instruction or in determining school policies or programs in secondary schools is not common. While parental involvement is generally assumed to be a positive factor (Henderson, 1981), it has not been carefully examined in school effectiveness studies. One early study found that the level of parental involvement in schools was positively related to achievement in schools serving poor minority children, and negatively related in schools serving affluent children (Brookover. *et al*, 1979). Salganik and Karweit (1982), in a re-analysis of the Coleman study of public and private schools, speculated that parental choice of schools led to greater acceptance of traditional school authority by parents and students, higher consensus on goals and behavioral norms between home and school, and hence greater commitment to the school and to academic tasks.

Experience demonstrates that parental support of their children's academic efforts is important to school success but the case for or against parental involvement in secondary schools cannot be made on the basis of the evidence reviewed here. Common sense suggests that it can be a strong positive factor but this may depend on the form of the involvement and the degree of consensus between the school staff and parents about goals, curriculum, methods, and standards.

School-wide Recognition of Academic Success

There has been no direct examination of the influence that different types of school reward systems, recognition programs or academic incentives have on achievement. Recognition and reward programs for students and staff are common in secondary schools and are being expanded in many schools in response to the reform reports. Rutter, *et al.* (1979) reported that the frequent use of praise and clear feedback on performance were strongly related to overall achievement. Many studies of elementary schools have identified school-wide recognition of academic success as an important factor (Corcoran and Hansen, 1983). Adolescents often choose to give their time and attention to activities other than academics. Jobs, friends, sports, music, extra-curricular activities, and sex compete for their attention. They often work hardest in areas where rewards are immediate and concrete and where their internal or peer-defined standards of excellence are applied. Hence their motivation to concentrate on the core academic demands of school is problematic. Appeals to future rewards (college, jobs, etc.) or to adult authority ('Do it or be punished') often seem to be ineffective. From this perspective, the provision of more immediate rewards and recognition makes good sense. The research support for the efficacy of school-wide recognition of academic success is not strong but the anecdotal evidence is persuasive.

Maximized Learning Time

Here the studies of effective secondary schools (Rutter, *et al.* 1979; Coleman, *et al.*, 1982) confirm findings from research on effective classrooms. Beginning classes on time, minimizing disruptions, reducing disciplinary problems, having better school and class attendance, increasing the amount of homework, and obtaining higher rates of engagement in academic activities have all been found to be related to higher achievement. An additional observation drawn from related studies using the 'High School and Beyond' database is that high rates of participation in co-curricular activities may also be a factor (Lindsay, 1984; US Department of Education, 1986). If these programs reinforce or extend academic learning, increase contact between students and teachers, or help students bridge the gap between academic work and their interests, they can be powerful supplements to the formal curriculum.

Policies and procedures that enhance, extend, and protect instructional time are important. Equally important are work norms that reinforce beginning classes on time, not wasting class time, assigning homework, tutoring, and participating in extra-curricular programs. Some of the behaviors that maximize learning time cannot easily be acquired but they can be modelled, solicited, and rewarded by thoughtful instructional leaders.

District Support

Only the California study verified the importance of district support. The continuing lack of attention to this factor was noted in the previous discussion of the limitations of the school effectiveness research. Discussions of applications of the school effectiveness model to school improvement have directed attention to the critical functions performed by the district leadership and central office staff (Cuban, 1984; Purkey and Smith, 1985, Corcoran, 1987). Empirical studies of school improvement also have identified district support as a critical factor in implementing change (Berman, 1981, Crandall and Loucks, 1983) but research provides little guidance on the forms or amounts of district support that are related to school effectiveness. At this point, districts are on their own in dealing with the questions of the proper amount of school autonomy and the best forms of central office assistance.

Collaborative Planning and Collegial Relationships

Three of the studies found evidence of collaborative planning and strong collegial relationships among staff and between teachers and administrators in more successful schools (Rutter, *et al.*, 1979; Lightfoot, 1983 and Lipsitz, 1984). This finding is confirmed by other studies of successful schools (Little, 1983) and research on school improvement (Berman, 1981; Louis, Rosenblum and Molitor, 1981). Such conditions are not common, however, in large secondary schools where people often work in relative isolation from their fellow teachers, where little time is provided for staff to discuss instruction, and where adversarial and competitive relationships are common. In his discussion of the relationships within high school faculties, Roland Barth concluded:

> The nature of relationships among the adults who inhabit a school has more to do with the school's quality and character and with the accomplishments of its pupils than any other factor.
> *(Education Week.* 1984: 24).

Collaborative planning requires school leaders who are willing to part-icipate and to listen. It also takes time, a precious commodity in public schools. Collegiality requires regular allocations of time; it does not happen naturally. Teachers need opportunities to engage in dialogue about curriculum and instruction. School boards and school administrators must come to the realization that organizational health requires the provision of such opportunities and that providing some 'slack time' in the system is not inefficient and need not threaten management prerogatives or detract from instruction.

A Sense of Community

Teachers often feel isolated and lonely. They frequently feel victimized by students, parents, and administrators. They often are held in low esteem by and receive little respect from these important groups. These attitudes about teaching are sources of stress for teachers and obstacles to their productivity. In successful schools, the reverse appears to be true. Teachers are respected, relationships are supportive and reciprocal, and there is a strong sense of community. Four of the five studies affirmed this finding. Finn (1984) described the phenomena this way:

Members of the school community share a belief structure, a valued system, a consensual rather than a hierarchical governance system, and a set of common goals that blur the boundaries between their private and organizational lives.

Creation of a sense of community is not something that occurs overnight or can be achieved simply by adopting new policy. It is the outgrowth of sustained efforts to build the collegiality and collaboration described above. But it is an important element in school success and should be held up as a value. The creation of a strong sense of community among the staff and between staff and students should be actively sought and actions that would jeopardize these relationships should be avoided. In many situations this would require both managers and teacher leaders to alter their styles and learn how to work together.

Clear Goals and High Expectations

All five studies confirmed the importance of this dimension of effectiveness — one of the original 'five correlates'. Other reviews of the school effectiveness research have stressed goal consensus (MacKenzie, 1983 and Rutter, et al.,1979). The California Assembly study (1984), Lightfoot (1983), and Lipsitz (1984) also reported that a shared philosophy or agreement on goals was characteristic of successful schools. Whether this was a true consensus or a working consensus is not clear and may not be important.

The meaning of high expectations, however, is not always clear. As Lipsitz (1984) observes: 'We lack a reasonable vocabulary for describing the differential expectations held by teachers that enhance student capacity to learn.' Speaking of realistic expectations may be interpreted as racism or sexism yet teachers must operate within the realm of the possible. There is a tension between the push for higher standards and the need of teachers to motivate individual students, but it is reasonable to ask that expectations across a school be high. The resultant academic press may help everyone. And expectations should not be linked to race, gender, or class.

Setting goals is easy, implementing them is more difficult. Goals must be kept visible and actually be used to set priorities and allocate resources. If the goals are kept front and center at all times and influence important policy decisions, then they are likely to be taken seriously by staff and students. Expectations must be discussed and shaped. Standards are the most obvious visible manifestation of expectations. If they are low, staff expectations are likely to follow suit. Raising standards and expectations is an incremental process in which demonstrated success plays a critical role.

Order and Discipline

All five studies provided further support for the importance of maintaining a task-oriented, orderly climate in schools. This has been a central theme of all effective schools studies and is another one of the 'five correlates'. The reaction often has been stricter rules, tighter enforcement, and a more punitive atmosphere. But adolescents also must learn self-discipline (Etzioni, 1982). This requires some structure but not an authoritarian atmosphere. Lipsitz (1984) says that many young adolescents are not ready for the independence offered in most secondary schools and this often leads to behavorial problems. The result is reliance on authoritarian control mechanisms which produce student alienation. Proper relationships must be defined in a school. Teachers must have the authority to keep order. But it is a climate of respect and responsibility that is desired, a climate in which adult-student relationships can be positive. School success is not likely to be fostered in a prison-like atmosphere.

Discipline is important but how it is achieved is equally important. Effective discipline may not be possible unless some of the other dimensions of successful schools are present or being worked on. Good discipline is a by-product of the culture of the school. Cooperation, consensus about goals and values, and strong leadership are needed to foster an affirmative discipline policy.

Other Significant Findings

The thirteen dimensions of school effectiveness defined by Purkey and Smith (1983) do not encompass all of the findings of the five studies reviewed in this discussion. The data suggest that there may be other dimensions that should be added to the framework if it is to be applied to secondary schools. Among these are:

1. Presence of a rigorous academic program.
    Rutter found that enrollment of a core of academically able students was related to effectiveness and Coleman reported that students took more rigorous courses in the more effective schools.

2. A high quality staff.
    Lipsitz and Lightfoot noted the significance of the quality of the teaching staff and the processes of their recruitment. Rutter found that it was important that teachers provided good role models for their students in terms of punctuality, behavior, dress, care of the facilities, and so on. Both Coleman and Rutter identified good classroom management practices as important to school success.

3. Good working conditions for teachers and students.

   Rutter, Lightfoot, and Lipsitz identified clean, safe, attractive physical facilities as important to attitudes and morale. They also noted that teachers were respected, listened to, and provided the discretion and autonomy needed by professionals.

4. High levels of discretionary effort by staff.

   Discretionary staff effort refers to the amount of work performed beyond what can be required by direct supervision. This includes work done at home, such as lesson planning and materials development, as well as tutoring and personal assistance provided to students. Three of the studies (Rutter, Lipsitz, and Lightfoot) identified this as an important process variable.

5. Positive teacher–student relations.

   Lipsitz and Lightfoot observed the importance of having teachers who liked and understood adolescents. Rutter and Coleman found better and more frequent student–teacher relations in more successful schools.

6. High levels of student participation.

   Rutter found that the proportion of students holding positions of responsibility was significant and Coleman suggested that the proportion participating in extra-curricular activities might be a factor in school success.

7. The use of data to assess progress.

   The California study found that more effective schools were clearer about their indicators of success, used data to assess their progress more frequently, and conducted diagnostic assessments of students more regularly.

8. A bias for action.

   Lightfoot describes a 'willingness to search for solutions' and Lipsitz observed that staff ingenuity was encouraged. The California study noted that the school staff had the autonomy to solve school problems.

These additional eight dimensions add to the emerging portrait of the successful secondary school. Taken together with the thirteen dimensions discussed above, they suggest a far more complex portrait than that provided by the 'Five Factor' theory or other simplified summaries of the school effectiveness research. The overall *gestalt* that emerges reinforces the notion that specific policies and practices may be less important than work norms or school culture, the 'ethos' that integrates policies and practices into a concerned and caring community of academic workers. Some of the work norms that have been identified as associated with school success are:

- high levels of trust
- high expectations
- cooperation and collegiality
- high levels of discretionary effort
- a concern for student welfare
- a belief in improvement
- respect for teaching
- concern for the weakest members
- a sense of collective responsibility
- careful use of time.

These norms are often embedded in specific policies and procedures but acceptance of, and adherence to them is due less to the presence of rules or regulations than to the nature of the work culture in the school. When asked about these behaviors, staff might reply: 'That's just how we do things here'. Purkey and Smith (1983) concluded that:

> ... there is a remarkable and somewhat disturbing resemblance between the traditional view of schools as serious, work-oriented and disciplined institutions where students were supposed to learn their three R's and the emerging view of modern effective schools.

Purkey and Smith apparently were disturbed because they inferred narrowness, rigidity, and a stress on control from the portrait produced from the findings. But as the above discussion suggests, successful secondary schools are modern workplaces, characterized by a culture that is task-oriented to be sure, but also supportive of initiative, creativity, and diversity.

Culture is by definition elusive, implicit, and taken for granted. But every organization develops a core set of assumptions, understandings, and implicit rules that govern daily behavior (Deal and Kennedy, 1982). The norms described above are similar to those found in all successful organizations (Peters and Waterman, 1982) and they are related to high productivity. They define the 'shared moral order' referred to by Cohen (1983) or the 'ethos' alluded to by Rutter and his associates (1979). Having a distinctive and strong academic culture allows a school to impose its values on students and to enforce work and behavioral demands. (For more complete discussions of school culture, see Anderson, 1982; and Rossman, Corbett and Firestone, 1988).

High schools, particularly large ones, do not always have a single dominant culture. Tracks, grades, peer networks, and extra-curricular programs create multiple sub-cultures. But in a strong school, these sub-cultures accept the core values of the school and complement them. Programs that do not grab students tend to lose them. This is especially true for disadvantaged students. It is a tragedy that the students who are most at risk often attend fragmented, weak institutions that lack direction. A strong school culture provides a sense of social cohesion, of being special. Support is provided as well as direction. This is one of the main insights to be drawn from the research on effective schools.

The effective schools research can be, and is being used, as its critics have suggested, to justify tighter administration, less discretion, more control, and increased focus on narrow measures of success rather than on the improvement of the quality of worklife for staff and students (Pratzner, 1984). Such actions seem to be at odds with the findings reported above. However, whether such actions are appropriate may depend on the conditions in the school and its stage of institutional development. Lightfoot (1983) suggests that schools develop into good schools in a series of six steps or stages in which different concerns are addressed. These concerns are:

Stage 1. Safety and Security
Stage 2. Attendance and Discipline
Stage 3. Basic Skills and Graduation
Stage 4. Post-school Preparation and Individualization
Stage 5. Intellectual Growth and Performance
Stage 6. Leadership and Responsibility

Unfortunately, current thinking about secondary school effectiveness seems fixated on Stage 3. This reflects its origins in studies of urban schools, the narrow criterion of effectiveness applied, and the pressing need for improvement in many schools. Focusing on basic skills testing and raising graduation requirements may be politically attractive steps but they are an inadequate formula for long-term school success. School reform requires attention to the dimensions discussed earlier in order to help schools move to higher levels of development.

Reform and Research on Secondary Schools

The topic of secondary school effectiveness — and success — is particularly timely because public attention in the United States once again is being directed to the critical examination of the purposes and the effectiveness of the nation's public secondary schools. The urge for educational reform appears to be a re-occurring event in American life, taking place at regular intervals of ten to fifteen years. During the last cycle in the early 1970s, studies by blue-ribbon panels, foundations, and national educational organizations concluded that American secondary schools were in serious trouble because they were inhumane and overly rigid. Schools were criticized as dull, authoritarian places whose offerings were often unrelated to either the needs of their students or their communities. More student choice, greater individualization of programming, more community involvement, better career preparation, an earlier school-leaving age, and smaller schools were among the remedies proposed (Timpane, Abramowitz, Bobrow and Pascal, 1976; Passow, 1977).

But neither the dire predictions of increased student alienation nor the recommendations for reform generated much public response. Perhaps the public was preoccupied with Vietnam and Watergate or perhaps the reformers' emphasis on student rights and increased choice did not coincide with more popular notions of the changes that were most needed. It must be remembered that these reports followed a decade of youthful activism and rebellion, first over civil rights and then in opposition to the war. Student rights and student choice were not popular issues by the early 1970s; the public may have been more interested in discipline and control in the schools. Moreover, a review of the reports and recommendations of this period conducted by staff of the Rand Corporation concluded that there were inadequate data to assess the costs or the likely impact of the proposals (Timpane, *et al.*, 1976). In the absence of either strong public or professional support, state and federal actions to implement the recommendations were weak and short-lived. Nevertheless, many of the recommendations were implemented in piecemeal fashion by the staffs of the nation's high schools (Cusick, 1981).

Beginning with the Paideia Proposal in 1982, a new round of reports and studies appeared in the 1980s and this time reformers found the public more receptive (Adler, 1982; Boyer, 1983; The College Board, 1983; The Education Commission of the States, 1983; Goodlad, 1983; The National Commission on Excellence, 1983; Task Force on Federal Elementary and Secondary Education Policy, 1983; The National Science Board Commission on Precollege Education in Mathematics, Science, and Technology, 1983; The National Academy of Sciences, 1984; Sizer, 1984). Too many students, these new critics contended, were simply drifting through the schools, unchallenged and unmotivated, getting by with as little work as possible. Sizer (1984) referred to this as 'the conspiracy of the least' in which overworked teachers and unmotivated students negotiated tacit understandings to minimize the work required to achieve passing grades. This insight into the internal workings of the schools has been supported by subsequent empirical studies of secondary classrooms (Powell, Farrar, and Cohen, 1985; Sedlak, Wheeler, Pullin, and Cusick, 1986). These studies have drawn increased attention to the tension existing between two widely-held goals for public education — academic excellence and universal completion of high school.

The reform reports present a comprehensive and, on balance, highly negative assessment of the health of public secondary education. The strong criticism has stimulated and focused growing public concern about the quality of the nation's 29,000 public middle schools, junior high schools, and high schools (National Commission on Excellence, 1983). Repeated media accounts of declining test scores, failure rates on minimum competency tests, school attendance problems, and increasing drop-out rates in some locales had laid the groundwork for public acceptance of the reports. The informed public was already aware that many youths were failing to gain basic academic skills and that the social cost in terms of government programs, delinquency and crime, and productivity was unacceptably high. Since few adolescents are believed to be intellectually unable to complete the minimum academic requirements of high school, policy-makers, parents, and educators have been asking why so many are failing. This concern has also raised the question of why some schools seem to be consistently more successful than others — the same question that set off the original school effectiveness studies in the early 1970s.

The findings from the effective schools studies and the theoretical work they have stimulated are contributing to the process of reform in secondary education in several ways. First, the research has raised issues of policy and practice heretofore neglected by policy-makers. For example, how much authority should school principals have? How does the amount of instructional time vary across schools and districts and how is it allocated and used? Are there sufficient rewards for academic achievement and growth? Is there collaboration between the administration and staff? Second, the school variables found to be related to achievement provide a framework for assessing the potential of reform proposals. Do the proposals of the reformers address the most critical issues? Are their proposals formulated in a manner that makes successful implementation likely? Third, the findings can be used to design organizational audits for use in schools. What are the strengths and weaknesses in a building? Are there deficiencies in critical areas? Similarly, the findings could be used to develop indicators of quality for state evaluations and regional accreditation procedures. And finally, the research has been used to design comprehensive school improvement interventions in states such as New York, New Jersey, and Connecticut and in large districts such as St Louis, Milwaukee, and Seattle.

The authors of the reform reports of the 1980s have tended to use the school effectiveness paradigm to define the issues. The priorities for attention included low academic standards, the lack of a core curriculum for secondary education, poorly articulated programs, lax discipline, ineffective instruction, poorly motivated staff and students, the lack of attention to thinking skills, poor working conditions, and inadequate educational leadership. Summaries of the reports and comparative analyses of their recommendations have been prepared by a number of organizations. (See Griesemer and Butler, 1983; Michigan Association of School Boards, 1983; Passow, 1984; Spady and Marx, 1984).

What impact has all of this dialogue had on educators struggling to improve secondary schools that experts and the public have agreed are in dire need of reform? In the view of many practitioners the dialogue has raised the correct issues. Both the effective schools research and recent reform reports have identified a set of priorities that ring true. For example, educators have not challenged the call for stronger school leadership and clearer missions for secondary schools or the demands that more attention be given to working conditions for teachers and students. But the discussions of the critical school factors are often missing two important ingredients. The first is a clear definition of what a particular factor or theme means in practical terms; and second, how does one create the desired conditions in a school where they appear to be absent or inadequate?

The data that form the basis for this book offer some remedies for both these shortcomings. Organized around six themes, the data suggest some concrete practices adopted by successful schools. These practices put flesh on what was previously only a skeletal outline of excellence. Viewed from another perspective, the examples bring dynamism to what some critics have suggested were static models. Equally important, in describing these exemplary practices, specific strategies are suggested that may help those who are willing to act and take the risks to make their schools exemplary. In short, the book offers some practical advice, grounded in the dialogue of reform, directed to those willing to search out and implement a vision of excellence for their schools.

Wehlage (1983) defined five outcome domains for their proposed study of high school effects. Noting that there were serious obstacles to research on high school effectiveness due to problems of measurement and conceptualization and disagreements over the purposes of secondary education in the United States, they suggested basic literacy, academic knowledge, higher order thinking, vocational competence, and social maturity as domains to be assessed. If these are the major outcomes of secondary schooling, they reasoned, does it not follow that they should be the basis for the development of criteria of effectiveness?

Taking a totally different approach, the Ford Foundation (1984) identified the capacity to address and solve educational problems as a key criterion of school success in its school recognition program:

> The central organizing concept was to recognize accomplishments and gains — not just improved achievement scores and academic growth, but also success in raising student attendance, reducing truancy and drop-out rates, increasing participation in extracurricular activities, easing racial tension, involving parents and community, and generally enhancing the quality of student life.

The same issues have arisen in discussions concerning the effectiveness of middle schools and junior high schools although basic skills test scores would seem to have a better fit with the missions of these institutions. To identify successful schools for her study of the education of early adolescents, Lipsitz (1984) defined seven criteria that she stated were so essential that they were 'non-negotiable'. Her minimum standards for successful schools were: scores on standardized achievement tests at, above, or approaching the district or county means; low absentee rates among staff and students; low incidence of vandalism; little or no destructive graffiti; low suspension rates; high parental satisfaction; and public reputations for excellence.

Hoy and Ferguson (1985) have offered an entirely different approach to defining organizational effectiveness in public schools. Drawing upon the work of social theorist, Talcott Parsons, they suggest four broad dimensions of organizational effectiveness:

1. organizational adaptation — the successful accommodation to internal and external forces for change;
2. organizational productivity — the extent to which the organization is successful in setting and accomplishing its goals;
3. organizational integration — the degree to which solidarity among the elements of the system is maintained and intra-organizational conflict is minimized; and
4. organizational commitment — the creation and maintenance of a system's motivational and value patterns.

When this framework is applied to the approaches previously reviewed, it is clear that most of the emphasis, the focus of debate, has been on productivity criteria, with marginal attention being given to commitment and almost no attention to the other two domains. Given the role that students play in determining the measures of productivity, typically test scores, and the problematic character of student motivation, this seems an inappropriate and unfair way to assess the effectiveness of schools. The approach taken by the Ford Foundation, on the other hand, stressed adaptation and neglected productivity concerns which seems equally inappropriate.

There is a wide range of opinion on the issue of effectiveness criteria and the reader probably could add to the criteria discussed above. For example, no mention was made of the development and demonstration of skills in the arts or in athletics, but these outcomes are certainly important to the public's judgments about the quality of schools. The fact is that the American public expects its schools to pursue excellence in all of these areas. The public's attitude about the relative importance of the social, personal, vocational, and intellectual purposes of education varies from community to community, therefore, the most appropriate criteria may vary somewhat from one community to another. Effectiveness is a construct, an abstraction that has no objective reality. It cannot be defined precisely because it means different things to different people.

Nevertheless, some general conclusions about criteria of effectiveness for secondary schools can be drawn from this discussion:

1. Multiple criteria should be used in order to cover the broad mission of the secondary school and to avoid the distortions created by reliance on single measures.
2. Insofar as possible the criteria should include measures of achievement for all of the major curricular areas and these measures should fit the school's academic goals.
3. The criteria may include both student outcome measures and indicators of school processes but the latter should be related demonstrably to student outcomes.
4. The performance and academic growth of students in different curricular programs should be examined and differences by gender, race, ethnicity, or social class analyzed. Time-series data should be used to show changes in both the distribution of opportunity and performance.
5. Indicators of 'civility', pro-social behavior, or the absence of anti-social behavior should be among the criteria used.
6. Attendance, participation rates, and other measures of commitment to the school should be included.
7. Measures of the school's internal coordination and the level of staff cooperation should be examined to assess its effectiveness at making efficient use of resources.
8. Evidence of the school's efforts to address problems and its capacity to adopt new programs or develop new approaches should be reviewed.

9. The time-frame for assessing effectiveness should cover at least three years in order to provide for evidence of sustained success.
10. Whenever possible multiple referents should be used, that is, performance should be compared to past performance, to performance of similar schools (e.g., in terms of student population, resources, size, and overall mission), and to state and national norms or standards.

The Secondary School Recognition Program, the program which generated the data from 571 secondary schools for this book, attempted to provide its reviewers with such data. The data collected and reviewed in the program generally satisfied the guidelines set forth above. Given the use of multiple criteria and both quantitative and qualitative data the schools selected may have been more representative of high quality public education than schools selected using narrow criterion measures such as performances of students on basic skills tests or Scholastic Aptitude Tests (SATs). However, the staff of the recognition program were unable to compile outcome data on all curricular areas or to obtain test data disaggregated by race, gender, or social class; nor were they able to provide data on the performance of similar schools.

The program staff have been explicit about the fact that their review process has not been scientific and systematic in the way that empirical studies are conducted. Nor have they claimed that the program resulted in the identification and recognition of the 'best' schools in the nation. Rather, they have relied on a broad set of criteria, drawn in part from the research on effective schools, and on the professional judgments of experienced educators whose views merit respect. Their goal has been to select schools whose unusual success make them worthy of respect and emulation. The program staff have actively resisted formal decision rules for the recognition of schools. However, there were formal criteria that determined which data were collected and influenced the professional judgments of panelists and site visitors.

These included fourteen attributes of success drawn from research on effective schools and used as criteria of quality in the recognition program. The fourteen attributes are:

clear academic goals
high expectations for students
order and discipline
rewards and incentives for students
regular and frequent monitoring of student progress
opportunities for meaningful student responsibility and
    participation
teacher efficacy
rewards and incentives for teachers
concentration on academic learning time

positive school climate
administrative leadership
well-articulated curriculum
evaluation for instructional improvement
community support and involvement.

The selection process also included an examination of educational outcomes that included test scores, attendance rates, drop-out rates, suspensions and other exclusions, and awards for recognition of outstanding programs or individual performance.

There were other more qualitative criteria employed in the program. First, there was the notion that successful schools are uniquely responsive to the communities they serve. This criterion helped program staff avoid the trap of defining overly-prescriptive models of excellence. For example, the program staff acknowledged the importance of leadership but remained neutral as to how leadership should be manifested. The same was true with school-community relations. Second, special attention was paid to the discontinuities in the information about the schools. If the teachers painted one picture of the school and the students a different one, the school was unlikely to receive recognition. Third, if the atmosphere and program of the school did not provide opportunities for success for all students, particularly those students most in need of support, the school was not recognized. Several very academically-oriented schools did not receive recognition for this reason. Fourth, candidness was treated as a virtue. Panelists admired school staffs who had addressed adversity head-on and had overcome serious obstacles. They were skeptical about school staff who indicated they had faced no obstacles and had no problems. Finally, unusually successful schools were also able to document a consistent track record. Trend data over time either revealed significant improvement or stable, high performance on indicators of student achievement, staff and student attendance, graduation rates, and good discipline.

Program Description

At the change of Federal administrations in 1981, the Department of Education was the focus of intense debate among politicians. What should be the role of the Federal government in public education? All parties were agreed that one critical role was leadership to foster excellence in public education. One response was a program developed to give recognition to unusually successful public secondary schools. In early June 1983, the first group of high schools and schools for young adolescents (junior high schools and middle schools) to be given national recognition was announced. From 1983 through 1985, 571 secondary schools (just over 2 per cent of the nation's public secondary schools) have received the Secretary of Education's flag, a symbol of excellence in education.

The stated purposes of the program are to identify and recognize unusually successful public secondary schools, and through publicity and other means, to encourage others to emulate their successful programs, policies, and practices. The staff of the program have worked with the individual states to set up a selection process that is fair and yet responsive to the diverse social and economic circumstances under which the nation's public schools function.

The first part of that process is the completion of a school nomination form by individual schools. There are three parts to the form. The first focuses on demographic characteristics of the school and includes information on enrollment, type of community, racial and social composition, and staffing. The second section focuses on answers to questions concerning the fourteen attributes of success drawn from research on effective schools and used as indicators of quality in the program. The third section, indicators of success, requests data on educational outcomes that include — but are not restricted to — achievement test scores. Other measures include attendance rates, drop-out rates, suspensions and other exclusions, and awards received for outstanding programs or individual performance. The nomination form also includes several questions that enable school staff to elaborate on factors contributing most to their success and obstacles they had to overcome to be successful.

The program has been administered by the Secretary of Education's office in cooperation with state departments of education. The state departments of education distribute individual school nomination forms and set up screening processes for review of school applications. Individual states are responsible for establishing selection procedures suited to the conditions in their state. In the 1982–83 school year, each state was permitted to nominate five schools in each of the categories: schools for young adolescents (junior high schools and middle schools) and high schools. In that year, forty-four participated and 496 nominations were submitted. In the second year, 1983–84, the procedure was altered and each state was given a quota for nominations reflecting its population and the number of eligible schools. During the second year of the program, forty-eight states, the District of Columbia, and the Department of Defense Dependent Schools participated and 555 nominations were received. In the third year, 1984–85, states were asked to nominate as many schools as there were senators and members of the house of representatives representing the state in the federal legislature. In that year, forty-nine states, the District of Columbia, and Department of Defense Dependent Schools were involved by forwarding 509 nominations.

The nominations submitted by the states have undergone a three-step review process. First, each year a national panel has been convened by the federal recognition program to review the nomination forms forwarded by each state. The eighteen-member panels have been broadly representative of constituent groups in public education with members from universities, professional associations, state departments, local school systems and the business community. The information provided by each school on the demographic characteristics of the school, the outcome criteria and the 14 indicators of success in the nomination form was carefully reviewed by the panel. Typically, this paper screening reduced the pool of nominations by approximately one half.

The second step involved schools receiving a site visit. These site visits lasted two days (only one day in 1983) and were conducted by visitors representing a mix of researchers, consultants, administrators, and other educators with extensive experience in secondary education. During the site visits, structured interviews were conducted with teachers, administrators, students and parents; observations were made in the building and classrooms; and detailed reports were prepared on each school. The site visit reports contain extensive information about how various school personnel perceive the strengths and weaknesses of the school and their roles and influence in them. The reports also contain vivid descriptions of the climate in the schools and activities in the classrooms.

In the final step of the selection process, the national panel reviewed these site visit reports and the school nominations, interviewed the site visitors about each school, and made recommendations to the Secretary of Education. As a final check, all nominated schools were reviewed by the Office of Civil Rights to ensure that they were in full compliance with federal civil rights laws.

The number of schools nominated, visited, and recognized each year are summarized below:

Table 2.1   Number of secondary schools participating in the program

Year	Schools Nominated	Schools Visited	Schools Recognized
1982–83	496	198	152
1983–84	555	263	202
1984–85	509	277	217

While the basic process of selecting schools for recognition has remained intact over the three-year history of the program, there have been a number of important changes that have strengthened the design. As with anything new, one learns that initial designs are not always optimal during the course of their implementation. The important message, however, is that the program staff learned from these early experiences and used their knowledge to improve the quality of the program. For example, in the first year, site visits were only one day in duration and little attention was paid to classroom processes because of time constraints. In subsequent years, the site visit was expanded to two days and an explicit schedule of classroom visits was initiated. The nomination form was also extensively revised after the first year of the program to more explicitly address the fourteen attributes of success. Even the attributes themselves were redefined slightly in response to insights gained by the site visitors. Nomination quotas at the state level were also altered to reflect more accurately the population and total number of eligible students in each state. Through experience, the recognition program staff also learned how to make better use of the panelists and site visitors and by intensifying training sessions were able to minimize individual differences in the conduct of visits and preparation of reports.

As with any program of this magnitude and visibility, there are a number of unresolved issues that continue to affect the process and the data being collected. Three of the more prominent issues relevant to this analysis are:

- creation of a national program
- promotion of quality and progress
- use of common forms for all schools.

Creating a National Program

The creation of any successful, large-scale program is a difficult feat. The positive response by the public to the recognition program far exceeded even the highest expectations of the US Department of Education. For a program of this scope to continue without legislative support, to operate on a small budget from the Secretary's discretionary fund, and to function with a small overworked staff is a tribute not only to those whose vision created the program but also the many people who contributed to its implementation.

An important part of building the program has been the establishment and maintenance of cooperation with the chief state school officers in the fifty states. They are responsible for providing the first round of nominations. The quality of the applicant pool is directly dependent upon their decisions. The program staff have worked closely with staff liaison representatives in each state to ensure that the goals of the program are communicated accurately to local schools. As the program staff have gained experience and public support, the state participants have been able to learn from their past efforts and appraise the adequacy of their judgments about schools.

Promoting Quality and Progress

An issue that resists simple solution is whether to recognize schools with only the best quality programs or to recognize schools that have not yet reached the peaks of excellence but have improved relative to their past. The program staff have recognized both but acknowledge that publicity in the early years spoke of excellence more loudly than improvement. More recently, a better balance has been achieved. However, it is a formidable task to define improvement. Improvement is an ambiguous concept and it seems that staffs of improving schools often are working so hard to achieve goals that they have little time to collect or reflect on information that bears on their success. In addition, there is little consensus about how to assess increases in test scores.

Common Forms for all Schools

If the program staff recognize that schools must respond to their local contexts, why has there been a common format to the nomination form and the site visit process? The assumption underlying this question is that important and unique characteristics may not be captured in a standardized format. The answer is that the nomination form and site visit process are open-ended enough to allow a school to highlight its unique identity. Rather than constraining schools, the program structure has provided enough flexibility for the full story to be told. There have been no set formulas or scoring formats employed by panelists when making their decisions. Indeed, the essay structures of both the nomination form and the site visit report have lent themselves to a wide range of responses by applicants. Several lengthy essay questions focusing on obstacles that have been overcome and factors that contribute most to the schools' success offer opportunities to highlight uniqueness in very clear terms.

These problems are not likely to be resolved to everyone's satisfaction. The operation of a national recognition program in a nation as diverse as the United States and one which delegates responsibility for public education to the fifty states is bound to generate disputes and differences in viewpoints. However, by showing a willingness to face up to the difficult issues and learn from both its successes and mistakes, the program continues to improve the data available for efforts such as this book.

Available Data

Data from each school were drawn from two scources: the nomination form completed by the school staff and the site visit report written by an experienced independent third party. A summary of the contents of the nomination form is presented in Table 2.2 and the site visit guide in Table 2.3.

Nomination Form

The data in the first (demographics characteristics) and second (indicators of success) sections of the nomination form, for the most part, were numerical in nature and were available for direct entry into a computer. The middle category of data, the attributes of success, were more qualitative in nature with prose descriptions that provided specific examples. In most cases, applicants were allowed approximately a quarter of a page (usually a paragraph or two) to provide an answer. In two cases, the question on what contributes most to the success of the school and the probe on how the school has overcome obstacles, a whole page was allotted for the answer. In these latter two cases, the additional space afforded school staff the luxury of providing detailed descriptions of their school activities. These questions provide particularly fertile sources for documenting important aspects of the school. The total length of the nomination form was seventeen pages, providing a wealth of information about the schools. A summary of the data collected on the nomination form is described in Table 2.2.

Table 2.2   Summary of Data Provided in School Nomination Form

A. Demographic Characteristics
    1. school enrollment by grade level
    2. district enrollment
    3. number of schools in the district by level
    4. number of recent immigrants
    5. urbanicity
    6. racial composition
    7. per cent of low-income students
    8. primary educational needs
    9. entrance requirements
    10. school staff numbers (administrators, teachers, specialists)
    11. principal and other administrator tenure

B. Attributes of Success
    1. clear academic goals
       a. instructional goals
       b. how identified
       c. how communicated
    2. high expectations for students
       a. graduation requirements by subject
       b. approach to fostering communication skills
       c. students in advanced classes by subject
       d. students exceeding basic requirements
       e. programs that develop study skills
       f. programs for basic skills remediation
       g. strategies to communicate high expectations
    3. order and discipline
       a. approach to discipline
       b. special programs
    4. rewards and incentives for students
       a. procedures for recognizing student accomplishments
       b. special features

Table 2.2 Continued

5. regular and frequent monitoring of student progress
   a. procedures for notifying students and parents of progress
   b. career and educational opportunities programs
   c. dropout/high risk student prevention programs
6. opportunities for meaningful student responsibility and participation
   a. participation in governance
   b. participation in community activities
   c. participation in co-curricular program
7. teacher efficacy
   a. teacher input in decisions
   b. staff development
8. rewards and incentives for teachers
   a. procedures for evaluations
   b. formal procedures for recognition
   c. special rewards/incentives
9. concentration on academic learning time
   a. procedures to ensure effective use of time
   b. homework policy
10. positive school climate
    a. description of climate
    b. how created
11. administrative leadership
    a. principal/staff communciation
    b. communication with other schools in district
    c. other examples
12. well-articulated curriculum
    a. procedures for sequencing in content areas
    b. procedures for sequencing across grade levels
    c. opportunities for planning and coordination with other schools
13. evaluation for instructional improvement
    a. program evaluation
    b. dissemination of evaluation
14. community support and involvement
    a. parent participation
    b. community participation
    c. school use by community
15. other
    a. most contributes to success
    b. obstacles overcome

C. Indicators of Success
   1. school achievement measures
   2. mimimum competency tests
   3. enrollment of graduates (college/vocational/military/employment)
   4. student and teacher attendance
   5. per cent of dropouts
   6. school program awards
   7. teacher awards
   8. school awards

Site Visit Guide

The site visit guide was designed to verify the information provided on the nomination form and to enrich a reviewer's understanding of the school. The site visit guide was organized around the collection of data from each of the major constituent groups involved in the school. In each case, site visitors were expected to ask the same set of questions and organize their report around the responses to those questions. The site visitors, all experienced in secondary schools and qualitative data gathering techniques, were also instructed to be observers and recorders of information. Their role was not as evaluators and they were requested not to make overall judgments or assessments of the visited schools. While there were set questions to be asked of each constituent group in the school, there was also ample opportunity to probe further on a given topic or to explore completely new channels. A summary of the information gathered for the site visit report is provided in Table 2.3.

Table 2.3   Summary of Data from Site Visit Guide

A. Teachers
    1. perceptions of current state of school strengths/weaknesses
    2. degree to which all student needs are met
    3. role in planning and decision-making
    4. opportunity to communicate about curricula/instruction/programs
    5. recognition for efforts and accomplishments
    6. program improvements

B. Students
    1. strengths of the school
    2. school responsiveness to needs of friends and peers
    3. weaknesses/improvements needed
    4. work and behavioral expectations
    5. recognition of student performance
    6. co-curricular activities
    7. opportunities to influence programs

C. Special Service Personnel
    1. integration of roles and functions
    2. communication with administrators and subject matter teachers
    3. contribution to school success

D. Parents/Community
    1. strengths of the school
    2. most important student learning experiences
    3. needs of all students being met
    4. access to principal and staff

E. Principal
    1. current assessment of the school
    2. efforts to sustain improvements and solve problems
    3. vision of the future

Table 2.3   Continued

F. Superintendent/Board Member
   1. factors most contributing to school success

G. School Setting
   1. informal settings
      a. lunchroom
      b. corridors
      c. playing fields
   2. physical plant
      a. buildings
      b. grounds
      c. graffiti
   3. Classrooms
      a. physical environment
      b. activities
      c. student/teacher interaction
      d. academic learning time
      e. climate

H. Additional Comments

All the site visitors convened as a group each year before making the school visits for two days in an attempt to maximize uniformity of the data collection effort. The authors were either participants or trainers for those sessions during all three years of the program. In these sessions, detailed discussions were held about balancing time commitments and maximizing exposure to the full school program. During the site visit, interviews with each constituent group typically lasted forty five minutes to an hour. The interviews were primarily conducted in group sessions with six to ten participants. Multiple interviews were held with teachers and students. While the site visitors were often constrained by school schedules, the short duration of the visits and the fact that principals usually sampled the interviewees, special effort was made to obtain as wide a range of perspectives as possible. For example, when interviewing students, separate sessions were often held with student leaders, average students, and those who were struggling in the school. Interviews with teachers were planned to tap the views of experienced and inexperienced teachers as well as the full range of subject matter specializations.

The site visitors' schedules were also arranged so that approximately half their time was spent observing informal and formal activities of the school. Most of this time was spent observing classroom interaction. Reports of those observations were written in narrative summary with guidelines to focus on:

   1   physical setting:
      architecture
      seating arrangements

         grouping patterns
         furnishings
         materials
         displays

2   activities:
         drill
         testing
         lecture
         discussion
         busy work
         critical thinking

3   student/teacher interaction:
         direct questioning
         indirect questioning
         feedback
         criticism
         praise

4   academic learning time:
         announcement interruptions
         discipline
         start-up activities
         direct instruction
         clean-up

5   climate:
         orderliness
         enthusiasm
         pace

The site visit report consisted of narrative summaries describing each constituent group's views of the school. The responses to each issue were typically a paragraph or two in length (about a half page) and the written reports were fifteen to twenty-five pages in length.

Data Compilation

From the above review of the data available on the recognized schools, it should be clear that some form of data reduction and management was necessary to work with these files. It was just impossible to review and summarize raw data from 571 cases on almost 25,000 sheets of paper. To reduce the burden of managing and analyzing this data, a coding scheme was developed to organize the quantitative data (i.e., demographics and outcome variables) into standard formats, and to reduce the qualitative text data to manageable size. This latter step was accomplished by first identifying the categories of information contained in the files and then developing a conceptual framework for their review. The list of variables to be coded derived in part from an assessment of the information available in the nomination form and the site visit guide, in part from what the literature on school improvement and effectiveness suggests is important (see Chapter 1), in part from consultation with other experts in the field (especially on the topic of middle schools) and in part from the authors' own practical experience and familiarity with school policies and issues. The authors spent a great deal of time discussing the merits of various variables and eventually agreed upon a list of over 200 variables. Several versions of this framework were tested with the files to determine if there was adequate information to assess each variable.

Codes were then created to permit reviewers to assess and summarize the narrative information in the files relevant to the conceptual framework. These assessments took two forms. The first was a simple dichotomous response (yes/no). Was a certain program, policy or practice reported as being in place in the school or not? The second type asked the reviewer to make an assessment of the relevant conditions in the school on a five point scale in which the mid-point, three, was treated as the typical practice or situation in American public schools, and a five was an absolutely outstanding example of good practice. Most of the variables of this kind were coded in the three to five range as might have been predicted given the unusual sample of schools.

Data for the schools in the first year of the program were coded by a colleague with whom the authors worked on a daily basis. Coding for schools in the second year of the program was performed by three graduate students who had previously taught in secondary schools. The coding for the final year of the program was performed during the summer by a group of five secondary school teachers. Several extensive training sessions preceded each round of coding. During those sessions the authors discussed in detail the intended meaning for each variable and the potential data sources for that variable in both the site visit guide and the nomination form. In the majority of cases, an assessment could not be made on a variable by simply reviewing the response to a single question. Rather, it required a careful review of several data points on both the site visit guide and the nomination form.

After careful training, the coders and authors coded several schools collectively. Coded data were compared to check for discrepancies and any differences were carefully discussed to maximize agreement and to standardize our understanding of what was being assessed. Early in the process the entire group again coded several schools together to compare results. Periodic checks were made by the authors throughout the process to ensure that reliable data were being obtained. On average, between two and two-and-a-half hours were spent coding each school. The results were recorded onto a fixed format coding sheet which could then be entered directly into the computer for systematic analysis.

Analysis Strategy

With the completed coding, the authors built a computerized data file with more than two hundred variables for each school. The first step in the analysis strategy was to review the frequency distributions on each variable. This allowed the authors to make some judgments about overall trends across the entire sample and to highlight the variables where schools scored particularly high. Many of these variables seemed to cluster together. For example, strong leadership was exemplified by frequent vertical communication, a clear sense of mission for the school, and a sensitivity to the needs of teachers. At a preliminary stage some bivariate relationships were investigated to test associations identified in other research literature. However, it was the perspective of the authors from the beginning that the strength of the database was not to be found in a systematic bivariate of multivariate quantitative analysis. Rather, the strength of the database lay in the capacity to tap the rich qualitative descriptions of exemplary programs and practices.

The patterns that emerged from these descriptions gradually evolved into six themes. Careful analysis of the data led the authors to conclude the common elements in these excellent schools are:

- active leadership
- professional work environments
- positive learning environments
- broad community involvement
- continuous school improvement
- service to all students.

The computerized database became an effective sorting mechanism to identify small subsets of schools with particularly outstanding examples in each of these six areas. These examples were then used to enrich and elaborate key aspects of the themes. Chapters 4 to 9 provide detailed reviews of the themes, using a range of concrete examples from schools in the sample.

Before these themes are developed, it is important to understand the character of these schools and the social contexts in which they exist. The next chapter sets the stage for the six themes by describing these schools using statistical indicators and by comparing the data from these schools against the thirteen dimensions of effectiveness outlined in the previous chapter.

Chapter 3

Profiles of the Schools

The diversity of social settings across American communities is far too complex to capture in a few statistics portraying the contexts of schooling. Yet, it is instructive to review the more commonly used social indicators to set the scene for these exemplary schools. These indicators highlight the diversity of the schools that have been recognized for their exemplary programs and practices and the communities they serve. The chapter begins with a presentation of a broad range of basic descriptive characteristics including demographics, organizational characteristics and outcomes. Comparable national data are offered when available. The comparisons suggest that these exemplary schools are generally representative and are not limited to more privileged or high-status contexts. The chapter concludes with a discussion of the degree of fit between the characteristics of these recognized schools and the thirteen dimensions of effectiveness identified by Purkey and Smith (1983).

Demographics

Three major characteristics are displayed in this category. The first focuses on the character of the communities in which these exemplary schools are located. Table 3.1 shows the distribution of schools across urban, suburban, and rural settings for both the recognition program and the nation as a whole.* The data indicate that the number of urban schools that have been recognized is in proportion to their national numbers. In contrast, suburban schools are over-represented and there is an under-representation of rural schools.

Several factors may explain the imbalance among the categories. First, while active efforts have been made to promote the recognition program in

---

*References to the original national data sources for the tables in this chapter are found on the last page of the chapter.

Table 3.1   Metropolitan status of communities

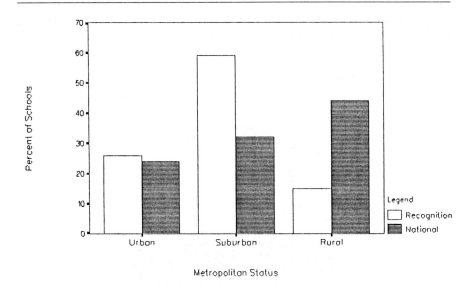

Metropolitan Status

all types of communities, suburban schools have responded more enthusias-
tically than rural schools. However, it should be noted that the chances of
receiving recognition once nominated were no less for rural schools than
those in the other two. Indeed, the proportion of nominated suburban
schools denied recognition has been higher than the proportions of urban or
rural schools. Second, the application process is time consuming. In small,
rural schools it is often harder to make time available to prepare the application. Third, some rural educators may have believed that their schools had
less chance of being recognized because their programs were less comprehensive than those in schools serving larger communities. Finally, the
communication channels to suburban and urban schools may have been
more effective. Although the distribution of recognized schools by
community type does not necessarily match national averages, the evidence
suggests that educational excellence is found in urban and rural settings as
well as in suburban sites.

The second comparison concerns the racial composition of the schools.
Due to the number of suburban schools in the sample, concern has been
expressed by some educational organizations that schools serving minority
students were under-represented. The pie charts in Table 3.2 address that
issue. While the data reveal that the recognized schools do not compare
exactly to the national data the numbers are not markedly different.
Minority students represent just over one-quarter of the nation's school
enrollment, while in this sample, they represent just under one-fifth. The
pattern of minority enrollment in the schools also is broadly representative,

reflecting the full spectrum from all-white to all-minority schools. Indeed, 54 of the 571 recognized schools had a majority of minority students. These data contradict the belief that excellence is only found in schools serving predominantly white student populations.

Table 3.2   Racial composition of schools

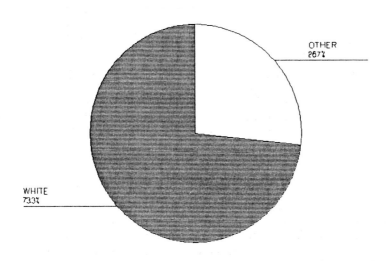

National

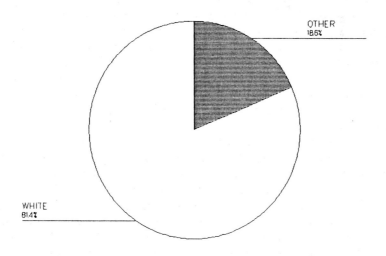

Recognition Program

The final demographic variable is an indicator of student socio-economic status. Based on the number of students eligible for free school lunches, this variable reflects the financial status of the students' families. The data in Table 3.3 display the proportions of schools in each of four categories defined by the percentage of low-income students. While the differences between the national figures and those of the program are not large, it is interesting to note the differences at the extremes. On one side of the table, the recognized schools are twice as likely to have small numbers of low-income students. On the opposite side of the chart, recognition program schools are one-and-a-half times as likely to have more than a quarter of their students in the poorest category. As with the racial data, these numbers reflect the broad diversity of students enrolled in outstanding public secondary schools.

Table 3.3   Students from low-income families

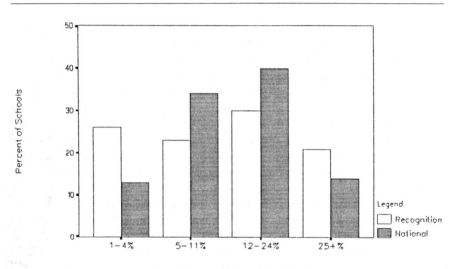

Percent from low-income families

By design, no per-pupil expenditure data were collected from these schools. These data were avoided so as not to bias judgments of review panelists about program quality. However, an independent study (Corcoran, 1986a) indicates that there was a relationship at the state level between resources and recognition. Data were collected on per-pupil expenditure for 82 per cent of the school districts in which these recognized schools are located (no data are available on school per-pupil expenditures). These per-pupil expenditures were then compared to statewide average per-pupil expenditures. In 63 per cent of the cases, the recognized schools were located in districts that spent above their state's average per-pupil expenditure. In sum, judgments about school quality appear to be related to resource levels even when no fiscal information is examined in making those judgments. This supports the commonsensical perception that school quality is linked to the level of resources provided for public education.

Organizational Characteristics

Data presented in this section focus more directly on the institutional characteristics of the schools. Six separate measures are reviewed in this section:

- school size
- school grade-span
- total number of secondary schools in the school's district
- student–teacher ratios
- principal's years of service
- graduation requirements.

The first variable focuses on the total enrollment of the schools. Separate figures are presented for high schools and schools for young adolescents (see Table 3.4). For the high school sample, there are marked differences in enrollment patterns between the sample and the national distribution. The recognized schools are under-represented in the smallest category (1–299 students) which reflects the under-representation of rural schools in the sample. On the other hand, the recognized schools are twice as likely to be found in the largest category. These differences are not nearly as striking in the schools for young adolescents. Overall, the data indicate that the recognition program schools tend to have larger enrollments than secondary schools in the nation as a whole.

The next variable focuses on grade level organization of the schools. At the high-school level, the two primary combinations are 9–12 and 10–12 with the majority of schools having the former organization. The data from the recognized schools look very similar to the national distribution (see Table 3.5). In the schools of young adolescents, there are a greater variety of grade-span combinations but the critical distinction is whether a school labels itself as a junior high or a middle school. As with the high school data, the proportions in the recognized schools are very similar to the national distribution (see Table 3.5).

The third organizational indicator concerns the number of secondary schools in the district. This is a proxy for overall district size and the bureaucratic complexity of the system. Some argue that schools in larger systems are more rigidly bureaucratic and have less discretion and flexibility than those in smaller districts. Along those lines, it is argued a more complex, hierarchical district bureaucracy makes it more difficult to develop strong school identities and to establish the levels of staff and student commitment that promote school success. Data are displayed in Table 3.6 comparing the

Table 3.4 Enrollment

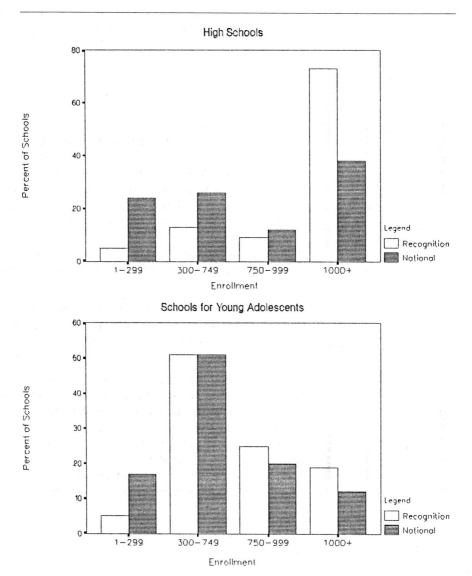

proportion of recognized schools that are the only schools at their level in their district with those that are one of a group of secondary schools in the district. Separate figures are offered for high schools and schools for young adolescents. While the data indicate that high schools are more likely than schools for young adolescents to be the sole school at their grade level in the district, the numbers reveal that in both cases, a majority of the districts represented have multiple secondary schools. These data run counter to the argument that successful programs are easier to maintain in small districts.

Table 3.5 Grade-span distribution

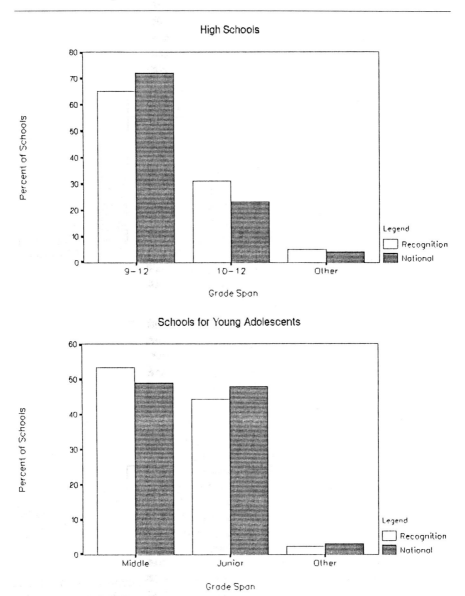

The next indicator presents evidence about an important staffing ratio. Table 3.7 compares teacher–student ratios in the schools for young adolescents with a national sample. No nationally comparable data were available at the high school level. The differences are striking. The recognition program schools allocate their resources to provide lower

Table 3.6 Single vs. multiple secondary schools in a school district

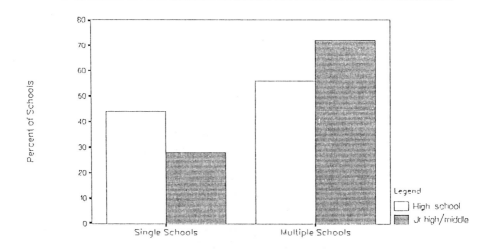

Table 3.7 Teacher:Student ratios (schools for young adolescents)

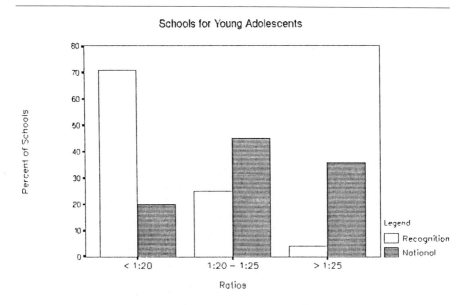

teacher–student ratios. Almost three-quarters of the schools have ratios of less than 1:20, whereas nationally only one-fifth have ratios below this level. The evidence here is very strong; these exemplary schools are committed to establishing favorable teacher–student ratios. It is also consistent with the a-forementioned finding that the recognized schools tend to spend at levels that are above their state averages.

Table 3.8   Principals' years of service

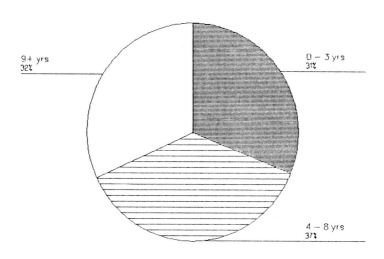

High Schools

9+ yrs
32%

0 — 3 yrs
31%

4 — 8 yrs
37%

Recognition Program

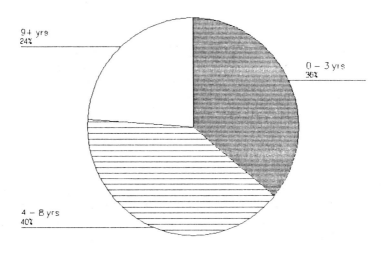

9+ yrs
24%

0 — 3 yrs
36%

4 — 8 yrs
40%

National Sample

Table 3.8   Continued

Schools for Young Adolescents

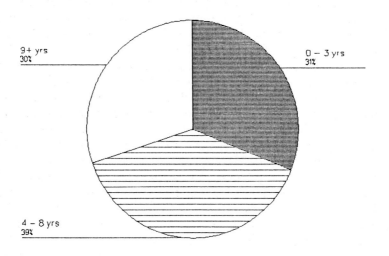

Recognition Program

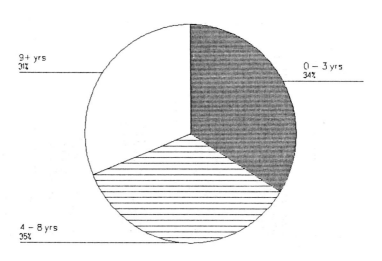

Notional Sample

Another interesting characteristic of the schools is the wide variation in the principals' years of service in the building. When dividing the principals into three groups by years of service, it is worth noting there is an almost equal proportion in each category in both the high schools and schools for young adolescents (see Table 3.8). Success does not appear to be affected by length of principal service; there are almost as many newcomers as there are long-tenured principals. Furthermore, when this indicator was matched with other success attributes (e.g., see Table 2.2), no associations were found between length of service and the attributes.

The last indicator in this category focuses on graduation requirements. Table 3.9 summarizes these data for high schools. Junior high schools and middle schools were not asked to provide these data. A summary such as this does not allow the few schools in the sample with extremely demanding requirements to be identified. However, it does portray overall trends. Several points about the data are worth mentioning. First, with the national focus on secondary education and the penchant for legislatures to raise course requirements for graduation, it is interesting to note that from 1983 to 1985 there were no significant increases in requirements among the schools receiving recognition in each of these years. Second, the formal course requirements in these schools are quite conventional — the averages for the recognized schools are no different than the averages reported for the entire nation. Clearly, it is more than just course requirements that are contributing to their success.

Table 3.9   Mean graduation requirements for high schools

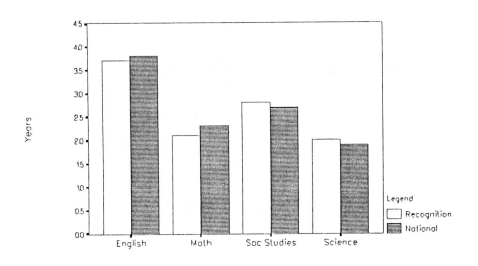

Outcomes

A wide range of outcome data were collected from each school including test score results, attendance rates, suspension rates, drop-out rates, numbers going on for further schooling, and special awards received by the school. The variety of test scores reported and the variation in presentation formats made it impossible to summarize them in any meaningful way. Likewise, reports of suspension rates involved such a range of definitions and presentation formats that it was not possible to make comparisons across the sample of recognized schools. The only comparable data available from the schools were student attendance figures, drop-out rates, and the proportion of students going on to college.

Table 3.10 summarizes student attendance data for the recognized schools relative to national data. Separate figures are presented for high schools and schools for young adolescents. The data are remarkably similar for both levels. Almost none of the recognition program schools reported average daily attendance rates below 90 per cent, while 15 per cent and 21 per cent respectively for high schools and schools for young adolescents, of the national samples had rates below 90 per cent. There was also a higher proportion of these schools with very high attendance rates. These numbers reflect what will be evident from additional information offered later in this report — these schools are exciting places to learn and students respond to that excitement by attending on a regular basis.

The last two outcome measures are reported for only the high schools. Table 3.11 displays the comparison of drop-out rates to national figures. These data provide one of the most striking differences across all the data. Students in the nation's schools are three-and-one-half times more likely to drop out of school than students in these recognized schools. A clear message is being sent to students by these schools — the staff in these schools care about students and are doing everything possible to maintain programs that meet their diverse needs.

The final outcome data reflect the proportion of graduates who enroll in four-year colleges or universities. The graphics in Table 3.12 provide clear evidence that the recognized schools are encouraging more students to pursue academic interests than are high schools in the nation as a whole. Not only are these schools doing a better job holding the enthusiastic attention of their students while they are enrolled in secondary school, they are also doing an excellent job of instilling a desire for learning that clearly is affecting their desire for post-secondary education.

This chapter has documented the diversity in the contexts for schooling both across America and across the sample of 571 exemplary secondary schools. Both the national data and the sample exhibit wide variation on a number of social indicators including demographics, organizational characteristics, and outcomes. While the sample of exemplary schools does not always match the profile for the nation as a whole, the data suggest that

Table 3.10   Student attendance

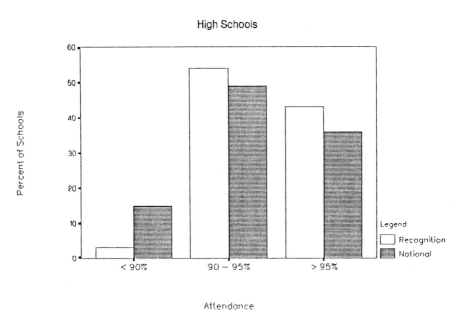

High Schools

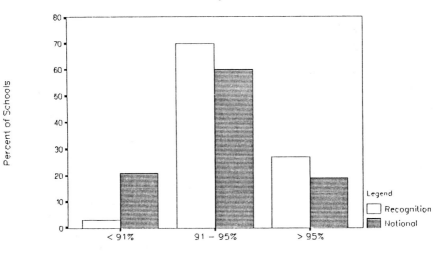

School for Young Adolescents

Table 3.11   High school dropout rates

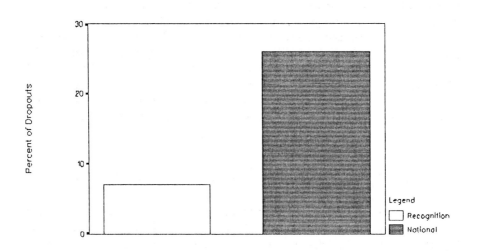

Table 3.12   Percent of high school graduates enrolling in 4yr colleges

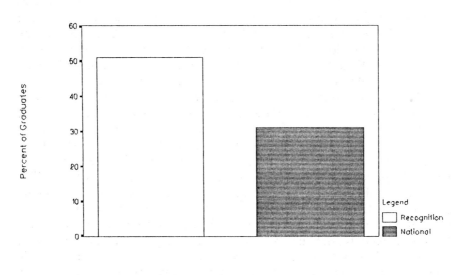

these schools are from across a wide range of contexts. Demographically, the recognized schools are located in urban and rural sites, as well as suburban ones; they serve minority populations as well as predominately white ones; and enroll students from all socio-economic backgrounds. The organizational contexts are equally diverse. Large schools and school systems as well as small ones have been recognized for excellence. A wide range of grade-level combinations are represented. The length of tenure of the building principals who lead these schools also varies. These schools report high attendance and performance, low dropout rates and high involvement of students in post-secondary school training. In summary, these good schools serve diverse social and economic settings and utilize a wide range of organizational arrangements.

School Findings in Relation to Effective Schools Framework

The data from the 571 recognized schools also offer a useful check on the validity and utility of the effective schools framework. This section reviews the fit between the characteristics of those schools and the thirteen dimensions of effectiveness identified by Purkey and Smith (1983). This comparison is presented in Table 3.13. The indicators used in the program have been categorized by dimension and the findings for high schools and schools serving early adolescents, i.e., middle schools and junior high schools, have been summarized in the table.

The data in Table 3.13 are drawn from both the nomination forms completed by the school staffs and the site visit reports prepared by independent observers. The latter are based on interviews and observations conducted in the schools. These two documents represent the data file for each school (see Chapter 2 for a full discussion of these data sources). The systematic application of Purkey and Smith's (1983) thirteen dimensions to the data from these 571 successful secondary schools is hampered because there was not always adequate data to assess all dimensions.

Some of the thirteen dimensions were adequately documented and well-developed in almost all of the schools. Strong instructional leadership, high levels of parent support and involvement, attention to recognition for performance, careful use and expansion of instructional time, high levels of collaboration and staff involvement, clear goals and high expectations, and good discipline were characteristic of almost all of the schools. The importance of these seven dimensions would appear to be strongly supported by the data from the recognized schools. For example, evidence of strong instructional leadership in the schools was found in the examples of the improvements that had been made and the problems that had been overcome. These self-reports were confirmed by the site visitors in their interviews with staff, students, and parents. However, the principal was seldom the only leader and was not always the critical one in the area of instruction. Department chairs and teachers also played significant leadership roles.

Similarly, the schools were characterized by high levels of parent and community support and by parent involvement in a limited, but important, range of school activities — fund-raising, school volunteers, extra-curricular programs, and the like. Parent involvement in instructional activities, such as tutoring, or in school planning and decision-making was reported in some sites but was less common.

The schools generally were attentive to the issue of rewards and recognition for both high performance and for improvement. Rewards were given not only for academics but for citizenship and other achievements. The schools went beyond the conventional means — honor rolls, honor societies, letters home, and scholarships — to use galleries displaying pictures of students of the month, award academic letters, convene academic periodic assemblies, and give tangible awards to students.

Learning time was often extended in these schools through the use of staff tutoring and personal assistance. This was done before and after school in many sites but some had relieved staff of non-instructional duties to make them available to students when they were not teaching. This was such a prominent feature of these schools that it seemed to the authors that the critical difference between a mediocre school and an excellent one may have less to do with how classroom time is used and more to do with the amount and use of discretionary time that extends the school schedule. High participation in extra-curricular activities also was encouraged and provided additional opportunities for learning. These programs were seen as extensions of the classroom and helped students bridge the gap between academic work and their interests. They also helped build positive relationships between teachers and students. School spirit was often described as a problem that required continual attention but most of the schools presented evidence that they were doing a good job of getting students involved.

Most of the schools were judged to have high levels of collaboration among their staffs and strong communal identities. Teacher involvement in both department and school decisions was more common than is generally found and teachers reported that they exercised considerable influence on these decisions. Staff attendance was much higher than average in these schools and staff turnover was lower.

Over 90 per cent of the schools had written educational goals and more than half regularly communicated those goals to staff, parents, and students. There was evidence that people were aware of the goals, supported them, and took them seriously. More than half were able to cite examples of how the goals affected programs, resource allocations, and other decisions. Expectations for performance were clearly high in these schools as evidenced by the standards set for promotion and graduation, their efforts to promote advanced or honors work, and the demands made on students in and outside of the classroom.

Table 3.13 Attributes of success: Relative strengths of 14 critical factors in unusually successful secondary schools

Attributes	Indicators	Conditions in high schools	Conditions in schools for young adolescents
Clear academic goals	• Presence of written goals • Evidence of actions toward goals • Consistency in statements of principals, teaching staff, and parents • Evidence of discussion and communication of goals • Identification of core values	• Over 90 per cent reported written goals and over 50 per cent reported established means of communicating goals to parents, students, and teaching staff. • There was evidence of action on goals in 50 per cent of the schools. • There was consistency in views of various groups in over 65 per cent of the schools.	• Over 90 per cent reported written goals and nearly 50 per cent reported established means of communicating goals to parents, students, and teaching staff. • There was evidence of action on goals in almost 50 per cent of the schools. • There was consistency in views of various groups in about 65 per cent of the schools.
High expectations for students	• Graduation requirements • Student reports on homework and work demands in class • School reports on changes in academic and behavioral standards. • Evidence of participation in academic competition. • Enrollments in honors or advanced placement classes.	• About 90 per cent of the schools were judged to set expectations and standards that were above average. • Formal graduation requirements varied but on the whole were similar to national norms. • Student reports on homework varied within schools from little to 3 hours depending on their course of study. There was little variation across schools.	• About 65 per cent of the schools were judged to set expectations and standards that were above average. • Student reports on homework varied within schools from little to $2\frac{1}{2}$ or 3 hours. There was less variation across schools.

Table 3.13 Continued

Attributes	Indicators	Conditions in high schools	Conditions in schools for young adolescents
Order and discipline	• Site visitor observations. • Applicants' description of climate • Identification of discipline as a problem area or an obstacle to overcome. • Data on suspensions. • Assessment of emphasis the school's climate (press).	• Orderly behavior was a strong feature of the schools with over 75 per cent rated as above average. • Discipline was identified as a problem by more than 50 per cent of the schools but nearly 75 per cent of the schools claimed to have resolved the problems. • Good discipline was seldom identified by applicants as a key factor in their schools' success.	• Orderly behavior rated above average in about 75 per cent of the schools. • Discipline was identified as a problem in about 25 per cent of the schools, but it was the problem most likely to have been resolved (90 per cent of the cases). • Discipline was identified as a major emphasis in about 40 per cent of the schools.
Rewards and incentives for students	• Student perceptions. • Applicants' descriptions of rewards and incentives.	• Nearly 75 per cent of the schools were judged to be above average in their attention to rewards and incentives for students.	• Nearly 75 per cent of the schools were judged to be above average in their attention to rewards and incentives for students.
Regular and frequent monitoring of student progress	• Applicants' descriptions of assessment and evaluation procedures. • Identification of testing procedures.	• About 60 per cent of the schools were judged to be above average in their procedures for monitoring student progress. • The proportion of schools using Minimum Competency Tests rose each year, from 70 per cent in 1983 to 80 per cent in 1985.	• About 60 per cent of the schools were judged to be above average in their procedures for monitoring student progress. • The proportion of schools using Minimum Competency Tests rose each year from 63 per cent in 1983 to 76 per cent in 1985.

Opportunities for meaningful student responsibility and participation	• Application information on student government, extracurricular programs and participation, and community programs. • Assessments of student autonomy in the school. • Student perceptions.	• Schools reported higher participation rates in extracurricular programs, about 70 per cent. About 25 per cent were judged exceptional in their efforts to increase participation. • Almost 65 per cent of the schools reported unusual or exceptionally active student governments. • About 50 per cent of the schools were judged to permit more student autonomy than is typical but only 10 per cent were judged exceptional on this dimension.	• Schools reported high participation rates in extra-curricular programs, about 70 per cent on average. Only 10 per cent of the schools were judged exceptional in their efforts to increase participation. • About 33 per cent of the schools reported unusual or exceptionally active student governments. • About 25 per cent of the schools were judged to permit more student autonomy than is typical but only 5 per cent were judged exceptional on this dimension.
Teacher efficacy	• Site visitor interviews with teaching staff. • Applicant reports of procedures for staff participation. • Assessments of the amount of teacher autonomy. • Assessments of teacher influence in the school.	• High efficacy was the norm, with over 90 per cent of the schools judged to be above average. • High participation in planning was reported in over 75 per cent of the schools. • Teacher autonomy was judged to be above average in 75 per cent of the schools and exceptional in about 10 per cent. • Overall staff influence was judged higher than average in most schools.	• High efficacy was the norm with about 75 per cent of the schools judged to be above average. • High participation in planning was reported in over 80 per cent of the schools. • Teacher autonomy was judged to be above average in about 66 per cent of the schools and exceptional in about one in eight.

Table 3.13 Continued

Attributes	Indicators	Conditions in high schools	Conditions in schools for young adolescents
Rewards and incentives for teachers	• Site visitor report on teacher perceptions. • Applicants' descriptions of policies and procedures. • Assessment of overall reward and incentive structure.	• Slightly less than 50 per cent of the schools were judged to be above average in their attention to rewards and incentives for teachers. Only a few were judged exceptional. • About 80 per cent of the schools described specific recognition policies or activities. • About 80 per cent of the schools provided opportunities for advanced study.	• About 65 per cent of the schools were judged above average in their attention to rewards and incentives for teachers. Slightly above 10 per cent were judged exceptional. • Almost all of the schools had specific recognition policies or activities. • Only a third of the schools described opportunities for advanced study.
Concentration on academic learning time	• Classroom observations. • Applicant reports on actions to increase instructional time. • Estimates of homework by students.	• Site visitors reported almost all classes began on time and worked to the end. 'On task' behavior was judged to be high in nearly 90 per cent of the schools. There were few disruptions. • Almost all schools reported having homework policies, but student estimates varied widely.	• Site visitors reported classes began on time and students worked to the end. 'On task' behavior was judged to be high in about 65 per cent of the schools. There were few disruptions. • Almost all schools reported having homework policies, but student estimates varied widely.

Positive school climate

- Attendance data for staff and students, data on discipline.
- Staff perceptions.
- Student perceptions.
- Site visitor observations on climate, teacher–student relations, facilities, etc.

- School climate was rated as exceptional in nearly 50 per cent of the schools and above average in almost all of them.
- School spirit was identified as a problem in about 40 per cent of the schools, but most claimed to have resolved it.
- Student attendance averaged about 94 per cent, with only 4 per cent of the schools reporting average attendance below 90 per cent.
- Teacher attendance averaged 95 per cent with only 1 per cent of the schools reporting average attendance below 90 per cent.

- School climate was rated as exceptional in 25 per cent of the schools and above average in almost all of them.
- School spirit was identified as a problem in about 15 per cent of the schools but most claimed to have resolved it.
- Student attendance averaged over 94 per cent with only 2 per cent of the schools reporting average attendance below 90 per cent.
- Teacher attendance averaged about 95 per cent with no schools reporting average attendance under 90 per cent.

Administrative leadership

- Interviews with staff and parents.
- Interviews with administrators.
- Applicant's description of administrative roles.
- Assessment of administrative involvement in instruction.

- Principals averaged over 7 years of service. Over 20 per cent had in excess of 10 years of service.
- Principals were judged to be highly involved in instruction in about half of the schools.

- Principals averaged over 7 years of service. About 20 per cent had in excess of 10 years of service.
- Principals were judged to be highly involved in instruction in about 60 per cent of the schools and their involvement was judged exceptional in about 15 per cent of the schools.

63

Table 3.13 Continued

Attributes	Indicators	Conditions in high schools	Conditions in schools for young adolescents
Well-articulated curriculum	• Applicants' descriptions of articulation procedures. • Site visitors' interviews with teachers in special programs.	• All applicants claimed to have articulation procedures and almost all claimed curriculum review procedures. • Communication among teaching staff was judged to be above average in more than 75 per cent of the schools and there were few instances of interdisciplinary teaching or inter-departmental cooperation.	• Almost all applicants claimed to have curriculum articulation and review procedures. Yet communication among teaching staff was judged to be above average in slightly over 50 per cent of the schools. More than 50 per cent of the schools reported some form of team teaching.
Evaluation for instructional improvement.	• Description of testing program. • Examples of uses of test data. • Mechanisms for evaluation described.	• Over 95 per cent of the schools reported use of standardized testing programs. • The number of schools using minimum competency tests measured from 70 per cent in 1983 to 80 per cent in 1985. • Over 90 per cent of the schools described formal curriculum review procedures. • Utilization of evaluations was judged to be above average in more than half of the schools.	• Over 95 per cent of the schools reported use of standardized testing programs. • The number of schools using minimum competency tests increased from 63 per cent in 1983 to 76 per cent in 1985. • Over 95 per cent of the schools described formal curriculum review procedures. • Utilization of evaluations was judged to be above average in about 40 per cent of the schools.

Community support and involvement

- Parents' perceptions.
- Teachers' perceptions.
- Applicants' descriptions of mechanism for parent, community, and business involvement.
- Assessment of overall community role in the schools.

- Communication of evaluation results to the public was judged strong in slightly less than half of the schools.
- Parent participation was judged to be above average in 80 per cent of the schools and exceptional in 25 per cent of them.
- School/community relations were identified as having been a problem by half of the schools but in 85 per cent of these cases, it was described as a problem overcome and turned into a strength.
- The activity of business and civic organizations was judged to be above average in over two-thirds of the schools and the data suggest growing involvement in the schools from 1983 to 1985.

- Communication of evaluation results to the public was judged strong in about 40 per cent of the schools.
- Parent participation was judged above average in about 60 per cent of the schools and exceptional in about 10 per cent.
- School/community relations were identified as having been a problem by 30 per cent of the schools, but in 75 per cent of these cases, it was identified as a problem overcome and listed as a strength.
- The activity of business and civic organizations was judged to be above average in about half of the schools.

Student discipline was generally very good as assessed by the number of suspensions per 100 students, student attendance, the school's own report on student behavior, and the site visitor's observations. Some schools reported that discipline had been a concern in the past but they had been able to resolve the problems.

On the other hand, the importance of several of Purkey and Smith's (1983) dimensions could not be clearly determined. These dimensions received only partial or weak support from the data on the 571 schools. There was some evidence of the building level autonomy implicit in school-site management but it was seldom formally acknowledged and there was apparently considerable variation in the amount of discretion given to the principals by district officials. While the school staff gave evidence of being permitted to develop policies and programs to meet educational needs, these policies were initiated at both the school level and by the district. School staff did describe considerable latitude for revising or developing curricula but there also was evidence of strong district influence in this area.

Support for the importance of staff stability also was mixed. There was low turnover among teaching staff as might be predicted by Purkey and Smith but there was high turnover among principals. Similarly, the data did not support the critical importance of school-wide staff development. These schools provided many staff development opportunities but the focus was typically on the individual teacher or the department rather than on the entire school staff and there was not always a clear focus to these efforts.

For two of the dimensions, curriculum articulation and district support, there was simply not enough data available to make an assessment. There is nothing about the recognized schools that suggests that these dimensions are not important but neither is there any empirical evidence to support their significance.

Summary

Successful secondary schools are clearly not static institutions. Their vitality and dynamism is not fully captured in these data summaries. Reviews of common social indicators such as demographics and outcomes or even comparisons with characteristics identified by effective schools research do not begin to capture the full story behind excellence in American secondary education. In these schools teachers, students, and administrators actively pursue school goals, addressing and overcoming obstacles that would deter others less committed to success. School leaders insist on high standards and are willing to take risks to meet them. They strive to create the best possible conditions for teaching, and, as a result are able to assemble talented, dedicated staffs. The hallmarks of these schools are caring, positive environments and the creation of strong, supportive relationships between adults and adolescents.

Vision. Respect. Incentives. Caring. Action. Outreach. These are the keys of success in these schools. What emerges from the analyses of data drawn from these successful secondary schools are six broad themes:

- active leadership
- professional work environments
- positive learning environments
- broad community involvement
- continuous school improvement
- service to all students.

Each of these themes is developed in one of the following six chapters. Each chapter uses narrative from the school files to show the flavor and character of excellence in the schools. However, the reader is cautioned not to regard these themes as a simple prescription for success. There is no single formula or combination of factors that will ensure success. The themes and the examples drawn from these successful schools are presented in the hope that they will encourage more dialogue about excellence and offer concrete examples for practitioners to consider as options for action.

The themes arise from analyses of data on school characteristics, reports by site visitors, and self-reports by the schools on factors contributing to success. They are consistent with the effective schools dimensions most frequently found in the schools. What distinguishes these themes, however, and the schools that model them is their focus on the importance to school success of people, their talents, their energies, their relationships, and their commitment to educational excellence.

The discussions of the six themes include examples of policies and practices taken from school nomination forms or site visitor reports. The examples illustrate the variety of ways in which the themes are realized in the schools. They demonstrate how they can be put into practice. These brief vignettes have been selected because they shed light on the dynamic and human dimensions of school success.

Original National Data Sources for Tables in this Chapter

Table 3.1   Metropolitan Status of Communities: Market Data Retrieval, 1985. (Unpublished data).

Table 3.2   National Center for Education Statistics (1985) *Condition of Education*, Washington, DC (p.26).

Table 3.3   Market Data Retrieval (1985), *1985 Educational Mailing Lists and Marketing Guide*, Shelton, CT.

Table 3.4   National Center for Education Statistics, 'Public Elementary and Secondary Schools: Fall 1982' *Historical Report (NCES 85–1–3)*, Washington, DC.

Table 3.5   *Ibid.*

Successful Secondary Schools

Table 3.6   No nationally comparative data are available.

Table 3.7   Valentine, J., Clark, D. C., Nickerson, N. C., Jr and Keege, J. W. (1981) *The Middle Level Principalship Vol. I: A Survey of Middle Level Principals and Programs*, Reston, VA: National Association of Secondary School Principals (p.49).

Table 3.8   *Ibid* (p.12).

Table 3.9   Education Commission of the States (n.d.), 'Minimum high school graduation requirements in the states, as of November 1985', *Clearinghouse Notes*.

Table 3.10   **High Schools**: National Center for Education Statistics, High Schools and Beyond — First follow-up, 1982. **Schools for Young Adolescents**: Valentine, J. *et al.* op-cit. (p.50).

Table 3.11   National Center for Education Statistics (1985), *The Condition of Education*, Washington DC.

Table 3.12   National Center for Education Statistics (1985), *Digest of Education Statistics*, Washington, DC.

68

Chapter 4

Leadership in Action: Setting the Direction*

Effective leadership played a critical role in the schools selected for recognition. Parents, students, and teachers were unanimous in citing the work of school leaders as a major and essential factor in the success of their schools. While other factors were seen as important to school success, typically leadership was credited with providing vision and the motivation to create and sustain the conditions that led to national recognition. School leaders initiated improvements and supported, encouraged and integrated faculty initiatives. They set the tone and were the prime forces in creating positive climates for teaching and learning.

The contribution of leaders to school excellence also has been a major topic in the research literature (Greenfield, 1987; Sheive and Schoenheit, 1987). Particular attention has been drawn to the role of principals as instructional leaders. Yet, many of the reform reports did not address the central question of how educational leaders influence instructional work in their schools.

Bureaucratic and Cultural Linkages

Two different schools of thought have dominated discussion of leadership in schools. The first, influenced by a long tradition of organizational research, suggests that schools are loosely linked organizations, providing leaders with only limited opportunities to influence teachers' work (Bidwell, 1965; Weick, 1976). This view was summarized by James March (1978): 'Changing education by changing educational administration is like changing the course of the Mississippi by spitting in the Allegheny'. Another perspective receiving considerable recent attention and interest has been spawned by the effective schools research. This literature argues that strong

---

*This chapter represents an expansion and revision of a paper by Bruce L. Wilson and William A. Firestone which appeared in the September 1987 issue of *Educational Leadership*.

leadership does have a significant impact on the quality of instruction (Brookover, Beady, Flood, Schweitzer and Wisenbacker, 1979).

These seemingly contradictory perspectives can be reconciled by examining the full range of linkage mechanisms in schools. Linkage mechanisms are structures, procedures, or ways of thinking that permit leaders to coordinate people's activities. Linkages can be viewed as tight when the activity of person A leads to some kind of desired activity by person B, or when person A has considerable assurance that person B will behave in a certain way. They are loose when the activity of person A has little relationship to the desired activity of person B, or when person A has little assurance that person B will behave in a desired manner. Linkages range from job descriptions to clique structures (of teachers as well as students), from schedules to unwritten rules about how to address students, from supervision conferences to informal conversations. While schools may be loosely linked organizations in the traditional bureaucratic sense, they make use of other linkages that were not fully examined in the past. By examining and orchestrating the full range of linkages, school leaders can provide strong support for effective instruction. Indeed, school leaders can enhance the effectiveness of instruction and over time can have a strong impact on the quality of outcomes.

Researchers agree that schools are more loosely linked than other work organizations. While they do not always agree on what the relevant linkage mechanisms are, most commentators focus on the lack of strong bureaucratic ties, especially those related to formal authority (Miles, 1981; Meyer and Rowan, 1978). Bureaucratic linkages are the formal, enduring arrangements in a school that guide its operations. These include its rules, procedures, and authority relations. One group of researchers refers to them as the 'prescribed framework' of the organization (Ranson, Hinings and Greenwood, 1980). They are the formal mechanisms designed to control the behavior of organizational members. But they comprise only one approach to coordination of work.

To understand the potential impact of leaders on instruction, however, one must move beyond bureaucratic linkages and consider cultural ones as well. The professional culture of the school is another factor that contributes to coordination. Cultural linkages include the system of collectively accepted meanings, beliefs, values, and assumptions that organizational members (teachers) use to guide their regular, daily actions and interpret their surroundings (Pettigrew, 1979). These linkages have been likened to the glue that holds organizations together (Deal and Kennedy, 1982). A full understanding of a school's culture and the leader's role in it requires an examination of its content — shared meanings — and the means of communicating that content.

Because organizational culture is more elusive than the prescribed frameworks associated with bureaucracy, it has rarely been considered as a locus of linkage mechanisms. Yet a growing business literature suggests that an important management responsibility is the creation of coherence between an organization's basic purpose and its larger environment (Deal and Kennedy, 1982; Peters and Waterman, 1982). Recent research in schools also suggests that culture influences organizational performance (Cusick, 1983; Lightfoot, 1983; Rossman, Corbett and Firestone, 1988). Strong cultures with appropriate content can promote excellence. Leaders can play an important role in creating, maintaining, or changing such cultures.

Cultural linkages, the tools that school leaders most frequently use to improve instruction, have rarely been examined in the past. But, like bureaucratic linkages, they are too weak to make a great difference by themselves. Before we can consider the interaction of bureaucratic and cultural linkages, we must first have a clear understanding of each linkage, how it affects instruction, and the role of the leader.

Linkages, Instruction, and School Leaders

The relationships between various linkages and instruction is established in a number of ways. Briefly, bureaucratic linkages establish constraints and opportunities on what, where, to whom, and for how long, teachers teach. Cultural linkages shape what teachers want to do or how they take advantage of those opportunities or deal with the constraints. Let's look at the possible effects of each kind of linkage on instruction.

Bureaucratic Linkages

The most common ways in which principals are thought to affect instruction are through the close supervision and evaluation of teachers' activities. These are viewed as the primary bureaucratic means of controlling instruction and recent literature emphasizes the importance of engaging in frequent supervision. State and local policies also emphasize supervision and evaluation and often define both the processes and the frequency with which they are to occur. Yet supervision is not a frequent activity (Newberg and Glatthorn, 1983; Morris, Crowson, Porter-Gehrie and Hurwitz, 1984). The state and local minimums often become the maximuns. Principals, overworked with administrative duties, often find it difficult to do more. Second, there are often no incentives for leaders to do more than pay lip service to the process of supervision. There are few rewards for giving supervision top priority, and there are few sanctions for doing the minimum. In fact, the easiest path is to negotiate a bargain with the staff that in effect says: 'I won't demand much if you don't give me trouble'. Finally, effective supervision requires follow-up work. Resources must be committed to activities that can improve noted deficiencies. Most leaders in school have had little experience in solving instructional problems.

This argument that supervision is, in fact, seldom the crucial bureaucratic linkage in schools that it is held to be does not mean that bureaucratic linkages have no value. Rather, more attention should be paid to bureaucratic linkages that focus on the indirect control of teachers' behavior. These are much easier for leaders to work with and may have more influence on teacher behavior. How instruction is carried out depends in part on the way that work is formally structured. For example, creation of common planning periods encourages cooperation and coordination. Use of departmental examinations insures thorough coverage of the curriculum. School leaders have considerable influence over key work structures such as these. By altering these and similar work structures, leaders can affect how teachers interact with each other and their attitudes about their work.

For example, the leader is a key factor in controlling organizational constraints on the amount of *time* students spend on academic tasks. Leaders can have a powerful impact by protecting classrooms from external interruptions and altering activities to maximize instructional time or contact between students and faculty. The policy at *Benjamin N. Cordozo High School* in New York City is to maximize instructional time. This has been accomplished in a variety of ways:

> The class passing time, period to period, was decreased and the time itself added to the length of the period. The home room period was shortened . . . The term-calendar was adjusted so that classes would start virtually at the beginning of the semester and continue to the very end. Testing and survey days that previously took a full day were reduced to half days and classes held for the remainder of time. The public address system is not to be used during instructional periods. In addition to the faculty conference, the principal's cabinet pinpointed the emphasis on time use and developed a series of supervisory approaches to encourage its maximization. Assistant principals followed up on this emphasis, coaching teachers in departmental conferences on effective strategies. Teachers were encouraged to tighten their classroom routines and classroom management. Where appropriate, teachers were encouraged to place homework on prepared handout sheets, rather than give it verbally or take the time to write it on the chalkboard. Where previously student social trips were taken on school days now these can only be taken during vacation time.

Second, policies about *class size* and the *grouping* of students have important effects on the way classroom instruction is delivered. By controlling the number of children in a particular room and the mix of gender, race, or ages, the school leader can influence the quality of instruction and, ultimately, student achievement.

Shaker Heights High School in Ohio offers a useful example. The proportion of black students in this school has increased over the past two decades from 8 per cent to over 40 per cent. Academic excellence has always been a hallmark of the school and the challenge was to continue that record of excellence with a changing student population. The first response was to create a tracking system that resulted in *de facto* segregation within the school and a negative reaction from the black community. A study by Western Michigan University found there was peer pressure to stay in the lower track, that it was too easy to get in and too hard to get out, that students felt you got less work in those classes, and there was a lack of bridges to move up. The result of the study was a set of fourteen recommendations that the district and school are trying to implement. One of the policies adopted was to open all levels of classes to all students who wanted in. The decision about the appropriate level was given to the students and their parents. Through involving a wide range of people, support has been garnered for improvements. As the site visitor commented:

> The issue is on everyone's agenda and there is a genuine concern about doing better. They have accepted it as their problem, one that they are willing to struggle with until they find some answers.

Leaders can also influence the working patterns of teachers by arranging physical space and free time to promote norms of *collegiality* and *experimentation*, both of which have been associated with effectiveness (Little, 1983). The overall success of *Princeton Junior High* in Cincinnati, Ohio was primarily attributed to the uniqueness of the organizational structure which facilitates collegiality and experimentation. Students are assigned to a five-teacher academic team. Each team consists of an English, math, science, social studies and reading teacher. One teacher is designated as the team leader and is responsible for chairing meetings of the team and other administrative responsibilities. All teachers on the team share a common daily planning period when discussions and decisions can be made on ways to better assist their students. The power of this arrangement is that teachers can plan together every day, they can achieve greater consistency, it is easier to share ideas and materials, there is no question about whether everyone is 'on board' on a given issue, and there is a stronger sense of mutual concern and support.

Leaders often have some discretionary *resources* (money, release time, faculty meeting time, materials) at their disposal and, through their judicious distribution, they can greatly enhance innovative instructional activities. Wealthy communities often provide more of these discretionary resources. However, the staff at *Byng High School*, a poor school with almost half of their students from low-income families, have improvised creatively and provide a model for less-wealthy districts. By using donated land, stockpiling building materials when a favorable price presented itself, and having construction work done by vocational students and maintenance staff, they have created a masterpiece facility. But more important than the physical plant itself is the pride engendered by the involvement of the entire school community. As one observer noted: 'The teachers don't think of themselves as poor, they think of themselves as resourceful'. In building such an image they have created a climate that is most conducive to learning.

Finally, *knowledge* and *skills* can serve as linkages. Leaders can encourage the use of previously unused or under-used skills within a classroom as well as networking those skills among teachers. Leaders can also encourage teachers to seek new knowledge and facilitate that activity by recommending training sessions, providing resources for attendance at conferences, or planning school in-service programs.

In suburban *Wyoming High School* (Ohio) declining enrollments has been a major concern, and the primary issue was how to keep excitement and enthusiasm alive at the same time. The faculty was projected to decline to twenty-five (from a 1983 staff of thirty-three) by the end of the 1980s. The principal has worked closely with the superintendent and the staff to plan for this decline while protecting the staff. A mock-up of the high school schedule under these conditions demonstrated that the curriculum would not be affected if some staff held multiple certifications and classes were somewhat larger. The district is supporting those teachers who are seeking additional certificates. The district also has supported other teachers in preparation for other jobs in the district or elsewhere. By working one-on-one with teachers to prepare for the future and involving them in planning, the principal has managed to maintain high morale and commitment to the school.

Bureaucratic linkages, or the structural arrangements that facilitate or inhibit productive instruction, have received a great deal of attention in the literature. As suggested earlier, too much attention is paid to the more direct means of control — supervision and evaluation — and less on indirect control of teacher behavior through manipulation of structural arrangements. We have suggested a number of ways in which school leaders can indirectly affect the quality of instruction through the alteration of work structures. However, that is only part of the answer. In addition, leaders also must pay careful attention to cultural linkages.

Cultural Linkages

Cultural linkages work on the consciousness of teachers by clarifying what they do and defining their commitment to the task (Firestone and Wilson, 1985: Rossman, Corbett, and Firestone, 1988). Task definitions create the standards and expectations that are so important for instruction. Commitment is an issue because supervision processes are weak and because so much depends on the level of discretionary effort of the teaching staff.

The creation of a strong culture requires a sense of shared purpose among the faculty, students, parents, and community. This is the foundation upon which many school staffs have built their success. As one site visitor noted, 'There is a consistency in the belief system'. As might be expected, an operating consensus about goals and values cannot be constructed simply by reviewing lists of formal goal statements or by reaching agreement on what to write down. In some cases, the written statements of goals prepared by the staff of these recognized schools are no different than those found in most schools; they are full of the same abstract platitudes and educational ideals. What is different is that the goals reflect a shared value system that is taken seriously and is translated into daily actions that affect day-to-day activities. *Colville High School* in rural eastern Washington offers a clear example:

> We have five 'desired student outcome goals' that were adopted by a school-community committee. They are reviewed annually, are in every year's staff handbook, and form the basis for all major curriculum decisions. They also form the basis for accreditation visits and evaluation of the total school program. These goals are communicated directly to all students by the principal each year and by all the staff before each semester's advisory session. They form the basis for all student scheduling and counselling sessions. The goals are elaborated in a weekly newspaper column by the principal and a quarterly newsletter to parents.

Why do goals come alive in some schools instead of being put in a file to be paraded out at accreditation time? Part of the answer to this question lies in the commitment of policy-makers and administrators to follow up and assess progress toward goals. These schools make use of data from multiple sources to regularly refine and redefine their goals, as accounts from two schools clearly illustrate:

> The school's goal setting begins with the principal's evaluation of year-end recommendations, evaluation by the community/teacher/student committees, student cabinet report, PTA Board recommendations, and parent/student questionnaires developed in conjunction with special projects. The district goals set annually by administrators are reviewed, as well as test results, later student achievement in high school, and community feedback. Proposed goals are directly related to identified student needs. While yearly goals are discussed in the first faculty meeting of the year and the department chairperson's first meeting, there is a continuing emphasis throughout the year upon revision of goals to meet changing student needs. (*Rosemont Junior High*, La Crescenta, CA.)

> The instructional goals have been addressed and developed through faculty meetings, class meetings, open meetings for parents, and teacher advisory meetings. Some of these goals were planned topics at faculty/Board of Education dialogue breakfasts. In every en-

deavor, whether it be academic or extra-curricular, these goals are explained, discussed, pursued and refined by students, teachers, and parents. (*Clayton High School*, Clayton, MO).

One of the turn-around schools attributes its success to a set of clearly written goals. In the words of the principal, 'Common goals are a must. All actions can be related to those goals, and everyone understands why things are being done in a certain manner'. An urban school facing many problems used resources from a Danforth Foundation grant to align its curriculum and governance structure with twelve democratic principles. The school maintains much of its success is attributable to a conscientious effort to apply these principles in every aspect of school life.

The other part lies in the schools' commitment to traditional values or their efforts to build a tradition. As the principal at *Cass Technical High School* in Detroit, Michigan commented:

> The major reasons for the success of Cass Tech lie primarily in its history, not in the last few years. The tradition of accomplishment is deeply ingrained in this school community. Students come to Cass Tech feeling the responsibility of living up to the school's reputation and strive to meet that responsibility. Solidarity is an excellent word to describe the Cass Tech connection. This solidarity held the school together through many transitions and evokes friendly responses world wide whenever the Cass association is revealed.

Perhaps the most important role goals can play is defining a clear vision for the school. One of the biggest challenges facing the nation's secondary schools is regaining a clear sense of their purpose or mission. The commitment to the concept of the comprehensive high school sometimes has meant that secondary schools have been pressured to try to be all things to all people — an impossible task. Far too often, this has led to lower standards and a watered-down curriculum. The primary commitment of staff and students has been to get through the day. By articulating a set of goals and using them to make choices and guide actions, schools establish a clear identity, a significant characteristic of these unusually successful schools, and build staff commitment to a common mission. These institutional identities vary markedly from school to school as these two quite different examples reveal:

> I am deeply committed to improving the quality of human interactions within our school and district. I believe we will continue to improve as long as we keep this as our highest internal value. Specifically, I believe every adult is a role model and must be aware of his/her influence on young minds. Ted Sizer said that when two or more of us are gathered, values are being transmitted. My goal is to send a clear message to everyone that caring, commitment, responsibility, love of learning, self-discipline, and initiative are

values that this school deeply, sincerely believes in. It is every person's responsibility to model these behaviors inside the classroom and outside, I want these modeled behaviors to so permeate our school climate that a peron cannot speak of the school without also describing these as 'what we are'. (*Seaholm High School*, Birmingham, MI).

The vision of this school is to use the scientific process as a fundamental learning strategy, a means through which to develop critical thinking and problem-solving skills, and a method for use in gathering and organizing data. Whether the subject is language, arts, social studies, math, science, or computer study, students are taught to approach the available learning through the discipline of science. By developing a command of the scientific process, skills of observing, classifying, hypothesizing, inferring, communicating, analyzing, and problem solving, students gain the desire and means to discover and learn throughout life. (*School #59 Science Magnet*, Buffalo, NY).

It is the clarity and power of the vision that establishes a unique identity for the school and strengthens the bonds of loyalty among members of the school community. It is important to stress that vision alone will not bring success to a school. Vision must be accompanied by action. In the above example of the Buffalo, NY, *Science Magnet* for seventh and eighth grades where the scientific process was used as the fundamental learning strategy, the school board worked closely with the local Zoological Society to build a school on the zoo grounds. Sharing jointly in the planning, financing, and designing of the school program, the zoo is available to the school on a daily basis. Students have experiences such as observing a bison giving birth and participating in a zebra autopsy and are able to do field work on a regular basis.

Another way that cultural themes contribute to commitment and define standards is through stories or rituals. Stories include myths and legends as well as actual events. They positively or negatively emphasize valued traits of members of the school community. The leader's goal is for the stories to reinforce preferred values. Regardless of their basis in fact, if such stories are told effectively, they become powerful tools for making people believe the school really works a certain way and that its members should act accordingly. Leaders can manage the flow of stories and other information about their schools.

An example of constructive stories that reinforce positive views of how to enhance discipline in the schools is reported by Metz (1978) in her study of desegregated schools. The principal had tried to communicate that such problems were rare individual outbursts that teachers could easily handle. A recalcitrant student said: 'I ain't going to study today, 'cause I don't feel like it'. The teacher just grinned and said, 'Well, I'm going to give you a book just in case you change your mind'. In five minutes the student was studying. Such a story carries the message of an important value which was prized in that school and the professional way in which that value was inculcated in the mind of an initially uncooperative student.

Rituals are another way of communicating the school's culture. These repeated ceremonial activities include assemblies, teacher meetings, and parent–teacher conferences. A leader can also create and shape rituals. By giving priority to academic assemblies or granting rewards for especially effective teachers, leaders can reinforce preferred behaviors. By using faculty meetings to discuss instruction, leaders can build collegiality and commitment to improvement. In some cases, leaders themselves may actually become a symbol. The principal's own deportment can symbolize to other adults and students in the school a new order in which education is taken seriously (Lightfoot, 1983).

The principal at *Northview High School* in Grand Rapids, Michigan, mentioned the annual ritual of an academic convocation as the most important thing the school does:

> Each May an outstanding honors convocation takes place which is sponsored by the school and parent–teacher organization. All students, grades 9–12, who have maintained a 'B' are honored in the school. Special awards are given to seniors who maintain a 'B + ' or better and to seniors who are selected as the top students in academic and practical arts areas. The speaker for the convocation is chosen from the faculty, and the ceremony takes place in a beautiful neighborhood church and is followed by a luncheon for the top senior honors students and their parents. It is truly a school/community affair with 700 parents and families filling the church.

Equally important in communicating the culture of the school are the specialized, informal communication roles that facilitate the transfer of stories and the operation of rituals. These include faculty gossips and secretarial sources, among others. Expectations of leaders are often communicated to others in this manner. Stories and rituals build meaning through the ongoing flow of communications that ensure they are appropriately interpreted. While a variety of people may fill those communication roles, the principal can structure situations to maximize the exposure of key story-tellers.

A creative example of the use of story-tellers comes from *Lincoln, Nebraska High School* where the principal has taken advantage of the enthusiasm of a group of parents as a way to communicate to the community the positive qualities of the school:

> This parent group works very hard at telling the school's story to the community. The members have produced a videotape describing

school programs, and they show this videotape to service organizations and other interested groups throughout the community in order to help people better understand the strong school program.

Finally, school leaders themselves are usually the central communicators of the culture. Anyone familiar with the day-to-day experience of being a school leader is acutely aware of the multiple, impromptu opportunities that exist to interact with teachers, students, and parents. By being more intentional and consistent in their use of these hundreds of interactions, leaders may be able to constructively influence the culture for instruction.

An excellent example of the power of communication in a school comes from *Redmond High School* in an affluent community outside of Seattle, Washington. Morale was poor among students and staff because of administrative turnover that resulted in inconsistency and lack of direction. Climate has improved significantly with stabilization of the administrative team. A primary tool has been improved communications. There are now clearly defined goals, objectives, and expectations. Communication with staff and parents has been increased through high visibility of administrators in halls and classrooms, non-evaluative classroom visits, and frequent visits to the faculty lounge. The institution of period-faculty meetings where the principal meets regularly with small groups of the staff to discuss areas of faculty interest has provided for greater input and interchange.

Two additional examples of how principals have translated their visions into constructive actions illustrate how programs for all students, not just the academically talented, can be created:

> This school enjoys an outstanding reputation for its work with the academically talented students. The number of National Merit Finalists and Commended Students, unusually high scores on Advanced Placement exams, successful academic teams, national and international winners in chemistry competitions, large numbers of academic scholarships, and so forth, justify the school's reputation for its work with the academically talented student. The principal's vision, however, goes beyond success with these very capable students. Even though these programs are being closely monitored and the school is in search of ways to improve them, the principal has a mission to see that the programs for all students are comparable to the ones for the academically talented students. The results are that in mathematics the enrollment has increased from 64 per cent of the student body to over 90 per cent. The chemistry course, entitled, 'Chemistry for the Other Half', has received national recognition. A full-time counselor was employed to work with no more than 15 students at a time to place order in their lives. Many of these students are responding positively in their academic studies. A new work-study program was implemented. This program brings the students in contact with the community. In add-

ition to adding courses, an in-service program to help teachers better work with the third-quartile students has been implemented. Teachers have had workshops in the Myers-Briggs Learning Styles, Rita Dunn Learning Styles, and Madeline Hunter Teaching Techniques. A program of having teachers visit each other within the building is in progress. (*Clayton High School*, Clayton, MO).

The principal holds a vision of a school without failure. He is working toward success and recognition for all students. This vision is realized by: (1) a triangular approach to school improvement. This involves teachers, students, and parents interacting with one another around priority learning goals; (2) seeking improvement in parent involvement; (3) continuing growth in curriculum and instruction, staff development is being offered to improve the skills of teaching for staff and the skills of learning for students; (4) continuing to place an emphasis on student self-concept and esteem to undergird a solid academic program; and (5) continuing to expand extra-curricular activities as a priority activity. To make places where every student can feel comfortable, establish relationships, and grow is a final priority. (*Sacajawea Junior High*, Spokane, WA).

A vision, a shared philosophy, forms the basis for decisive action and the creation of a shared moral order. These are essential ingredients of successful schools. They often are the result of strong leadership and they lead to the creation of a community in which educational leadership and progress can be sustained.

No single linkage is likely to have a dramatic impact on the instructional program. Rather, effective school leaders use a number of relatively weak means of control or coordination of teachers over the course of the school day and year. The problem is that these interactions are so numerous and disconnected that their focus is often blurred. The leader's task is to develop a clear vision of the school's purposes, a vision that gives primacy to instruction, and then to employ it consistently during these frequent interactions. The evidence suggests that the recognized schools use bureaucratic linkages to create opportunities for teachers to act on that vision, and, at the same time, use cultural linkages to ensure that the vision can become part of the teachers' own professional culture.

Two further issues need clarification. The first focuses on leadership styles and the second on who provides leadership in these schools.

What is most striking about this collection of schools is the diversity of leadership styles. No one leadership style appears to be dominant. Great differences are exhibited by principals and others in leadership positions in how they lead their schools. What seems to matter most is the fit between the style of the principal and the various subcultures in the school community. In some cases, there are dynamic, powerful principals who seem to be everywhere and orchestrating everything; for example, at *Dixie Hollins High School* in St Petersburg, Florida:

> The teachers credit the principal with the good morale among the faculty. They indicated that he was so positive and upbeat that it was impossible to get down on kids or on the school....Parents, students, and faculty give much credit to the principal. He is always around, he is positive, fair, color blind (a racially diverse school), firm, and consistent. He keeps looking for new projects and new ways to improve the school.

In other cases, the principals are collegial and low-key, relying on persuasion, delegation, and their ability to select and develop strong faculty members, as in this report from *Artesia High School* in Lakewood, California:

> [The principal] was excited about the fact that the school has returned the dignity of the teaching profession to teachers. Teachers at this school are not burned out, on the contrary, are excited and stimulated. Again, teachers are buying into this school and are in control of the school's destiny. They know they are accountable for their actions and must assume responsibility. This is her 'role-reversal' theme. There is clear leadership emerging and developing among the faculty because of the fact that they have had assignments in terms of school reform and are responsible for the success of these particular actions. She thinks there is an impressive 'critical mass' of leading faculty at the school in a position to make even more exciting things happen.

The reference to leadership throughout this discussion rather than to the principal has been intentional. While it is acknowledged that the principal is a primary force, leadership in secondary schools tends to be dispersed. Seldom do all of the desired qualities or all of the required energy reside in one person. In most of the schools, there are a number of people who can and do take leadership roles at different times. Assistant principals, department chairpersons, team leaders, deans, and senior teachers may play significant leadership roles in various situations. These examples run counter to simple versions of the 'great man/woman' theory. The example at *Metro Secondary School*, an alternative school for dropouts in Cedar Rapids, Iowa, illustrates one form of dispersed leadership:

> There are three assistant principals, called 'lead teachers' who divide the administrative and counseling functions. Teachers have immediate access to each of them. These people are highly visible in the building and are always available to the staff. The staff feels that they are encouraged to provide input on school policy, programs, curriculum, and activities almost on a day-to-day basis.

Teachers actually develop the courses and the programs, adhering to district guidelines, and subject to approval by the lead teachers. There are periodic meetings of teachers and administrators to develop strategies to work on motivational and behavioral problems of students. Teachers participate in developing in-service programs. There is frequent referral and cross-counseling between teachers and lead teachers. They feel they work together as a 'team' or 'family'. Teachers know their fellow teachers quite intimately. Each Friday morning, teachers meet as a group to discuss various aspects of the school's program with lead teachers and the principal.

Administrative leadership also may be provided by a team whose members work cooperatively on a common agenda as illustrated by the administrators at *Theodore Roosevelt High School* in Kent, Ohio:

The administrative team believes the following basic ideals are critical to sustaining improvement. 1) Happy people produce good results. 2) That which is reinforced will tend to happen again. 3) The best way to communicate is one-to-one, face-to-face. With these ideas in mind, the administrative team attempts to do a great deal of managing by walking around. It is felt that being visible is very important, therefore, each of the six administrative team members expects to accomplish the following each and every day: 1) Spend between 7:45 and 8:10 each morning walking from classroom to classroom in a designated area of the building, talking to teachers. 2) Being in the halls at a designated location between each period of the school day. 3) Spending at least one other hour a day walking round the building.

In other schools these 'leadership teams' include department heads, members of school improvement committees or advisory councils, and respected members of the faculty. Such teams may be structured formally or informally. What is clear is that many individuals take on leadership roles in successful schools, that the leaders change with the issue or situation. However, the principal is always a key actor, developing and supporting these other school leaders, and orchestrating their efforts into a harmonious whole that moves the school closer to its goals. At the heart of this harmony is the ability of formal leaders in these schools to recognize the strengths of a diverse set of people and to encourage those people to make maximum use of their skills. Good leaders develop other leaders.

The message from the files of these successful schools is quite clear: effective leadership in creating and maintaining quality programs and practices is of central importance. Much of the success is associated with the quality of leadership. It is equally important, however, to understand that the character of this leadership is complex. The examples cited above document that leaders in these schools not only effectively use the more commonly mentioned bureaucratic devices of rules, procedures, and authority relations to establish or reinforce a set of desired behaviors on the part of staff and students, but they also are attuned to the importance of cultural linkages — those activities that provide a consistency to the belief system and consensus about the direction in which the school is headed. It is the ability to focus all the brief interactions and weak leverages around a vision of the school that contributes to the dynamism of these educational organizations. No one style offers a solution. Nor is it a single individual who provides the answer. By attending to the full range of linkages in the school, matching leadership style with the character of the school community, and recognizing the leadership potential of staff, the formal leaders in these schools have made major contributions to their success.

Chapter 5

Conditions of Teaching: Motivating the Staff

During the latter half of the 1980s, the attention of educational reformers in the United States shifted from raising academic standards and tightening the accountability of educators to improving the quality and productivity of public school teachers. Often collectively criticized by the public and the media as less than competent, lacking in commitment, preoccupied with narrow self-interests, and responsible in one way or another for the inadequate achievement of American students, teachers were suddenly heralded as the new engine for progress in public education. Policy-makers came to the realization that good teachers and good teaching were the essence of effective schools.

The 1983 report of the National Commission on Excellence in Education and subsequent reform reports reflected this belief when they raised concerns that 'not enough academically able students are being attracted to teaching'. They called for higher entry standards, higher salaries, better working conditions, and new opportunities for advancement for teachers. However, the initial thrust of the reform movement following the reports was to raise the standards for entry into the profession and to improve teacher education. Workplace issues were ignored. The problems of inadequate conditions for teaching in the schools were seldom discussed in the initial stages of the reform movement, the exception being ill-fated attempts to introduce merit pay plans or master teacher programs.

To launch the second wave of the reform movement, the Carnegie Forum (1986) issued a dramatic call for the creation of 'a profession of well-educated teachers prepared to assume new powers and responsibilities to redesign schools for the future'. The report recommended restructuring schools to provide more professional work environments for teaching, freeing teachers to determine how best to meet the needs of their students and fulfill state and local goals while also holding them more accountable for student progress. The education report of the National Governors Association (1986) echoed these recommendations, citing better work environments, higher salaries, more policy influence, and career ladders as needed reforms in teaching. In both cases, it was argued that better working conditions would attract and hold better people and that teachers would be more effective if their conditions of work were changed.

By 1986, there was growing evidence that talented teachers were leaving the profession, and particularly leaving the public schools, because of poor working conditions as well as inadequate salaries (Schlechty and Vance, 1983; Sykes, 1983; Chapman, 1984). There also was evidence from national and state surveys that the existing teaching force was less than satisfied with their roles and with conditions in schools (Bacharach, Bauer, and Shedd, 1986; Centre for Public Interest Polling, 1986). Such evidence focused the attention of policy-makers on the improvement of teaching environments. Questions about what configuration of working conditions in the schools would elicit the desired responses from teachers and how these conditions could be created became major public policy issues in the second half of the 1980s.

Research on Environments for Teaching

The recommendations for the reform of teacher working conditions and the survey findings were substantiated by the effective schools research. A reanalysis of effective schools studies, conducted by Rosenholtz (1985), concluded that the schools identified in the studies as effective were more successful at recruiting and holding talented teachers. Principals in these schools, she contended, created conditions under which teachers received more support, were encouraged by their colleagues, felt more confident about their eventual success, and enjoyed greater psychic rewards. These conditions contributed to greater success with students and hence increased psychic rewards for the teachers who were thus motivated to work even harder. According to this analysis, the most vital resources in effective schools were the effort, commitment, and involvement of their teaching staffs and leaders who understood the importance of creating good conditions for teaching.

Other effective schools analysts reached similar conclusions and called for increasing the influence of teachers over school policy (Bird and Little, 1986); giving teachers more control and discretion over matters affecting their work (Corcoran, 1986b); providing more opportunities for teachers to interact with their professional peers (Little, 1983); and increasing their involvement in staff development (Purkey and Smith, 1983). Both the reform and research literatures suggest similar sets of propositions about the ideal or desired environments for teaching.

The primary characteristics of this ideal work environment for teachers include:

1. shared goals and high expectations of success to create strong communal identity;

2. respectful and dignified treatment as professionals by superiors and by parents and students;
3. participation by teachers in the decisions affecting their work;
4. regular opportunities for interaction and sharing with colleagues that promote a collective identity;
5. recognition and rewards for their effort and achievement;
6. opportunities for professional growth; and
7. decent physical working conditions.

These seven conditions are believed to have an enormous impact on the behavior and attitudes of teachers and to be essential to high levels of teacher performance. These factors have been shown to have positive effects on teacher attendance, level of effort, commitment to the school, sense of efficacy, and job satisfaction (Rosenholtz, 1985; Firestone, 1985). They are seen as part of a *gestalt*, and taken together, they provide a model or a definition of a professional teaching environment. To some observers, they constitute the agenda for the reform of the school as a workplace.

Conditions of Teaching in the Recognized Schools

The quality of their teaching staffs was highly valued by administrators, parents, and students in the recognized schools. Good teaching was the most common response to questions asked on the nomination form about the conditions contributing most to school success. Students and parents also frequently told site visitors that it was the quality of the staff that was the most important factor in understanding why their schools were successful.

The information available on the schools reveals that large numbers of the teachers had won state, regional, and national awards and honors and that their students, with their assistance, regularly won similar academic honors. While complete data on the credentials of the school staffs were not available, many of the schools reported high percentages with master degrees or better. The staff also reported that they worked hard. Although the data on the level of effort of the staffs are soft and incomplete, the impression gained from the descriptions of the programs, the teacher interviews, and site visitor observations is one of high levels of discretionary effort and high levels of teacher participation in extra-curricular activities. Most of the schools were proud of their low staff turnover. Indeed, a serious concern in some schools was how to replace aging individuals whose credentials, backgrounds, and intellectual abilities were not readily available in today's market. In sum, the staffs in the schools were regarded as highly competent, many of them had won distinction themselves and through the work of their students, they held impressive credentials, and they worked hard. They were experienced, dedicated professionals.

These secondary schools had been effective in recruiting, retaining, and motivating talented teachers and administrators and their leaders believed that they would continue to be more successful than other schools in the highly competitive marketplace for good teachers. Why were they so confident? Clearly national and state reputations for academic quality were factors in a few cases. Schools with long traditions of excellence and reputations for quality based on student selectivity or National Merit results and SAT scores, regularly recruit new staff from neighboring school districts and sometimes are able to avoid hiring inexperienced teachers altogether.

However, the vast majority of the recognized schools, although highly successful, were neither selective nor blessed with national reputations. Clearly other factors accounted for their apparent ability to recruit, hold, and motivate outstanding teachers. One high school principal expressed views held by many of his peers when he told a site visitor that it was not salaries or reputation that most attracted teachers to his school but the professional environment and the better working conditions. The opportunity to work with talented professionals, to exercise greater discretion over both course content and methods of teaching, and to have more time to work with students and develop curricula were critical factors in his view.

Do such conditions help schools attract and hold talented teachers? Is the principal correct that good working conditions are critical? Obviously, salaries are also important and most of the recognized schools were able to offer salaries that were highly competitive within their regions. In general, these schools were well supported by their communities and their per-pupil expenditures were typically above average for their states. However, the critical differences appear to be those factors identified by the principal and also discussed in the reform reports. These schools are most clearly distinguished by the excellent working environments they provide for their staffs. Their experience appears to substantiate the recruiting power of providing good environments for teaching. They also demonstrate that the provision of good conditions for teaching is not beyond our grasp and that it does not necessarily require radical restructuring of the public schools. Examples from the recognized schools are offered for each of the seven primary characteristics of positive work environments.

Shared Goals and Communal Identity

One of the hallmarks of these schools is a strong sense of communal identity, a sense of belonging to a professional community and an institution whose goals and values are shared. Satisfaction is derived from being part of a group that has clear direction and high *élan*. The example from *Millard North High School* in Omaha, Nebraska, illustrates how this feeling can be established in a restructured school:

> The building of the strong staff began by working with volunteers from the existing staff and then going through an extensive screening process in which the principal personally talked with

many individuals about their reasons for wanting to come to the school and how they would be expected to behave when they got there. For example, staff were told clearly that they would be expected to know kids personally, to be in the halls, to be accessible and to be available to the kids for a full day. This challenge resulted in a good deal of self-selection. Once staff were chosen, the question of identity and tradition were dealt with in joint staff planning. The staff met, discussed exactly what would be required and reinforced one another in always holding high expectations for students and demanding excellent performance.

Many of the middle schools have developed a staff consensus that is based on an understanding of the needs of early adolescents; staff at *Shoreham-Wading River Middle School* in Shoreham, New York expressed that philosophy as follows:

For students, the school is truly child-centered. Students know that their individual teachers care for them and will spare no effort to deal with their individual needs. Each student has a teacher advisor to whom he/she can turn for academic and emotional support. The advisor in turn can effectively communicate with parents and work cooperatively with them in the interests of the child. The student finds herself/himself in a supportive, open, and friendly environment in which she/he is guided to develop her/his potential and to make a successful transition from childhood to adolescence.

Respectful Treatment as Professionals

A second factor was respect for teachers and for teaching, a sense of dignity that comes with being regarded with esteem by colleagues, students, and community members. Over and over again, teachers told site visitors that respect for teaching was important to school success. This quotation from a site visitor report on *Metro Secondary School*, Cedar Rapids, IA, is typical of their comments:

This school truly operates in a highly-skilled, professional 'team' fashion. The teachers are very homogeneous and treat each other with high regard, dignity, and respect. They are all totally involved in every student and in the school's wide range of activities and events, both on and off the campus. Their lives are very much meshed with the lives of the students.

Another example from a site visitor illustrates the respect the building administrator at *Westchester Middle School* in Chesterton, Indiana, has for teachers' judgments about their work and when they do it:

(Teachers) feel that the school administration allows them to make responsible judgments and act in accordance with those judgments. When I asked the teachers who made most of the important decisions about curriculum, budget, discipline, instruction and resources, their responses were unanimous: 'We do'. One teacher told me, 'In this building, the teacher is the school executive'. One feature of the school seems to illustrate that point well: during a planning period, teachers may leave the building. 'Good teachers plan all the time', the principal told me. 'Why should they have to do it for 48 minutes between 10 and 11 a.m.? They'll be better teachers if they can use that time to get to the bank and make the deposit they need to cover the mortgage payment. I just treat them like the adults they are'.

Participation in Decisions

A critical feature separating professional work environments from other work environments is the amount of discretion and influence that professionals exercise in carrying out their work. To the extent that teachers feel they have some autonomy and control over what they do, there is likely to be a stronger feeling of being a professional. An example of such a situation comes from *Amity Regional Junior High* in Bethany, Connecticut:

Curriculum guides are written by teachers and are comprehensive descriptions of instructional objectives and content activities. Curriculum assessment occurs on a planned cycle and is directed by teachers . . . . The responsibility for the discipline policy is shared by teachers, administrators, and the Board of Education. Teachers are deeply involved in the identification and evaluation of issues affecting the school. We have standing committees addressing discipline, attendance, computers, energy, community volunteers, and substitute teachers. Two new committees this year deal with social/emotional needs of students.

In such an environment the teachers have a greater sense of control over their work life. The site visitor, commenting on *Amity Junior High*, suggested:

Teachers have been given great liberties in teaching strategies and experimental ideas. The two teaching teams have a common planning time which gives them an opportunity for developing a mini school-within-a-school program. They decide grouping patterns, the schedule, the length of classes and the rotation of classes. I found teachers were using the liberty they had in very effective ways. I felt from my observations that the faculty knew they had ownership over the way this school is run.

89

A high degree of influence over curriculum is particularly important to secondary teachers who equate their professional standing with their knowledge of content. Teachers did share in curricular decision-making in many of these schools. The following vignette from *Niskayuna High School*, Schenectady, New York, describes how balance is achieved between the desires of teachers for discretion and influence and the need of the district for focus and articulation:

> The faculty feel that they play the critical role in curriculum development and review. Teachers are involved in the district's periodic review of curriculum. They also feel they are influential on other instructional and programmatic issues. In general, they see themselves as the initiators. Each department does its own curriculum planning. Summer support is provided for new projects. Individuals and departments prepare proposals in response to an RFP. There is review at the department level first, then a district committee reviews them, rank orders them, and funds them to the limit of the budget. Examples of recent projects: a new marketing course, a law course, a photography program, an environmental design class which has since grown into a commercial art program, new computer classes, revision of the electronics curriculum, experimental English courses, and so forth.

Teachers in these schools have many opportunities to work together and to discuss issues of instruction and school policy as the example from *McCluer High School* in Florissant, MO illustrates:

> At all levels, teachers have opportunities to discuss and to provide significant input about all aspects of the school program. For example, every teacher is a member not only of a department but also of an advisement team. Within a subject matter department, a teacher also works with others whose teaching assignments are similar. At the same time, every teacher functions as an advisor and belongs to a cross disciplinary advisement team. A structure exists which allows teachers time to share: 1) their speciality content areas, 2) student and parent feedback, and 3) need for change.

This example illustrates not only the high degree of participation, but also the importance of the collective nature of that process — the next important working condition.

Collective Responsibility

A common characteristic of secondary teaching is that individual teachers have considerable flexibility in choosing how they interpret and implement curricular guidelines and instructional strategies within their classroom. A *laissez-faire* atmosphere often prevails, in which everyone does their own thing, often in splendid isolation. Rather than being uplifting, this kind of autonomy may be demoralizing (Lortie, 1975). Teachers feel that they must rely solely on their resources and skills to solve problems. The alternative to this isolating and alienating form of individual autonomy is a sense of collective responsibility and accomplishment. A collegial culture directed by common goals can create a strong sense of personal efficacy. One site visitor, describing *Mrachek Middle School* in Aurora, Colorado, offered an example of how this works:

> There are many formal, and even more informal mechanisms for communication, planning, and development. First, there is a common planning period for all teachers in each team. Second, each team meets once/week with the learning coordinator and selected members of the resource team to plan, discuss, coordinate, or whatever. Third, the team organization, itself, fosters communication and planning among members within teams. Fourth, the open corridor architecture of the school fosters an open environment which forces teacher interaction, cross class observation, and so forth. Teachers physically cannot isolate themselves in a classroom; there are no doors to shut! From year to year, the members of each team are rotated, so over time, the ethos of the program and cohesion among the staff is strengthened and reinforced — cliques are harder to form. The teachers said that because of all the above, there is constant communication among teachers, within teams, across grades and across subject areas. The teams also 'force' interdisciplinary discussion.

Princeton Junior High in Cincinnati, Ohio, offers yet another example of the important role that teaming can play in creating the desired collegial ethos:

> A team structure, according to the teachers, permits a great deal of autonomy in the way teachers function. A team can even decide to schedule an independent field trip without disrupting the rest of the school. Team meetings are an especially important source of peer support for good teaching. One teacher said 'The expectation that you will be a good teacher is communicated clearly but subtly by your faculty colleagues'. It is clear, that the teachers expect one another to act professionally and competently. They are willing to help one another, but as one teacher put it, 'We have little patience with people who don't want to be good'.

The teachers in this school believed that the most important decisions were made by the team and were simply facilitated by the principal. The style of administration encouraged this notion. The teachers said: 'You don't feel threatened, yet you know someone is in charge'. They felt that they were trusted to do a job and expected to do it, so they did it.

Recognition and Rewards for Teaching

Another important factor that is often neglected is recognition of good teaching and high levels of effort by staff. Discussions of the rewards for teaching can bring laughter from teachers. A common complaint of many public school teachers is that their best efforts and their accomplishments go unrecognized and unrewarded. When something goes wrong in a class, teachers say, they are held responsible, but when things go well, they are usually ignored. Motivation erodes and effort declines when individuals are not recognized and rewarded for their performance.

Recognition means being singled out personally as a contributor to the school. One of the important features of the working conditions in these successful secondary schools was the attention given to teacher recognition. For example, at *Clayton High School* in Clayton, Missouri:

> Teachers are recognized during faculty meetings when 'promising practices' are shared. Teachers are honored when selected by seniors to read their names at graduation. The PTO sponsors a 'Find the Good and Praise It' project. This project encourages parents to compliment teachers for their successes. Outstanding teachers are honored by being featured as speakers at a special lecture series.

And at *Westchester Middle School* in Chesterton, Indiana:

> The hallmark of this school is the extent to which everyone's activities are recognized and rewarded. Teachers are constantly receiving short notes from the principal (usually handwritten) thanking them for something special they may have done, no matter how small it may have seemed to them. Many times the thank you comes from something they didn't even think had been noticed. That, then, became the word used most often by the teachers to describe life in the schools: they are noticed.

Teachers often told site visitors that the most important recognition came from their peers. In some schools, even peer recognition was not left to chance as at *Metro Secondary School*, an alternative school for dropouts, where:

> On Fridays, the first order of business at staff meetings is to discuss positive activities which occurred that week. At that time, staff members praise each other for exemplary teaching, effectively working with a difficult student, and for special accomplishments made throughout the week.

Some schools offered teachers more tangible awards to show their appreciation. These included merit pay, stipends for professional development, promotions, and higher rank or status such as team leader or curriculum coordinator. For example, *Hixson High School* in Tennessee offered its teachers a range of rewards including:

1. 'Teacher of the Year': $600 award sponsored by a local foundation. Selection is by vote of the faculty.
2. Outstanding Teacher Awards: Ten teachers are selected by vote of peers, students, and administrators for excellence based on criteria selected by the teachers. The Carnegie Grant received by our school in 1984 awarded these teachers $100 each.
3. Kathy King Award: Each month one teacher is selected to receive an award named in honor of a deceased teacher who displayed dedication, love, and concern for students.
4. Career Ladder: Referring to the state's merit system, teachers who qualify are awarded monetary bonuses that range from $2,000–$7,000.

Another high school in the midwest rewarded four excellent teachers annually with cash awards of $5,000 each. Cash awards were usually part of a broader strategy to recognize outstanding teaching as in this report from *Niskayuna High School* in Schenectady, New York:

> Staff say that they are both appreciated and recognized. They feel the students and their parents are appreciative and mentioned notes and feedback from returning students. The evaluations done by the administrators and chairpersons are often complimentary. There is a merit system which has been in place for 25 years. Teachers enter the plan voluntarily and can earn up to $2,000 in merit pay. There are two district publications which give recognition to the activities and successes of teachers — one internal and one for the community. There is a liberal policy on attending conferences and being active professionally. There is support for course development and summer work on curriculum. The district still provides sabbaticals. The parents provide a teacher recognition day. In sum, the staff members feel that the community and the administration value their efforts and as a result try to provide good conditions for teaching.

Recognition when combined with the other conditions that make up a positive work climate can build staff commitment to the institution and enhance their willingness to make extra efforts on behalf of their students. Indeed, appreciation from current and former students was almost always mentioned by teachers as a particularly satisfying form of recognition.

Professional Growth

Another important factor is the opportunity for personal progress and growth. Working with stimulating people can contribute to personal development. So can effective in-service programs, opportunities for pursuing advanced degrees, sabbaticals, serving on curriculum committees, and similar professional activities available to many teachers in these schools.

Artesia High School in Lakewood, CA is an example of how intensive and focused staff development can be:

> There is a very definite and active staff development plan which includes: (1) weekly staff development presentations in areas of instructional improvement; (2) monthly staff meetings for large group staff development workshops; (3) all teachers and administrators participated in Madeline Hunter's Research Based Instruction; (4) teachers participate in weekend retreats for special training. The list of in-service is very extensive.

Indeed, the list was extensive: fifteen in-service activities were listed for one year.

Many of the schools reported involvement with the Madeline Hunter program to improve instructional effectiveness or with school effectiveness based on the research of Ronald Edmonds and others. In many cases, such training was provided for most of the staff and used as a major vehicle for improvement, as illustrated by *Castro Valley High School*, CA:

> A second aspect of the staff development program this year is the enrollment of 24 teachers and 1 administrator in a six day series in the Clinical Teaching/Supervision methods developed by Madeline Hunter. With the other staff members trained last year, we will soon have all administrators and a majority of teachers trained in this methodology.

Some schools offer a rich variety of programs for their staffs as in *Jennings Junior High School*, MO:

> JJHS has an ongoing staff development program which consists of both teacher and principal initiated activities. Planning takes place in a variety of ways. In-service activities have grown from teacher surveys, sign-up sheets, teacher input and feedback sheets turned into the principal, state department opportunities, . . . and teacher initiated interests. District policies require teachers to reach a certain standard of professional development activities and most teachers at JJHS exceed and double this standard.

The nomination form listed twenty-two major staff development sessions held for the school's staff including seminars with Madeline Hunter, Tom Good, John Block, and Ronald Edmonds and programs such as the Bay Area Writing Project, TESA, the Missouri Mathematics project, and Assertive Discipline.

Physical Conditions

Physical conditions in schools are also important and, in some cases, can influence the climate and character of the school and its program. The age of the facility does not seem to matter, but its condition does. Like everyone else, teachers want to feel safe and secure, they want to have usable and comfortable work space. Some of the facilities housing the recognized schools are old, a few are even somewhat run down due to lack of maintenance. Other buildings are new. Some were designed to provide excellent conditions for teaching, with good office and meeting space, a variety of instructional areas, and pleasant common areas. For example, *Mariemont High School* in an affluent Ohio suburb was described as:

> ... beautifully maintained. The outside is brick and inside the walls are attractively painted with murals (student produced) everywhere. The floor is carpeted, the building air-conditioned and the furnishings are appropriate and attractive. The facility contains a swimming pool, large gym/weight room, 450 seat auditorium/theater with a small theater space, common areas, large playing fields ... Teacher offices are located in the middle of the pods according to academic discipline. The library is on two levels — the windows facing out on beautiful wooded areas.

Clearly teachers working in such spacious, attractive, and well-designed buildings have an advantage.

Design of facilities can affect the climate of a school. For example, the layout of *Lindbergh High School* in Renton, WA was credited by the site visitor with helping break down the student alienation often found in large schools by giving physical definition to a house plan:

> The building is placed on a gradual slope with various levels and yet easy access to all instructional areas. One never gets the feeling that 1300 students attend. As you walk through the halls at Lindbergh and visit various parts of the building you are impressed by what appears to be a small homelike setting.

Design can also affect instructional effectiveness. Sometimes negative effects must be overcome as in the case of *Maudlin High School*, SC:

> The building itself was designed to enhance the curriculum in career education, art, industrial arts, and pre-vocational training. Open classrooms were set up; a science lab was designed to accommodate use by two or three classes simultaneously, and the library at the center of the building was entirely open. It was hoped that this design would serve to foster interdisciplinary work among the various departments. Seventeen experimental courses were designed for this new facility. Test scores indicated that this

approach was not successful in our community . . . Ultimately it became apparent that there was a real dichotomy between philosophy and practice. As a result, the faculty was forced to re-evaluate its response to the community's needs. Extensive redesign of the building was undertaken, and the school returned to a more traditional orientation. The library, which had become a commons area, was enclosed with plexiglass walls. The science lab was designed for use by specific science classes, and classrooms which had previously been open areas were enclosed to house a more traditional classroom.

Simply providing clean, well-maintained workspace can also make a difference, especially if the efforts build pride and the staff know that extra efforts are being made. For example, at *Colville High School*, a small rural school in Washington, staff make the best of an inadequate plant:

Our school is twenty-five years old. There has been minimal funds for capital improvements because we plough every available cent we have into instruction. Our shop facilities, our PE facility, and our science facilities are barely adequate. We have five portable classrooms out back to help us house all of our kids. Yet this school is neat and clean and well kept. We end each day with a '5 minute clean-up period' so our custodians can spend less time in basic picking up and do more buffing and cleaning.

Unusual architecture also can be a source of pride, as evidenced by the description of *McComb High School*, MS:

This is the most beautiful building I have ever been in. The building is very old and is in the art deco style. When the school needed remodeling, the students lobbied for the old building to remain and for the remodeling to be done around the original structure. There are curved stairways, walls of glass brick and wooden floors. The students selected some super graphics to blend into the current architecture, including their school mascot in the entrance way surrounded by names of all the school activities . . . There is not one scrap of paper on the floors or a fingerprint on the walls.

In some cases, the improvement of school facilities played a critical role in turning a negative situation around, as in this case at *Kennebunk High School*, ME, where it took a decade of legal and political struggle to replace woefully inadequate facilities:

There is no question that the new facility has caused a big upswing in morale and pride among both the staff and students. Previously we had no cafeteria, science labs that were antediluvian, inadequate physical education and athletic facilities, and an overall crowded condition which limited our options and put a strain on a very creative, involved faculty.

What appears to cut across all these conditions is the sense that teachers have been given greater discretion in how they conduct their work and use their time. This creates an ethos of professionalism. As a consequence, teachers in these successful secondary schools report greater rewards for the effort they invest which serves only to reinforce continued effort. By combining a number of these conditions, leaders in other schools are going to enhance the prospects for success.

The Reform of Working Conditions

There are currently two divergent models of management reform competing for the attention of public school policy-makers (Cuban, 1984). One approach emphasizes control, uniformity, coordination, and minimum standards of quality. Often this model fosters increased centralization, routinization, and hierarchy in order to raise student test scores. The effective schools research has popularized the image of a trim, efficient school bureaucracy that tightens the links between the central office and the classroom through goal setting, district testing, curriculum alignment with the tests, definition of scope and sequence in curriculum guides, mandated use of standardized materials and timetables, and rigorous monitoring and evaluation systems. This strategy employs a familiar and comfortable top-down model and it is attractive to policy-makers because it seems to permit swift and efficient responses to public demands for improvement. This perspective is reinforced by demands arising from state testing programs, state curriculum mandates, and accountability laws. There is only limited staff participation and discretion in this model and the options open for consideration by staff and the direction of the acceptable decisions tend to be tightly controlled.

The other model of management reform stresses initiative, motivation, and professional standards and it encourages greater autonomy, responsibility, and discretion for teaching staff. Typically, advocates of this approach argue that school staff, sometimes in cooperation with parents, should set their own agenda, develop their own plans, and have considerable discretion in the use of district funds, developing curricula, and organizing school programs. Often labelled school-site management, this bottom-up approach is championed by many school improvement consultants, reformers seeking to upgrade the teaching profession, and some teacher organizations. Staff participation and ownership is a central factor in this approach.

Obviously there is considerable room for compromise between these two extremes. Yet discussions of school effectiveness and improvement often present the ideal types as though they were the only real options. To some district policy-makers, participation by teachers is perceived as a loss of control to teacher unions that inevitably leads to lowered effort in the classroom and reductions in overall school effectiveness. Union leaders may also oppose some forms of participation for fear that it will weaken staff loyalty to the union or make scapegoats out of teachers if and when problems arise, as they inevitably do. Conversely, to some advocates of school-site management, only radical restructuring of the schools is sufficient to guarantee true professionalism for teachers and they prefer to ignore the role and responsibilities of administrators and school boards. In some of the school improvement literature, the district appears to wither away entirely. Clearly, progress toward reform in the schools requires serious exploration of the middle ground in this debate and consideration of approaches that borrow from both ideal types.

The schools described in this chapter and many of the schools that have been recognized have been functioning with great success in this middle ground. They have tried to provide the best working conditions for teachers that their resources would permit. They have involved their staffs, treated them with respect, given them opportunities and time to work together, and granted them considerable discretion to carry out the educational mission of the school. It is not necessary for policy-makers or researchers to speculate about what good working conditions are, they can be found in these schools. That such conditions make a difference is evident from the consistent success many of these schools have experienced and the unusual levels of staff commitment and effort that have contributed to this success.

Chapter 6

Learning Environments:
Motivating the Students

A significant characteristic of unusually successful schools is a deep conviction by all or most of the adults associated with a school that all of the students can be motivated to master essential skills and content (Brookover, Beady, Flood, Schweitzer and Wisenbacker, 1979). This conviction is a critical source of the high levels of energy and commitment to tasks by staff and students in these schools. It is the basis for the development of high staff expectations for student behavior and achievement and high academic standards in the classroom. The importance of high staff expectations for student performance has been well documented by the effective schools research (Edmonds, 1979; Purkey and Smith, 1983; and Rutter, 1983), and, not surprisingly, it is strongly supported by the analysis of the testimonial data provided by staff and students from the schools in this study and by the independent reports of the site visitors who visited the schools and interviewed their staffs.

Academic standards are one manifestation of staff and community expectations for student performance. The character of academic rewards is another. Decisions about what student behavior or performance should be rewarded, the frequency of such rewards, and also their importance are influenced by staff expectations. These three aspects of a school's culture — expectations, standards, and rewards — are closely linked. When expectations are low, standards also tend to be low and the use of rewards diminishes or the rewards are devalued. Conversely, when expectations are high, standards also tend to be high and rewards are more frequent and more likely to be used to motivate students to work up to their potential. These three factors — high staff expectations, high academic standards, and the effective use of rewards — are critical to student motivation and, hence, essential building blocks in the success of these schools.

Expectations, Standards, and Rewards

In studies of effective schools, expectations refer to the attitudes of staff, parents, and students about the latter group's potential for academic achievement. When expectations are low, it means that members of the school community expect less effort and less achievement from students than they would of another group of students, perhaps with different racial or social characteristics. Conversely, high expectations mean that the staff expect and demand more from students than is typical of other schools serving similar populations. Rutter *et al.* (1979) maintained that secondary schools were characterized by rising or falling spirals of expectations:

> The initial teaching task is shaped by the attitudes, behaviors, interests, and capabilities of the children in the class. Teacher actions then influence children's behavior, which in turn modifies teacher behavior, which then further impinges on the children. In this way, spirals of either improving or deteriorating behavior (and attainments) seem to be built.

Other researchers share this view of the significance of positive expectations held by teachers. Brookover (1981) contended that teacher beliefs about the students' ability to learn and about potential achievement were critical factors in determining school effectiveness. Good (1982) explains these findings as follows:

- The teacher expects certain behavior and levels of performance from students with particular past achievement, reputations, social or cultural background, etc.
- As a consequence, the teacher behaves differently toward these students.
- The differential treatment is perceived by the students and affects their work effort, aspirations, and self-concept.
- If the differences persist over time, and the students do not resist, behavior and achievement are significantly affected.
- With time, the students conform more and more closely to the behavior expected of them.

In the case of low-income and minority students, the spiral of declining expectations may be reinforced by their awareness that education does not bring the same benefits to members of their group that it does to members of majority or affluent groups. The realities of economic or racial discrimination undermine motivation and effort in school and this also contributes to lower staff expectations and the viciously declining cycle described above. Failure to understand the social and economic realities facing different groups of students, and their influence on student attitudes, can lead to misplaced effort, frustration, and failure (Ogbu, 1978).

The standards set for behavior and academic performance in a school reflect the expectations held by individual teachers, by the school staff as a whole, and by the community. Standards set for the content and skills to be taught, the acceptability of student work, promotion or graduation, and awards reflect the staff's view of what it is possible to achieve with their students. Performance standards are the minimum acceptable levels of student effort and achievement that will result in a 'passing' score, credit for a course, promotion, or graduation. In most schools, teachers retain the ultimate responsibility for determining what is a 'passing' score in a test or in a class. While their decisions are undoubtedly influenced by school or district policies about promotion and graduation criteria, testing, textbooks, or student assignment, they are influenced most by the expectations that they and their colleagues hold for their students.

Sometimes teachers are vague about standards and how they will be applied in their classrooms, leaving it to the students to guess where to place their effort. Some teachers make normative decisions in advance about how many students will earn 'A's or 'F's in their classes. Sometimes there is considerable variation in standards among teachers and students face different situations in each classroom. Successful schools are characterized by efforts to set clear expectations and standards and to apply them uniformly.

In some departmentalized situations, there may be commonly used tests that provide some measure of uniformity. Or department heads may regularly review work samples to ensure that standards across classrooms are similar and appropriate. Or they may review teacher-made tests to ensure that they are adequate. Sometimes, but more rarely, there are guidelines for assessment that influence how teachers carry out this critical function. In various ways, the staffs of these schools strive to maintain their high standards and to ensure relative uniformity in the way that standards are applied across their schools.

Most commonly, there are simply opportunities for teachers to discuss standards and strong professional norms that define what is expected of the staff and, therefore, what is expected of the students. In schools where there is teaming, teachers may regularly work together to develop tests and even share the responsibility of grading them. The increased focus on writing and the popularization of holistic scoring has contributed to greater consensus on standards at least in this curricular area. Teachers from different departments may grade the same student product but apply different criteria. This helps build uniform standards and expectations and to ensure that school-wide standards are clear and applied to all students. These techniques help create a strong academic climate and an 'ethos' of high expectations and reduce the confusion that secondary students typically experience when faced with varying standards.

There has been little direct examination of how different student recognition and reward systems affect student performance or overall school effectiveness. Some of the school effectiveness studies found that the frequent use of praise in the classroom and the frequency of the opportunities for students to be recognized or rewarded were typical of more successful schools (Rutter *et al.*, 1979 and Lipsitz, 1984). Many of the studies of elementary schools reported that school-wide recognition of academic success was an important factor in school effectiveness (Corcoran and Hansen, 1983). Nevertheless, the contribution of activities such as academic honors ceremonies, public recognition, teacher notes to parents, and other forms of recognition and reward in schools is not clear from the research literature. Yet such programs are common in the schools examined in this study and were perceived as important by both staff and students in these schools.

Adolescents often choose to give their time and energy to pursuits other than academic work. Jobs, friends, sports, music, and sex compete for their attention. They often work hardest in the areas in which the rewards are immediate and concrete and where their internal or peer-defined standards of excellence are applied. Appeals by teachers and parents to future rewards (Do it to get into college or get a higher salary) or to adult authority (Do it or suffer the consequences) often seem to fall on deaf ears. From this perspective, the use of more immediate and tangible rewards makes good sense. The files on the exemplary secondary schools are full of descriptions of creative practices that are based on this reasoning.

Expectations and Standards in Successful Secondary Schools

Many of the schools included in this study could properly be described as 'turn-around schools'. In years past, these schools had poor reputations, negative learning environments, and mediocre or low educational outcomes. As one site visitor noted, what stands out most in these schools is the dramatic shift in academic expectations. This change in attitude is often the initial step on the road to excellence. The first step in the turn-around schools was not usually directed toward changing teaching strategies, nor toward revising curriculum, but instead sought to alter the attitudes of staff toward the students and thereby develop a climate that was more conducive to learning.

One such school is *Ribault High School* in Jacksonville, Florida, which experienced dramatic improvements in discipline, attendance, and academic achievement between 1979 and 1983 (the year in which it received recognition). It took drastic measures to alter staff expectations at Ribault. In 1979, all of the teachers were asked to re-apply for their positions or request transfers. As a result, nearly two-thirds of the staff were replaced with teachers who wanted to be at the school and who believed that the students there could succeed.

The result of staff commitment to a set of common expectations often resulted in startling differences from the norms of public education as it is experienced by low-income students. Describing an ethically-diverse high school in California, a site visitor wrote:

> Students (knew) clearly both the academic and behavioral expect-
> ations in each of the eleven classes (visited). Assignments were on
> the chalkboard. In nine of the eleven, classroom rules were dis-
> played on a wall. In all of my years observing classrooms, I have not
> seen eleven classes begin immediately after the tardy bell as I did at
> Logan. Absenteeism and tardiness are uniformly taken seriously by
> teachers and students. It is a bone of contention among some
> students, usually followed by a grudging acknowledgement that the
> school is serious about teaching. (*Logan High School*, Union City,
> CA).

Visitors to the schools often were surprised by student accounts of what was expected of them. The students clearly understood that high achievement required high levels of effort on their part and that they seemed proud of the high expectations expressed by the staff. In fact, they often praised their teachers for making them work harder than they might have if left to their devices. A classic example is found in a conversation reported by a site visitor with a student who had recently transferred into one of the schools:

> I had a boy say to me that he had moved into the school from
> another place. In the other school, the teachers told him he was no
> good, worthless, and never going to amount to anything. When he
> started the same behavior pattern in his new school, a teacher
> pulled him aside and said, 'Look, we don't behave like that here. If
> you want to be accepted in this school, you act this way'. The boy
> claimed, 'That saved my life', because they never told him he was
> worthless. (*Eastmont Middle School*, Sandy, UT).

Students also reported that they regularly had homework, although the reported amounts varied considerably among students within schools as well as among the schools. However, many of the schools had demanding policies that set standards for the teachers as well as students. For example, at *Pioneer High School* in Whittier, California, where three-quarters of the students are Hispanic and nearly a third are from low-income families, the formal policy requires:

> ...an average of 15 to 30 minutes of homework per class...be
> assigned Monday through Thursday and, if necessary, on
> Friday.... Homework will comprise 15 per cent of the grade and
> must be graded and returned to students. The policy is monitored
> by surveying students and identifying teachers who are not en-
> forcing it.

In a school in a depressed area of Massachusetts in which nearly half of the students were from low-income families, daily homework was mandated for all major subjects (*New Bedford High School*, New Bedford, Massachusetts). Courses that could not meet this standard were reduced to minor credit. In this school, as at *Pioneer*, homework was part of the student's grade in a course and the policy was enforced by the administration.

A student at *American High School* near Miami, Florida, captured the flavor of rising expectations when she said:

> Teachers are on you all the time to do better. Even when you think you are working hard, they expect you to keep improving. They keep adjusting the goals upward.

The staff at *American High School* had made it their number one priority to raise academic expectations. They told the site visitor that:

> Fundamental changes in school policy have allowed us to establish an academically demanding climate with policies and procedures that strongly support student achievement. All students are pushed to achieve their maximum academic potential, regardless of what that potential is. Students are no longer allowed to select academic classes which are below their ability level. Four years ago, students completed their own schedules, and were allowed to select courses satisfying the minimal requirements. Students and parents now receive individualized counselling prior to scheduling.

Similarly the staff at *Jamaica High School* in Queens, New York expressed the strong convictions that their students (40 per cent Black and 20 per cent Hispanic) would prosper most in an environment in which standards are stressed and maintained. They had created seven different curricular institutes which permitted their students to develop and pursue their interests:

> Students are encouraged to enroll in specific areas of concentration, earn special diploma endorsements and accumulate extensive credentials for a cumulative folder and better than 89 per cent do indeed exceed the basic diploma requirements. Students, when admitted, selected a concentration: math-science, humanities, finance, computer science, honors program, college discovery, or work-study.

The courses of study in these institutes at *Jamaica High School* were demanding and rigorous, but were designed to stimulate the students, raise their motivation, and prepare them for success after high school:

> A Math-Science Institute member takes a minimum of five years of science, four and one-half years of mathematics, a term of electronics and must complete a research report for competitive submission which includes one summer's experience of study or work. The Humanities major, in addition to other requirements, is enrolled in art, Latin, keyboarding, produces the school newspaper,

participates in extensive out-of-school activities and experiences (Model Congress, Law Team, Debate, Academic Olympics). . . . To allow participation in one or more of these areas, the school day has been extended to 10 periods; all students are programmed for a minimum of 7 subjects, the motivated and talented for 8. Modified classes have been eliminated. The honors level in English and Social Studies is a Humanities curriculum.

Staff expectations can be affected by the size of a school as well as its student population. Describing *Colville High School*, a school in a poor rural area of Washington state, its principal wrote:

Many teachers and students honestly believe that smaller rural schools cannot match the education offered by larger urban or suburban schools. Put quite simply, they confuse quantity with quality. The toughest initial task here at CHS was to convince our staff and students that despite being small and rural, we could develop excellent programs to meet the needs of all the students we serve by focusing on doing fewer things, but doing them better than anyone else. Changing this attitude was *at least* a five year project.

High expectations are expressed in a variety of ways in these exemplary secondary schools. School staff seem more willing to accept the responsibility for enhancing the learning opportunities for their students than is typical in other public schools. This commitment runs counter to recent descriptions of American schools that portray participants who merely go through the motions (Sizer, 1984) and who make tacit bargains between students and teachers that exchange reductions in work demands or standards for better classroom behavior (Cusick, 1983). Teaching staff in the recognized schools, on the other hand, generally appeared to expect their students to conduct themselves in a manner that maximized learning. This attitude was reflected in their work demands on the students and their expectations about attendance and behavior.

Rewarding Students in Successful Secondary Schools

Higher expectations and standards are also frequently coupled with strong reward systems. It is not enough to simply increase demands on students. There is also a need to recognize their accomplishments. The school used diverse and multiple means to provide this recognition. At *American High School*, for example, structures were created to reward the positive behavior that was the result of encouraging high expectations as documented earlier:

The program for recognizing outstanding student accomplishments begins in grade nine with a special assembly sponsored by parents for all ninth graders who have done well during the first hectic and often traumatic year of high school. At the end of each year there are assemblies for each grade level to recognize and honor those students who have achieved superior levels of success. There is a special Hall of Fame to which the academically most outstanding seniors are inducted.

Reporting on his interviews with students in a Connecticut middle school, a site visitor wrote:

> Recognition for student achievement is a high priority item with this faculty. They have certificates for high achievement given every month with copies of certificates and pictures of the students posted in the corridor outside the main office. Students are recognized in every class by displaying work on the walls, special teacher recognition awards, thank you notes, happy grams, and personal acknowledgement. Parents told me of many incidents when teachers called them to report school success. The principal makes it a point to recognize outstanding achievement through the morning announcements. I also found that many of these acknowledgements came in the form of improvement letters to those who might not be as academically talented. The school walls are literally saturated with student work . . . (*Flood Intermediate School*, Stratford, CN).

Similar academic halls of fame were observed in many of the schools, including the high schools, and are worth further elaboration. As one reflects back over his/her experience in secondary school, often the most vivid recollections are of ceremonies and rituals. These are integral parts of life in any institution and their importance to effectiveness has received increasing research attention (Peters and Waterman, 1982; Deal, 1985).

Most of the schools use both formal and informal means to recognize achievement (and to encourage even higher levels of performance). For example, at *Theodore Roosevelt High School* in Kent, Ohio:

> Extensive efforts are made to send students congratulatory letters and notes for all types of achievements. Whenever a student earns a place on the honor roll, is selected to an office, earns a spot on an athletic team, and so forth, a positive communication is sent to the student at his home. Also, a student recognition luncheon program has been initiated. Each month an academic department is asked to select the 24 students most worthy of recognition. These students are invited to a luncheon which is partially paid for by a community service group. Students are bussed to a local restaurant where they are served a delicious meal. Following the meal they are praised and a rap session takes place. Within the school, lists of achieving students are posted, names are read over the public address system, and so forth.

At *Nyssa High School* in rural Oregon emphasis is on recognition of student performance through policies and programs such as:

- Student of the month
- Subject area recognition monthly
- School year subject area awards
- Nights of excellence: four times a year ceremonies at sports events for students from each grade and their parents
- Semester honor rolls and pep assemblies
- Academic letters, the same as athletic letters
- Bulldog cards for good behavior that are mailed home
- Reward tickets for free ice cream for good citizenship
- Class president awards.

At *Linn-Mar High School* in Marion, Iowa, the rewards include:

'Student-of-the-Week' recognition, displays of student work, Student Appreciation Day, athletic team GPA records, academic display case, perfect attendance awards, and published student work are a few additional examples of rewards and incentives. We have a written document 'Going For The Gold'. The purpose of the Going For The Gold program, as outlined in a brochure distributed to students the first day of school, is to focus on the positive things students do all year long. It's also an attempt to show in one location or pamphlet all the things we do to promote positive behavior.

Two new programs are described as follows: (1) The America's Impressed Card, good for two admissions to athletic and one fine arts activity, may be obtained by students who raise their grade .5 from the previous semester or maintain a 3.85 or higher for two semesters in a row. Students who have a school year of no classes or study hall truancies or unexcused tardiness may also qualify for the card. The first students who qualified last spring were sent their cards September 26th, (2) The #1 Club features certificates and pins that may be awarded by staff and administration for special performance above and beyond the normal expectations. Each month two students can be nominated by each department for the award. Ten finalists will be selected by a faculty committee to receive the final award.

These examples typify the variety of efforts being made to raise expectations of academic performance and to recognize student achievements. Nothing symbolizes the changing climate in American public education better than one high school that prints the names of its honor roll students on all of its sports programs.

Standards in public secondary schools fell during the 1960s and 1970s as a result of changes in college admissions practices, pressures to reduce dropouts, erosion of teacher authority, grade inflation resulting from both parental pressure and bargains with the students, and an emphasis on minimums rather than excellence. These lower standards also reflected society's expectations about the potential of a changing student population. Many of the schools in this study resisted this trend and maintained their high expectations and standards. Others suffered the consequences of lowering standards, but struggled to restore academic integrity to their programs. Their stories demonstrate that expectations can be altered and standards can be raised. Opportunities for student recognition and rewards can be created. The schools and their staffs have demonstrated that it is not necessary to bargain for mediocrity.

Chapter 7

Public Involvement:
Reaching the Community*

The relationship of the community to the educational enterprise has evolved as American society has moved from a rural, handcraft economy to an industrialized one. With the advent of scientific management and the rise of the professional educator, the community has had less significance as a critical actor in defining educational agendas. Indeed, Seeley (1981) has gone so far as to suggest that the basic problem with education is in the design of the system. Public education has become a professionalized, bureaucratized, governmental enterprise attempting to deliver education as a service. Making the service-delivery system more efficient will not help it improve. Seeley suggests that what is needed is to make education more of a partnership in which individual families and communities can exert their voices and demonstrate their loyalty. Without such structural change, Seeley warns that public education may lose the required public support.

In contrast to this grim prognosis, there is evidence that some families and communities are actively involved in the educational process (Wilson and Rossman, 1986) and that such involvement is positively linked to school performance (Henderson, 1981). In other words, schools with higher community involvement are associated with better learning outcomes. In this era of reform many scholars are calling for increased collaboration between schools and other groups (Barth, 1980; Comer, 1980; Lombana, 1983). The recognized schools offer useful examples of how that has been accomplished and how bonds between the school and community have fostered excellence.

A central part of all definitions of community is the family. Social scientists have repeatedly documented the relationship of family background to school performance. The findings are well known. Family demo-

---

*This chapter represents an expansion and revision of a paper by Bruce L. Wilson and Gretchen B. Rossman which appeared in the June 1986 issue of *Phi Delta Kappan*.

graphic characteristics, including such things as intact households, occupation, income, and education have a direct and positive impact on student learning. What has been less often documented, but what recent evidence suggests can explain the correlations between social background characteristics and school performance are the internal dynamics of family life. As Dornbusch (1986) reports,

> Student activities and relationships with their parents predict grades more surely than do all the other indicators — parental education, family income, ethnicity, gender, and family structure — put together.

Or, as Epps (1983) notes:

> It is not class position that determines a family's educational competence; rather it is the quality of life within the home that makes a difference.

Yet, as Hobbs (1978) points out, in describing the ecosystem for children:

> Examining the scene from age six on up to about sixteen or seventeen, you will notice something very peculiar: The two clusters of activity, called family and school, have almost no overlap and few or no connecting lines.... Many schools regard parents as a nuisance; many parents regard schools as forbidding places in which they have no legitimate interest.

That negative perspective may be extended to the community at large. There is often an 'us and them' mentality when educators talk about people who are not educational professionals. Indeed, Morris, Crowson, Porter-Gehrie and Hurwitz (1984), in a study of urban principals, found an important part of the job to be buffering teachers from community members.

At the same time, the benefits associated with parent involvement can also be realized with the larger community. Involvement of the community helps its members better understand the world that students face in school. It also offers them insights into the problems of making such a complex organization more productive. Greater understanding brings increased public support at the polls and helps pass school budgets. Involvement by the community communicates to students the importance of the learning process. If outsiders are willing to devote their energies to helping schools improve, there is increased probability that students will become more committed to the process as well. Community members can also bring new resources into the schools. Community organizations can provide volunteers, tutors, equipment, space, and access to new experiences for students and staff.

In spite of the research linking community involvement to school success, staffs in schools have not made extensive efforts to collaborate with their communities to improve the quality of education. Several factors may help explain this lack of collaboration. First, there is a problem of defining the 'community'. As Goetzels (1978) points out, the term is so familiar that people take its meaning for granted. However, the term is used in a variety of ways. Goetzels goes on to note that no fewer than ninety-four definitions of the term 'community' can be found in the sociological literature. More important than the lack of clarity about definition may be the failure to recognize the complex role of communities in the educational process. Most Americans no longer identify with a single geographically-localized, self-contained, autonomous community but rather are a part of multiple, geographically-extended, loosely-knit, overlapping communities. Furthermore, school and school district catchment areas are such that they are not contiguous with other social and political communities.

Not only is the concept of community complex, but so too are the collaborative arrangements. Jones and Maloy (1986) point out two key features of school-community collaboratives that inhibit their smooth functioning. First, there are 'multiple realities', or interpretations of the meanings of activities and events, as perceived by the various actors (Schutz, 1967). While most groups want schools to succeed, they also want schools to emphasize some purposes more strongly than others. For example, the business community wants socialization skills, respect for authority, specific vocational skills, and support for capitalism. The higher-education community places priority on independence, creativity, and intellectual curiosity. Schools are already overburdened with too many goals and they lack systematic means for prioritizing them. Collaboratives only tend to exacerbate the problem. Second, collaboratives are not frequently established in organizations that are satisfied with their performance. Rather, they are created to address problems. The hope is that the additional resources and new perspectives generated by the collaborative may help solve the problem. Yet, the problem in search of a solution is typically so ill-defined or structured that collaboratives only increase problems rather than create solutions (Mitroff, 1983). For example, the introduction of bilingual programs has not resolved the apparent language problems in many schools. Often the response is outside the boundary of regular school procedures or activities to be implemented (e.g., multilingual teachers and materials are not readily available).

Nevertheless, partnerships exist in which there is a clear definition of community, in which there is consensus about the mission (i.e., multiple realities are minimized), and a clear definition of the problem or factors that are getting in the way of accomplishing that mission is known and accepted by all involved. Useful illustrations may be drawn from data among these recognized schools:

It is 8.45 on a cold Tuesday morning in Detroit. Twenty-seven boys and girls from the ninth and tenth grades are shoving books into their backpacks, jostling one another, chatting and laughing in their hurry to leave school. Where are they going? To a local nursing home to sing Christmas carols in French, Spanish, and English to the elderly residents.

By third period, some half a dozen parents and other community members are in the school. A scientist from a local engineering firm is helping out in a physics class; the director of a repertory theatre is teaching a unit on Shakespeare to the sophomore English classes; two mothers are reshelving books in the library, while three others are setting up for a teachers' tea to be held at lunchtime.

By 7.30 that same evening, the school is full once again. Down at the end of the science wing, the Boy Scouts are meeting in the chemistry lab for a session on 'kitchen chemistry'. In another part of the school, a woman is teaching a class for parents called 'Interpreting Modern Rock Music: A Guide to the Teenage Years'. And in the gymnasium, a group of adults is installing a new set of bleachers donated by a local lumber yard.*

What makes a school like this unusual? First, the barriers between the school and the neighborhood have been reduced. Students move out into the community to lend their enthusiasm and concern to all sorts of projects and organizations. And community groups participate in the activities of the school, either by giving their time or by using school facilities for community events. Frequently, the entire community works together to plan and carry out projects of interest to everyone.

However, more important than specific activities are the feelings, beliefs, and values that are generated. These local experiences demonstrate how people can be drawn effectively into the daily life of the school. Their involvement builds commitment and loyalty. It creates a special identity for the school that includes the surrounding community. The ethic of mutual caring that is created multiplies the effectiveness of the school and integrates the school into its community.

Although such examples may be unusual, they are far from unique. Indeed, our analysis of data from these exemplary schools suggests that collaborative links such as these are frequently found. As we reviewed the available data, five major strategies for opening schools to their communities and encouraging the forging of creative links were evident: the use of community members as human resources, as public relations advocates, as fiscal resources, as a means to involve students in community service activities, and as catalysts for building a sense of identity for the school. Each is described below with specific examples from schools in the database.

---

*This example represents a composite of several schools.

Human Resources

First, these exemplary schools actively recruit the human resources of their communities. Whether they are parents or not, community members are viewed as potential contributors to the school in a variety of ways. Citizens are recruited as volunteers for clerical duties, to serve as nurses' assistants, to come into classrooms to teach special skills, and so on. Extensive opportunities are made available for volunteers to give of their time, experiences, and good will. A typical description of such a volunteer program comes from *Caddo Middle Magnet School* in Shreveport, Louisiana:

> Active support is provided by the many volunteers who serve on advisory and steering committees, meet with the superintendent regularly to offer help and represent our needs, serve regular hours in the office to relieve the volume of contacts there, and assist in screening youngsters for hearing.

Another program, developed in *Twin Peaks Middle School* in Poway, California, is called the Grandpeople Program. This project is for people who are not parents of school children, primarily retired people:

> They teach art and science, reading and spelling. They help small groups build special projects in the shop, and they assist in the reading program. They serve as consultants, and even more important, as confidants of the youngster with whom they work.

What are the results of a program such as this? The school reports that the elderly participants find their lives revitalized. The teachers observe their students being more courteous and caring. The students express their appreciation for the additional personal attention and help they receive. The principal of *Richardson High School* (Texas) summarized such volunteer programs as follows:

> The goals of a volunteer program are to assist teachers in non-professional duties, to offer individual help to students, to enrich the school program by making available the talents and resources of the community, and to stimulate an informed community to more active support of public education.

Public Relations

The second way in which these exemplary schools build links to the larger community is through the use of aggressive public relations campaigns that rely on parents as promoters, communicators, and decision-makers. Strong parent organizations are the norm in these exemplary schools, and the schools take advantage of that extra good will. Volunteers in these organizations write and disseminate elaborate newsletters that inform the community of school activities.

For example, *Shoreham-Wading River Middle School* in Shoreham, New York, has divided the school attendance area into seventeen zones, each with a chairperson responsible for relaying information to parents in that zone and for bringing the concerns of those within the zone to a monthly meeting with the principal. A visitor to *Lincoln High School*, Nebraska, describes how the school has taken advantage of the enthusiasm of a group of parents:

> This group works very hard at telling the school's story to the community. The members have produced a videotape describing school programs, and they show this videotape to service organizations and other interested groups throughout the community in order to help people better understand the strong school program.

Rather than hide school crises from the community, these exemplary schools have turned the community into a resource to help solve problems. Many of these schools place parents on committees that make important policy decisions about the curriculum, staff development, and new programs. *Lakeside High School* in Atlanta, Georgia, which was recently desegregated, fought against white flight through honest two-way dialogue intended to deal with fears and concerns over the rapid changes in the student population. The school maintains this dialogue through such means as meetings in home, parent/teacher organization meetings, cluster meetings, school open houses, truth squads, and rumor clinics.

Another example of creative promotion through community involvement comes from *Keokuk Middle School* Iowa. Community organizations are invited into the school for a day of recognition and appreciation. A special Grandparents' Day, a National Association for the Advancement of Colored Peoples' Day, a Ministerial Association Day, or an American Association of University Women Day — all feature student tours, lunch for participants, a place for the organizations to meet, and other activities tailored to specific needs. Such activities bring many adults into the school who would not otherwise visit. The students are also exposed to a wider range of adult role models.

Fiscal Resources

Exemplary schools tend to have staff members who are adept at attracting financial resources from the community. Beyond the usual support for athletics, local business will also contribute funds to awards for citizenship, scholarship, and attendance. The community can be spurred to participate in large-scale projects that require time and money. The principal of North *Davie Junior High School* in Mocksville, North Carolina, reported:

When our school opened, several things were needed. The town became involved in an extensive landscaping and school beautification program that involved the total cooperation of students, parents, community members, members of the faculty and staff, and the student council.

In *Roosevelt-Lincoln Junior High School* in Salina, Kansas, local businesses and individuals donated $8,000 for staff development and training for a new teacher advisory program. The *High School for Creative and Performing Arts*, an urban, largely black, magnet school in Cincinnati, Ohio, reported that the community contributed more than $400,000 in a single year to supplement funding from the board of education in order to finance a performance program that reached more than 200,000 people.

Community Service

Not only do the staff members at these exemplary schools invite community members into their classrooms, they also invite themselves into the community. Students visit local nursing homes and establish relationships with the elderly; charitable organizations enjoy the youthful exuberance expressed in jogathons, bikeathons, and walkathons; and students help local recreation departments with many activities. *Roosevelt-Lincoln Junior High School*, for example, sends musical ambassadors into the community several times a year; its students officiate at the Special Olympics and take part in an adopt-a-grandparent program. The parent/teacher organization at an elementary school in Brunswick, Georgia, commissioned members of the *Glynn Middle School* Industrial Arts Club to design and build new playground equipment.

Community groups are also encouraged to use the facilities of these exemplary schools for their meetings and social events. The Boy Scouts, the Girl Scouts, blood banks, and adult and continuing education programs are housed in school buildings. The continuing education programs, sometimes called 'community schools', are open to students, parents, or other school patrons.

For many of these schools located in smaller communities, local social activities revolve around the school. In Hudson, Ohio, where both the junior high and the high schools were recognized as exemplary, the district philosophy is that the community owns the school facilities and residents have a right to use them. Instead of having the local government run the Community Education and Recreation Department, the school district takes on that responsibility.

These activities are not different in kind from those that take place in most secondary schools. But what sets these exemplary schools apart is the frequency with which the community and the school cooperate, the high level of participation, and the degree to which the activities are considered central to the school.

Building an Identity

The final way in which links to the larger community are created is by the building of an identity that consciously takes advantage of the characteristics of that community. For example, Shaker Heights, Ohio, has placed signs along the roadsides leading into the city that declare: 'A community is known by the schools it keeps'. Such activities are more symbolic than substantive, but they have the effect of galvanizing parents and other residents into becoming advocates for the schools. As the principal of *Wilbur High School*, Washington noted, the community develops a much stronger sense of ownership in the schools if citizens become actively involved in decision-making. Attachment to the schools can be fostered in many different ways, from flying schools flags all over Conway, South Carolina, as a means of pro-moting the spirit of the local high school, to reinforcing the thirst for knowledge that characterizes the larger community. This latter strategy is evident in *Ames Junior High School*, Iowa whose principal writes:

> This is a town in which generations have come to learn and create [it is the home of the state university]; it is a town of people who thrive on what they learn and want to share it with others. Our school works to re-create that atmosphere.

Yet another example of reinforcing a school's identity comes from an appeal to tradition at *Cass Technical High School* in Detroit, Michigan. This strong sense of tradition helps sustain local enthusiasm and motivate new students. The efforts of a very strong alumni association aid in this effort:

> The major reason for the success of Tech is primarily its history . . . . Our graduates watch out for Tech and honor the institution and its role in dramatic ways. For example, when awarding first prize to a student in the state contest for National History Day, the Michigan Secretary of State cheers, 'That's my school!'.

Summary

The collaborative activities that these exemplary schools built and sustained are generally recognized as important for the overall success of schools (Purkey and Smith, 1983). The establishment of more collaborative links with the community brings concrete benefits to schools and their staffs. First, collaborative links with the community strengthen the technical aspects of the school. Community people represent an enormous pool of expertise that creative school people can tap. Community people thus multiply the resources of the school, and so improve programs at little additional cost.

Second, strong community involvement makes schools more accessible and attractive places and builds political support across constituencies. As people come to know the schools and to feel that they can contribute to their success, ignorant criticism diminishes. During the 1960s and early 1970s schools tended, for many reasons, to close themselves off from close scrutiny. Since people tend to be critical of and suspicious about institutions they do not know, support for schools was low. The 1985 Gallup Poll makes this point: 'Those individuals most closely in touch' with the schools — and presumably most knowledgeable about them — perceive them more favorably (Gallup, 1985). A personal anecdote may make this point more cogently. We have a friend who had not walked the halls of an urban high school for more than a decade. When her daughter applied to Central High School, one of Philadelphia's public academic magnet high schools, she and her husband visited with some trepidation. Fearing violence and chaos, they were astounded by the busy orderliness and friendly sense of purpose they saw all around them. The only time they heard raised voices was when two students were arguing about a physics problem. When community members come to know a school, they inevitably understand the problems and pressures and often become more sympathetic advocates for the school; thus forging links to the community helps maintain the legitimacy of the school in its larger, surrounding environment (Meyer and Rowan, 1977).

Third, participation in school activities by adults other than school staff communicates an important message to students. If adults are willing to take time from their schedules to help schools, it must be an activity of some significance (Becher, 1984). Students see by the examples of other adults that schools are important places and students should take their work in them seriously. There is no better way to communicate the importance of education than by the example of giving time.

Finally, collaborative activities shape the school–community culture that encourages a sense of concern about the quality of life that is so often missing in today's harried, noisy world (Davies, 1985). Fostering all kinds of involvement of school staff members in the community and of community members in the school sends a message to the school's neighbors. It says, 'We care about you, we want to know you, and we want you to know us'. Such messages form an important part of the school's culture. In powerful ways, they link the school to the neighborhoods it serves. This bonding demonstrates to students that people care about them and that they, in turn, should care about the community. When people feel cared for and valued as human beings, they feel connected to the organization. Commitment is high, bonds are strong, and extra energy is available (Deal, 1985).

Let us add one final note to principals. As reported earlier, recent research suggests that principals spend a good deal of time buffering teachers from the outside environment (Morris *et al.*, 1984). When principals do this, however, relations between school staffs and the community often suffer. Many of these exemplary schools had poor school–community relations in the past. Indeed, this was listed as one of the five most pressing problems they had to overcome. Yet, it is also one of the problems most susceptible to solution, since twice as many schools reported converting school–community relations from a problem to a strength than was true of any other problem area. The staffs and community members representing these schools have taken available resources and built schools into places that are special. They have followed no single recipe. Rather, they have mixed a complex set of histories and traditions that link the school and its surroundings into a culture of caring. In so doing, they have built support and good will for the school, as well as expanded the learning opportunities for the school's most important constituents: the students.

Chapter 8

Institutional Vitality:
*Improving the School**

This is a school where people could give up. They have excuses
available — lack of supplies, large classes, an unsupportive bureaucracy, red tape, the list could go on. But they haven't. They have
found new ways to get things done. They have become entre-
preneurs in the effort to maintain a tradition of excellence. The
principal, the faculty, the students and their parents seem to be
determined to succeed in spite of the obstacles. They are tough, re-
silient, and admirable people. (*Benjamin N. Cardozo High School*,
Bayside, New York).

People are the key to successful improvement initiatives as the testimonial
from *Benjamin Cardozo High School* illustrates. Phrased another way, 'The
search for excellence in schools is the search for excellence in people' (Clark,
Lotto, and Astuto, 1984). Good results are not attained by merely adopting
new technical gimmicks or incremental curriculum reforms. Significant
progress requires re-examination and improvement of organizational
basics: work norms, management practices, staff competence, classroom
standards, and so on. How can such changes be accomplished? In particular, how can they be achieved without significant new resources?

There are educational programs that, according to their promoters and
advocates, can turn academically-inferior schools into effective ones if the
staff simply follow the prescribed recipe or use the recommended techniques. Unfortunately, such claims tend to be exaggerated. Experience with
federal and state supported programs to improve public schools in America
has demonstrated that there are many ways to fail and that what works bril-

---

*The literature review described at the beginning of this chapter relies heavily on a
booklet by Thomas B. Corcoran and Barbara H. Hansen entitled *The Quest for Excellence: Making Public Schools More Effective* and published by the New Jersey School
Boards Association, 1983.

liantly in one setting may fail in another. The specifics of context are critically important in determining what to do and how to do it (Corbett, Dawson and Firestone, 1984; Berman, 1981). Each school and school district represents a unique situation presenting different dilemmas to those who seek to design and implement solutions to school problems. Even schools facing similar problems may require different approaches to their resolution. There don't seem to be any quick and easy paths to school improvement.

Furthermore, the organizational structure of schools itself encourages resistance to the adoption of new practices or changes in routines. Powerful forces operate to preserve the status quo. Communication among teachers and between teachers and administrators occurs less frequently than among employees in most other work settings. Goals tend to be vague and different groups of staff members, even inadvertently, may have different goals. Teachers are isolated from one another by their classroom walls and by busy work schedules. Administrators are preoccupied with daily demands from students, parents, and others that pull them away from supervision. Little time is provided for planning or for acquiring or practicing new skills. The organization does not help school leaders bind people together in a common work effort and it often is difficult and frustrating to try to introduce new practices or alter regular routines. As a consequence, new ideas abound in the literature and in the rhetoric of reformers, but the basic structure and routine of schools seem to remain unchanged from year to year.

Undoubtedly, factors other than organizational structure contribute to this situation. So many new ideas and techniques enter the educational marketplace and clamor for attention, all claiming to be supported by research, that educators and board members may be understandably reluctant to alter their policies and practices. Often these new approaches are poorly defined and lack proper field testing; in short, their claims are not supported by convincing evidence. Efforts to protect the 'consumers' by 'validating' programs or conducting quasi-experiments with alternative educational approaches have produced mixed results.

Fortunately, a decade of studies on improvement efforts and the diffusion of innovations provide some insights into the 'do's and don'ts' of school improvement. The major obstructions to school improvement cited in the literature are:

1. The assumptions that the problems of effectiveness are primarily technical and can be solved with new curricula or instructional techniques and the related assumption that this technology can be transported from district to district and school to school with little alteration (Berman, 1981);
2. The lack of consensus about goals, poor internal communications, and weak incentives for cooperation that are typical of public secondary schools. These organizational aspects of schools make it

difficult to spread new practices within a school or to transfer ideas or techniques from school to school. The larger the school or school district, the more severe these problems will be, which is why improvements often are easier to implement in small schools and small districts (Crandall and Loucks, 1983; Miles, 1981);

3. The assumption that improvement can be attained by training individual teachers or administrators who then will implement the new ideas in their schools with little or no support. This assumption underlies the enormous workshop industry in education and is one rationale for the many conferences and meetings attended by educators (Miles, 1981);

4. The use of top-down approaches to decision-making and planning that often fail to involve the individuals who are closest to the problems and fail to develop understanding or commitment among those who must implement the proposed changes (Bassin *et al.*, 1979; Berman, 1981; Louis, Rosenblum and Molitor, 1981);

5. Political interference during the implementation process from interest groups or board members or an abandonment of the program because a leader departs (Pincus and Williams, 1979); and

6. The lack of competent external assistance to school staff who must implement the program or the failure to provide such assistance for a long enough time period (Crandall and Loucks, 1983; Louis, Rosenblum and Molitor, 1981).

These are some of the negative lessons to be drawn from research on school improvement. Fortunately, there are some positive findings as well. Clark, Lotto and Astuto (1984), in an insightful synthesis of two separate traditions of educational inquiry (generally labelled as school effectiveness and school improvement) summarize the positive findings in seven attainable attributes, which may be characterized as follows:

1. *Commitment.* Good schools project a *raison d'être*. Collectively the staff has arrived at an agreed set of behaviors and outcomes that are sufficiently specific to acculturate new organizational members and control the behavior of veteran members. They are organizations with a sense of themselves.

2. *Expectations.* Good schools and school systems are populated by confident people who expect others to perform to their personal level of quality. Teachers expect students to achieve. Students know they are expected to achieve, and they expect, in turn, to have involved, competent teachers. Principals are surprised by teachers who fail. Teachers are surprised by administrators who ask little of themselves and others.

3. *Action.* People in good schools do things. They have a bias for action, a proclivity for success, and a sense of opportunism. They plan for now, seize decision options when they arise, try new ideas,

drop bad trials, and play within their strengths. Good school systems and schools have learned how to avoid talking new ideas to death. Good schools invent a structure and improve their practice.

4. *Leadership.* Peters and Waterman (1982) pressed the point that 'innovative companies foster many leaders and many innovators throughout the organization'. People with high levels of efficacy and expectancy who are trying and experimenting cannot be restricted to designated leadership positions. Effective educational organizations spawn primary work groups and individual 'champions' in unusual numbers. The designated leaders create an environment for trial and a tolerance for failure so that leaders can emerge and be sustained at all levels of the school system.

5. *Focus.* Good schools pay attention to the task at hand. Student achievement in the classroom commands the attention of teachers and administrators. More classroom time is allocated to academic learning: more allotted time is engaged academic learning time for students. Staff development programs concentrate on classroom-oriented skills and understandings.

6. *Climate.* At a minimum, good schools maintain an orderly and safe environment for students and teachers. But they are much more orderly. Time after time observers report that the organizational climate in successful schools is obvious but hard to specify. Successful schools work for all people in the building. They are not schools for students; nor are they schools for teachers and administrators. They work for adults and children and adolescents.

7. *Slack.* Good schools have a reasonable level of human resources and slack time. [There is] time for teachers to participate in staff development activity and to incorporate new practices into their already crowded professional lives. Good practice is facilitated by a reasonable level of organizational redundancy, slack at the classroom level, tolerance for failure, encouragement of experimentation, and the capacity to invent and adapt innovations.

Are secondary schools more resistant to improvement than elementary schools? It is part of the lore of educational research and development that secondary schools are more resistant to change. Studies of school improvement and change by Rosenblum and Louis (1981) and Berman and McLaughlin (1977) found this to be true, but the apparent rigidities were not explained. A number of explanations have been offered since, including:

- the larger sizes of the institutions,
- isolation due to departmentalization ('loose-coupling'),
- the dominance of curriculum content,
- the larger proportion of males in the secondary work-force,
- lower parental interest,
- the greater attention given to professional autonomy,

- lower goal consensus and a lack of a schoolwide perspective among staff,
- the weaker role of the principal in instruction, and
- less accountability for results because of their multiple goals.

Yet secondary schools do change. During the 1960s and 1970s many new programs and policies were successfully introduced (Cusick, 1981). Reforms that created new clientele or were more easily monitored were most successful. New programs, new course requirements, or changes in scheduling are examples. Reforms requiring teachers to use new content, new methods, or to work harder were less successful (Tyack, Kirst and Hansot, 1984). Recent examination of change in secondary schools re-affirm these conclusions. Hall and his colleagues (Hall and Guzman, 1984; Hord, 1984; and Rutherford and Huling-Austin, 1984) visited eighteen high schools across the country. They found:

- there was a high rate of innovation,
- most innovations were minor,
- organizational and curricular innovations accounted for two-thirds of the changes,
- there were no clear patterns in internal leadership of change, and
- department leadership was ineffectual.

They concluded that the notion that high schools could not change was a myth. They further concluded that many of the recently proposed reforms are of the type that high schools are able to implement.

Are there improvement programs that work? During 1983, Farrar, Neufeld, and Miles (1984) conducted a snowball survey to identify school improvement programs in secondary schools based upon the effective schools research. They identified thirty-nine programs in twenty-five states serving 2378 buildings. There were thirty-five programs involving over 700 secondary schools and twenty-three of the programs were comprehensive school-wide programs. The programs relied heavily on results of studies of elementary schools, citing Edmonds' work most frequently (Miles, Farrar and Neufeld, 1983). The programs typically involved formation of a planning team, conduct of an organizational assessment, identification of needs, development of a plan, and creation of task groups to implement the program. The programs often used approaches from the field of organization development. The amount of external assistance, training, and cost varied widely. About half of the programs involved voluntary participation of schools and their staffs.

Impact data were only anecdotal as most of the programs were new. Most claimed success — 'clear impact in about 60 per cent of the schools' — but no data were provided to support the claims. The analysts, nevertheless, found the impact information sufficiently impressive to reach an optimistic conclusion about the potential effects of these programs. Noting the problems of designing interventions for secondary schools from a research base on elementary schools, they nonetheless were impressed with what the developers had done and with the amount of impact reported (Miles, Farrar, and Neufeld, 1983). Evaluations of programs in New York City (MEDARP, 1983), New Jersey and Pennsylvania (Research for Better Schools, 1982), and a number of district programs (Purkey, 1984; Fruchter, 1982) also show promising but mixed results. Evaluators report serious implementation problems and some faculty resistance. There is little hard evidence of impact on school performance. Nevertheless, the processes have been successfully installed in many sites and some schools report an impressive list of accomplishments in terms of changes in policies, programs, or procedures. As Farrar, Neufeld, and Miles (1984) have observed, the examination of these programs raises more questions than it answers. The effective schools movement has unleashed a flood of energy and good intentions. Some creative programs are being designed and put in place. But little is known about their impact on the schools or on student achievement. They should be monitored, shared, and improved, or their inability to meet expectations may produce more cynicism about public education and an irreversible loss of public confidence.

The schools in this sample are not immune to the problems faced by other public schools in America. As part of the nomination process, the staffs at each school were asked to write reflective essays about the obstacles their school had faced during the last five years and the degree to which these obstacles had been overcome. The most frequently mentioned obstacles (in order of frequency) were:

- inadequate facilities
- declining enrollments
- inadequate funding
- poor school–community relations
- poor discipline
- lack of school spirit
- low attendance
- lack of clear academic standards
- drugs/alcohol and
- complacency with past accomplishments.

Several important conclusions can be drawn from the answers to this question. First, while each school faces a unique set of obstacles (with more than fifty different categories of obstacles mentioned), there are a few common obstacles that most school staffs must address. Nearly two-thirds of the staffs identified inadequate facilities, declining enrollments, and financial constraints as obstacles to improvement. Second, most of the schools encountered multiple obstacles along the road to success, with the average number listed between five and eight. Third, the most pressing obstacles are those over which school staff have little direct control. Declining enrollments, inadequate facilities, and financial exigencies are issues arising from the larger environment in which the schools function. Fourth, there is little variation in what schools perceive as being their obstacles when factors like school size, racial composition of the student body, or metropolitan status of the surrounding community are considered.

The schools also provided information on their approaches to these obstacles and the success they had in addressing them. It is noteworthy that the areas in which high schools reported the greatest amount of positive change were student discipline, school–community relations, student attendance, academic standards, and school spirit. Junior highs and middle schools reported significant improvements in school–community relations, revisions of curricula, student discipline, and school spirit. These problems do not necessarily require significant new resources and generally fall within the scope of the authority and action of school staffs. They also are critical barriers to raising academic achievement. Problems relating to the use of drugs and alcohol, single-parent families, and the overcoming of staff and community complacency were also frequently mentioned but appeared to be more intractable.

What sets these schools apart from most American secondary schools is their persistence in addressing the problems and the creativity of their responses. Rather than viewing problems as constraints, many of these schools treated them as challenges. To borrow one slogan, their staffs have a 'can do' attitude. They didn't just sit back and wait for answers to appear. Rather, they aggressively searched for alternative solutions. Some examples help illustrate this point.

Van Buren Middle School, an urban school in Albuquerque, New Mexico, with a very diverse student population was confronted with a general malaise among the professional staff, described as follows:

> The teachers seemed to lack direction as there was no sequential curriculum or one designed to meet the needs of the diverse student population. The teachers also felt a severe problem was their delegation to the state of 'powerlessness' as decisions were made at the top of the school hierarchy and formally passed down with little or no support or guidance.

A remarkable turn-around in this school in recent years was spurred by changing the entire philosophy of the school from one of no participation beyond minimal expectations to one of participatory management. A curriculum was developed with teacher input that provided for proper sequencing of subjects as well as providing programs which would meet students' educational needs. The development of a school improvement team gave teachers a sense of power and a legitimate formal avenue to not only express concerns but to demonstrate their own creativity.

Since financial problems plagued a large number of schools, the responses from two school systems faced with severe budget cuts offer excellent examples:

Hudson, OH, School District was faced with an overnight 20 per cent reduction of the local tax base when the major employer in the community unexpectedly filed for bankruptcy. The school district aggressively mounted a campaign to deal with the problem. As the superintendent noted, 'We're very much a proactive place rather than a reactive one'. The community quickly lobbied the state legislature to negotiate a state loan fund for school districts that have 10 per cent or more of their tax base reduced by the demise of local industry.

Falbrook Union High School, CA, recently moved from the position of a well-funded school to a poorly-funded one, and was required to cut teachers and programs. Despite these problems, the school continues to enjoy success because of the dedication to professional excellence and the harmony and cooperation of the faculty staff. From the teacher in the classroom who maintains high student achievement, to the gardener and custodian who do double-duty to maintain the appearance of the campus and the classroom, there has been no let-down in performance. In fact, the lack of funding has had a beneficial effect; as the problem was recognized, there was a rally of support. Board members, parents, students, faculty and staff wrote letters to the governor and legislature, volunteers came to help on campus; contributions from boosters increased. The staff, board and community worked together in seeking solutions that would result in a minimal disruption to the quality of education.

Another school from a very poor district with a large minority population, in coping with inadequate facilities, built a showcase facility out of almost nothing. As the site visitor commented:

One quickly forgets when entering the grounds that this is a poor school. The teachers and students don't think of themselves as poor, they think of themselves as resourceful. By using donated land, stockpiling building materials when a favorable price presented itself, and having construction work done by vocational students and maintenance staff, they have created a masterpiece of construction and architecture . . . that would be the envy of a large metropolitan school. As a result of the student investment in the campus, it is clean, well-maintained, graffiti-free, and pridefully upgraded. (*Byng High School*, Ada, OK).

Declining enrollments at *Southwood Junior High* in Miami, Florida, were reversed by the development of a center for the arts which provides a diversified program in art, drama, dance, music, and photography. In a few years, the student body has increased by 25 per cent and in the process has attracted a group of students from throughout the city.

The reverse problem, a period of expansion where there was a campaign to build new schools, required a different tack at *Linn-Marr High School* in Marion, Iowa:

> A period of rapid growth (50 to 100 students per year) five years ago meant a focus only on 'bricks and mortar', that is, making sure facilities were adequate for the number of students. To redirect the focus an extensive staff development program was initiated with specified learning and skills activities all directed toward an improved curriculum.

Not only have many of these schools faced declines or expansions but also significant changes in the composition of the community. A fairly common problem is the increasing senior citizen population which often lobbies against tax increases that support local school improvement initiatives. The staff at *Roscommon High School*, MI, described their situation as follows:

> The population of the school district is changing. Currently, approximately one-third of the community residents are retirees. This number is growing and the passage of a millage vote favorable to the district is becoming more difficult. An adult education program with emphasis on enrichment courses for older adults was implemented. The objective of this program is to attempt to serve the educational needs of the adults and retirees of the district and to gain their support.

Hoover Middle School in Albuquerque, New Mexico, was forced to deal with another common problem, school-community relations. However, rather than the usual issue of how to get more active community support, this problem revolved around getting teachers to accept and eventually solicit parental input in areas previously considered the teachers' domain. Once administrators were able to convince teachers that involving parents meant that teachers would have access to additional welcome services, new skills, and resources, it was necessary to organize a parent liaison to more effectively handle the growing number of requests for parent assistance. Another piece of the solution was to get teachers to accept that parents' presence provided a critical link to the home–school partnership that excellent schools must have. As a result, a mutually satisfactory relationship exists between the community and the school, with constant positive reinforcement between both groups.

Another school, coping with high turnover of administration, staff, and students found it difficult to create a cohesive organization until the program was structured around four guiding principles:

1. *Direction:* the administration organized a consistent set of policies, particularly with respect to discipline.
2. *Cooperation:* key decisions in scheduling, teacher assignments,

teacher evaluation, and curriculum and budget are implemented through the input and efforts of teachers and administrators alike.

3. *Communication:* an effort to 'win back' students led to an all-out campaign of establishing clear and fluid lines of communication between the school and community.
4. *Flexibility:* the school strives to meet the needs of a diverse and changing student population by having the curriculum under constant review. (*Seoul American High School*, Seoul, South Korea).

This problem-solving approach also was applied to work with individual students. The following examples illustrate some of the ways in which these schools focus their resources on problem students and attempt to turn them toward success:

One especially useful technique seemed to be 'Targeting Sessions'. These meetings to discuss a 'problem' student are held for not more than 15 minutes in the morning, before school. No student is discussed during this initial intervention meeting for more than 15 minutes, and the product of the meeting is a 'plan for consistent treatment by all of the student's teachers and counselors in order to help him/her succeed'. According to the teachers I interviewed, these target sessions keep the discussion focused on improvement and problem resolution, rather than gripes and student shortcomings. (*Westchester Middle School*, Chesterton, IN).

Student assessment teams are comprised of the assistant principal, one special education teacher, reading specialist, guidance counselor, and the regular classroom teacher where the student assessed is assigned. This team was designed to identify students who did not qualify for special services but who are experiencing frustration, conflict, or special problems in the regular classroom. Their assessment team receives referrals and meets every two weeks to brainstorm for ideas to better reach each individual student. 'We've had a lot of success with the approach'. 'We can — together — address questions like "Why isn't this student clicking?" — or "How can I better motivate him/her or change my teaching techniques to reach him/her?"'. Teachers who may be experiencing success with a particular student where other teachers may not are reported to be sharing techniques during this process. A follow-up conference to check on each student is always held. (*Princeton Junior High*, Cincinnati, OH).

The story from *Jean Ribault High School* in Jacksonville, Florida is a model for any school with a multitude of problems to follow. Their motto says it all, 'From Concrete Jungle to Model School'. A series of steps were taken to change the image of the school, including:

- forcing all teachers to reapply to teach at Ribault, and in the process replacing two-thirds of the staff,
- encouraging teachers to set high standards (the school operates on the premise that students will rise to the level of the highest expectations being set) and pushing students to work hard to meet the standards,
- creating academic pep rallies that stimulate student achievement,
- running Saturday tutorial sessions to improve test scores, and
- designing and hosting a fine arts festival that enriches the cultural life of the school and community and develops good consumers of the arts.

The staff from *Artesia High School* in Lakewood, California, summed up their·drive for improvement as follows:

> The year 1982–83 became the year of focus on the public schools. There was a great deal of anxiety and guilt being shared by every element of the educational community. [Some of the public concerns were that] students don't know how to think and teachers are burnt-out. It is the philosophy of this high school that no one really subscribes to failure as a way of life. Mediocrity is not the goal. If we believe this to be true, then it follows that we had an obligation to raise the expectancy level for students and teachers, to create an orderly atmosphere in which education could become a reality, to give students and teachers an active voice in those decisions which affected their world, to support and train teachers for better delivery systems, to respect the potential of each student and the professionalism of each faculty member. A consistent plan of improvement training and accountability began in 1980. This plan included consistent participation, teacher training, staff development, master teachers who modeled effective instruction, and ongoing evaluation of teachers and program. We began not only to ask the 'what' questions, but the 'why' questions. As a result, the critical mass of trained personnel has grown. Teachers are coaching teachers. Students are receiving better instruction and therefore achieving more.... Teachers and students are taken seriously by one another and by the administration. A new model for school management has evolved which includes 'role reversal'; the administration has become the model, the trainer. Education is alive and well at our high school.

These unusually successful secondary schools face up to their problems. They are truly 'can do' organizations that refused to succumb to ready rationalizations for performances that are below expectations. They see problems as challenges to be overcome. Underlying this attitude is the support of their communities, particularly parents and board members who expect success but also give their school staffs the leeway and resources necessary to achieve it.

Chapter 9

Equalizing Educational Opportunity: Serving At-Risk Youth

The pervasive and continuing relationship between educational achievement and the ethnic and social background of students in the United States continues to be one of the major problems facing American society. The public schools are expected to provide the primary channels for social and economic advancement, but, in spite of decades of special funding and targeted programs, there has been only limited progress towards the reduction of the pernicious relationship between learning and family background. Almost all measures of academic outcomes, such as scores on standardized tests, graduation from high school, and participation in upper-level classes, continue to be strongly correlated with ethnic background and social status.

Breaking through this educational barrier has always been an important goal for social reformers. However, it has become critical to the cause of social justice in the 1980s because mastery of the basic and higher-order cognitive skills has become increasingly significant for entry-level employment and economic advancement. Blue-collar jobs are declining in number and being replaced with service jobs that, at a minimum, require good verbal communication skills and the ability to read and compute. More importantly, advancement from low-paying, entry-level positions requires even higher skill levels. The close relationship between educational attainment and economic opportunity poses a difficult dilemma for a society promising equal economic opportunities for all citizens.

The preceeding chapters have described school policies and practices associated with educational success, but in this chapter, the focus must be shifted to the efforts of educators to devise strategies that succeed with all students. A number of the schools in our sample serve significant populations of poor and minority students. As indicated in Chapter 3, more than a fifth of the schools reported that 25 per cent or more of their students were from low-income families. This chapter examines the special efforts made to meet the needs of these students and to raise the level of their educational achievement.

Demographic Changes

The label 'at risk' is often used as a euphemism for poor and minority students whose levels of achievement are lower than the general student population and whose drop-out rates are much higher. This is the most common usage. But the term is sometimes defined broadly to include all students whose behaviors limit or jeopardize their success in school — students who exhibit discipline or attendance problems, students who become pregnant, students who use drugs, and students who are alienated.

The numbers of such children have been increasing during the 1970s and 1980s. More children are living in poverty. The traditional structure of American families also is rapidly changing and single-parent families are the norm in some communities. Hodgkinson (1985), in his widely-read demographic report, concluded that the public schools are enrolling increasing numbers of children who:

- were born to teenage mothers
- were born to parents who were not married
- lived with one parent
- came from poor households
- were from minority ethnic and racial backgrounds.

These are the children most likely to fail in school.

Hodgkinson's forecasts and those of others suggest that these populations are likely to grow both in absolute numbers and as a proportion of the total school-age population. This is a cause for concern, not only for ideological reasons, but because the projected growth of populations who are difficult to educate and to employ might reduce the nation's economic competitiveness. Continued failure to effectively educate such children will increase the demands on scarce public resources, and could lead to the emergence of a dual society with a large, minority underclass who are poorly educated and economically at risk.

Educating 'At-Risk' Youth

In the mid-1980s, the attention of the educational reform movement was directed to the problems of students who were not succeeding in school and whose skill deficiencies put them economically and socially at risk. In 1985 and after, a series of reports was issued by prominent civic and business organizations seeking to draw the attention of educational leaders and policy-makers to the growing numbers of the educationally disadvantaged and to the danger that the reform movement, through its efforts to raise academic standards, might inadvertently increase the failure and dropping-out rates, thereby increasing the social and economic vulnerability of this population (Education Commission of the States, 1985; Institute for Educational Leadership, 1985; National Coalition of Advocates for Students, 1984; National Governors Association, 1986; and Committee for Economic Development, 1987).

Creating better secondary schools for children from poor families presumes some knowledge about schools that are effective with such students. Here educational policy-makers faced a dilemma. Public pressure required action, but policy-makers had no reliable roadmaps. Literature reviews and personal discussions with researchers suggested that few public secondary schools had been systematically successful with such students. Prescriptions drawn from the effective schools research were promising departure points for identification of problems and the design of school improvement programs, but, having been derived from studies of elementary schools and suffering from serious conceptual and methodological limitations, they offered few specific suggestions for action. There were no simple or surefire formulas for increasing the educational success of 'at-risk' students at the secondary level.

There were frequent media reports of secondary schools that had been 'effective' with at-risk children, but, upon closer examination, these reported achievements often turned out to be limited, e.g. improving discipline or attendance, raising basic skills to national norms, or related to some unique circumstance such as a large middle-class minority enrollment. No researcher had identified a non-selective American public high school in which the relationship between achievement and social status had been eliminated or even significantly reduced. Nor had a school been identified in which large numbers of low-income students were regularly successful at higher levels of learning such as advanced placement courses. There were simply no models to emulate.

Researchers examining alternative schools, small, special programs typically serving marginal students with serious discipline, attendance, and academic problems, did offer some specific suggestions for improvement based upon their examinations of successful programs. The following characteristics were found to be related to success in alternative programs (Gottfredson, Gottfredson, and Cook, 1983; Gold and Mann, 1984; Wehlage and Rutter, 1986):

- small size that facilitated personal relationships between students and staff
- strong collegial teacher cultures
- teachers who believed that such students could succeed
- development of positive peer cultures
- individualized and cooperative instructional strategies
- a curriculum emphasizing active student roles, student decision making, and content related to the needs of the group
- development of strong social bonds to the school community
- high levels of parent involvement.

132

Alternative programs were identified that had reduced delinquency, improved attendance, and improved student attitudes, but the numbers of programs and students were small and there was only limited evidence of sustained academic improvement.

Clearly, the best remedies for the educational problems of 'at-risk' students would be stronger and more effective public schools. From this perspective, all of the organizational and programmatic attributes described in the preceding chapters have special significance for these students. The US Department of Education supported this position in its 1987 booklet, *Schools That Work: Educating Disadvantaged Children*, that recommended among other things: strong instructional leadership, an orderly climate, raising academic standards, building character, and reaching out to parents. From this perspective, it is important to understand how successful secondary schools deal with 'at-risk' students. Such schools are likely to provide models of 'best' practice, and, although the best may fall short of what is needed, these schools are an important source of knowledge about the education of such students.

Examples of such schools and their progress are illustrated below. Each of the schools described has initiated a variety of programs to address the needs of at-risk students. Their leaders and staffs have worked on many fronts at once, including building more positive peer cultures and school climates, raising expectations, strengthening incentives, intensifying instruction, expanding support services, involving students in planning, and reaching out to parents and the community. Descriptions of these diverse strategies and the results that have been reported were extracted from the information provided in the school nomination forms and the site visit reports.

Ribault Senior High School, Jacksonville, Fl.

Called a jungle by the news media, and once regarded as the worst teaching assignment in Jacksonville, this large urban high school became a widely publicized lighthouse school in less than five years. Ribault students are a prototypical 'at-risk' population, predominantly black (99 per cent) and largely poor. The steps taken to reverse the situation at Ribault included:

- appointment of a new principal;
- changes in the staff, all teachers had to re-apply in 1979 and two-thirds were replaced by people who wanted to be at the school;
- increased parent involvement as a result of parent contacts and intensive public relations;
- introduction of academic competition programs and academic pep rallies to help students prepare for the state test;
- introduction of a strong, clear discipline code, a student dress code, and generally higher standards and expectations;

- Saturday tutoring in math and language arts for the state test;
- use of retired teachers as volunteer tutors; and
- visible activities such as a fine arts festival, a science fair, and a math field day to alter the school's image and raise community and student expectations for success.

The passing rates on the mathematics section of the Florida state test went from 20 per cent to 83 per cent in four years. The number of students continuing their education at post-secondary institutions increased. Ribault received many state and national awards and considerable public attention which helped build the belief among staff and students that educational success was possible and could be sustained.

West Mesa High School, Albuquerque, NM

This large school, serving a predominantly Hispanic student body, was in disarray in 1978 with a negative climate, frequent disruptions, and low morale. A new administration was brought in to restore order and then a second administrative change was made to foster a positive climate, higher expectations and improved academic programs. This renewal process took over 5 years, but it paid large dividends. The effects were dramatic: improved discipline (suspensions declined from 12 per cent in 1980–81 to 2.2 per cent in 1983–84), better attendance (a 6.5 per cent increase to 93.4 per cent), the percentages of students passing the state proficiency test increased from 75 per cent to 93 per cent, and the percentage going on to college rose from 7 per cent to 29 per cent.

To achieve these results, an array of new policies and programs were introduced at West Mesa, including:

- new attendance and discipline policies;
- PACK — Program for Academically Capable Kids — for students with GPAs of 3.0 or higher and who exceed graduation requirements in core subjects;
- MESA — Mathematics, Engineering, and Science Achievement — for minorities who exceed requirements in math or science (80 kids);
- core subjects offering developmental courses for students reading at 5th grade or below. Students moved out as they improve skills;
- diverse procedures to recognize academic success: notes home when grade point averages exceeded 2.5, honor certificates, newspaper articles, academic dinners, and so forth; and
- a nationally recognized alternate school, the LIFE Center that matches teaching style to learning style.

In addition, comprehensive services were made available for low achieving students such as Chapter 1 reading, a school support team, student health care services, a redesigned counseling center, and career programming and vocational educational programs. Building improvements also were made, including addition of a fine arts complex and a media-library center.

Colville High School, Colville, WA

This small (only 436 students in 1984), predominantly white, high school in a rural poverty area of Washington enrolls 40 per cent of its students from low-income families. As a result of ten years of introspection and hard work, Colville has overcome the low expectations often associated with small, rural schools. The principal described the problem as follows:

> Many teachers and students honestly believe that small rural schools cannot match the education offered by larger suburban or urban schools. Put quite simply, they confuse quantity with quality. The toughest initial task here at CHS was to convince our staff and students that despite being small and rural, we could develop excellent programs to meet the needs of all students we serve by focusing on doing fewer things but doing them better than anyone else. Changing this attitude was *at least* a five year project.

Among the steps taken to raise achievement at Colville were: (1) adoption of a demanding set of graduation requirements, (2) expansion of instructional time by elimination of study halls and scheduling special activities before or after school, (3) a homework policy that demands it be assigned, scored, and learner feedback provided, (4) an emphasis on student and staff responsibility for conditions in the school, and (5) an expanded student extracurricular program and an active effort to reach uninvolved students. Assistance to students was also expanded and intensified:

> All CHS teachers in the academic core conduct special 'help sessions' for students needing additional help and provide 'second chance testing' on the noon hour for those students who fail examinations.

A Learning Support Center also serves 15 students daily and provides one-on-one instruction.

The design and implementation of these new initiatives were aided by bimonthly brown bag in-services for the staff to discuss curricular and instructional issues, use of effective schools research to assess and improve the school's climate, and a principal who treats teachers as professionals. As a result of these various efforts, CTBS and SAT scores have improved and enormous pride in Colville High School has developed.

James Logan HS, Union City, CA

The student population at Logan is diverse, 39 per cent are white, 14 per cent are black, 26 per cent Hispanic, and 21.4 per cent Asian. Thirty per cent of the 2420 student enrollment was categorized as low-income and 12 per cent designated as having limited proficiency in English. While the staff and students at Logan did not face the dire conditions experienced by some urban schools, attendance and achievement were declining and the school's public image was poor. The actions taken to improve the situation included: a new emphasis on basic skills utilizing math and reading labs and staff development, an enriched curriculum and a strong curriculum review process, closing the campus and tightening discipline, an expanded ESL program, an attendance improvement program, stronger supervision and accountability, staff development to improve teaching, more student involvement, and teacher and student involvement in the school improvement process.

The changes have been carefully planned and implemented and students, as well as staff and parents, have been involved in planning and decision making:

> We have had a school site council for a number of years that includes students elected by students. The site council is composed of staff, parents, and students and acts in an advisory role to the principal regarding the implementation and monitoring of the school plan. We also have a Student Curriculum Council which deals specifically with curriculum questions and develops proposals for curriculum change based on assessment data which the students gather themselves. This has resulted in a large number of changes in both required and elective course offerings in the school. A third group established this year to deal with improved food services has been an advisory committee to the food service department. This committee meets on a regular basis with the district supervisor of food services and has been instrumental in solving problems as well as providing the opportunity for student groups to sponsor special activities.

More adult supervision and administrative visibility have helped strengthen discipline in the school and have contributed to its business-like atmosphere.

Not surprisingly, there has been great improvement in discipline and in school attendance (from 83.9 per cent in 1979–80 to 92 per cent in 1982–83). Drop-outs declined and test scores improved steadily. The number of students attending post-secondary institutions also has increased and strong emphasis has been placed, through a MESA program, on preparing minority students for engineering and science careers.

New Bedford High School, New Bedford, MA

An extremely large high school, enrolling over 3000 students in 1984, New Bedford serves an economically-depressed area with high unemployment.

The student population is 78 per cent white, 16 per cent black, and 6 per cent Hispanic. Nearly half, 44 per cent, are from low-income families. The principal wrote:

> Because of the educational, social, and financial limitations of our community, support and understanding from parents and other city residents for the traditional role and values inherent in a high education cannot be *assumed* in New Bedford. Therefore, a major emphasis has been focused on a variety of parent outreach programs and on sharing goals and needs with our neighbors, the community at large.

He went on to say that the school must deal with '. . . parents who want their straight A college-capable daughter to leave for a factory job on the 16th birthday', and with situations in which '. . . the senior with a College Board Math score of 800 may be the first member of his family ever to have gone beyond the eighth grade'.

The school staff have had to be creative to meet such needs and to cope with the budget limitations imposed in the early 1980s by Proposition 2 1/2, a state-wide tax reduction measure. A wide array of special programs were initiated to make full use of all resources (federal, state, and local) available to the school. These included peer and adult tutoring, Chapter 1 reading, bilingual education, student resource centers in each academic area, participation in Upward Bound, special programs for drop-outs, co-op students, pre-vocational students, pregnant teens, and an alternate school.

C.F. Vigor High School, Pritchard, AL

At the end of the 1970s, Vigor High School was a depressed school. The pattern was similar to other schools serving predominantly black, low-income populations. The student population at Vigor in 1984 was 30 per cent white and 69 per cent black; over half of the 1864 students were eligible for the federal free lunch program and almost all of the students were from lower-status families. Test scores were low. Student participation in activities had declined. The public image was poor. This was the aftermath of rioting that had accompanied desegregation. By 1984, this school was receiving widespread public acclaim for its turn-around. The major elements in the rejuvenation of Vigor were:

- an innovative ninth grade remedial program in core subjects, the competency-based VEBA program, that involves a team and a counselor and emphasizes English, mathematics, social studies, science, and career awareness;
- initiation of AP classes in four subjects: English, American History, biology, and chemistry;

- firm discipline, including penalties for tardiness and internal suspension, using a structured program called Retract;
- post-school day classes in math and English conducted by staff volunteers that meet twice a week; and
- introduction of computer training.

As a result of these innovations, there were improvements in attendance and discipline and large increases in the percentages of students passing local competency exams; in five years, the percentage passing county competency tests in reading and math rose from 42 per cent to 94 per cent and from 47 per cent to 85 per cent, respectively. There also were increases in the numbers of students taking PSATs and in their scores. There were accompanying increases in college attendance.

The principal believes that it is the people at the school who made the difference. He attributes the school's success to the involvement of people in planning and a positive attitude that encourages people to try harder.

Utterback Junior High School, Tucson, AZ

Utterback Junior High School, a small school in a low-SES neighborhood of Tucson, Arizona, was affected by court-ordered desegregation in 1978. Neighborhood children were bussed out and Anglo students were bussed in. Angry white parents sent their children to private schools and enrollment declined. In 1982, because of teacher talent in the fine arts, the school developed a Creative and Performing Arts magnet to attract Anglo students back and remain in compliance:

> During the summer of 1982, the faculty and staff created, designed, and implemented the Creative and Performing Arts Magnet component to highlight an outstanding academic curriculum. The pride in Utterback is evident. The feeling of ownership in a program is experienced by the faculty.

Total enrollment increased by over 25 per cent following development of the magnet program. Anglo enrollment has increased by 34 per cent, thus bringing the school into compliance. Still, nearly half of the students were from families below or near the poverty level and nearly half were minority students. However, the school's indicators of success with all students began to improve:

> Daily absences have been cut in half, from 44 students absent daily in 1981–82 to 22 absent daily in 1982–83. Student discipline problems have gone from 98 per cent of the students referred in 1981–82 to 40 per cent in 1982–83.

One of the more creative steps taken was an effort to foster more active student leadership and participation:

Utterback JHS offers an organized program to foster student participation in government. At the beginning of the school year, class time is provided to teach students how student government functions and how to run for office. All students are encouraged to participate. Academic credit is given to all student council members through their social studies classes. The council meets daily. Their functions include: (1) fund raisers for school improvement; (2) input on school policy; and (3) design and implementation of programs to promote school morale.

There was not simply one solution to the school's problems; many changes were made. Among the actions taken were: adoption of a new discipline policy, development of curricular options, introduction of a study-skills program, use of a performance orientation in both fine arts and academics, encouragement of activities involving staff and students, and increasing faculty control over curriculum.

Shaker Heights High School, Shaker Heights, OH

Shaker Heights High School is located in an affluent suburb of Cleveland, Ohio. It is well-known nationally because of its reputation for academic excellence as evidenced by the success of students on Advanced Placement tests and the large number of National Merit awards received by its students. A well-equipped school with an outstanding faculty, Shaker Heights once served only upper-middle-class, white students, but over the past twenty years the student population has changed. By the early 1980s, nearly 40 per cent of the student body was black. The black students generally came from working-class families and many lacked the educational backgrounds or aspirations of the students the school had been accustomed to serving.

In response to the change, the school developed a complex tracking system in all core subjects, known as the levels system. The policy was intended to protect academic standards and the rigorous curriculum. Unfortunately, it also created *de facto* segregation in the school's classrooms as the upper levels were wholly or predominantly white and the classes in the lower levels largely black. This policy was challenged by local civil rights groups and, after a thorough study of the system, the school decided to open up the levels system by letting students and their parents determine which level was appropriate. While this reform has not eliminated the achievement gap, it has increased the numbers of black students taking higher-level classes and stimulated the school staff to search for better ways to serve these 'new' students and accelerate their academic progress.

Staff at Shaker Heights encourage students to enroll in classes that challenge them. They express concern about students who are content to do remedial work or to drift through their coursework. A counselor noted that the school offered a rich array of extra-curricular activities and these were often the best means of helping a marginal student get involved in the school and learn the value of academics. Staff at the school are also concerned about those whose attendance and lack of involvement mark them as potential drop-outs. To help these students, the school developed several innovative programs in the 1970s and early 1980s. A counseling and tracking program, PUSH-EXCEL, modeled after the Jesse Jackson program, was developed to keep students on track and to help parents support their children. An after-school homework center was opened for students who needed a place to get some help with their work and maybe even a quiet place to do it. An alternate school was developed in a refurbished area of the school to provide a more structured environment for students who found the freedom of an open campus too much of a temptation or got lost in the hustle and bustle of the larger school. A job placement program was developed to help those whose economic needs competed with their completion of high school.

Shaker Heights is seeking to maintain its high standards, while still effectively serving an increasingly diverse clientele. Reducing the achievement gap between white and black students is the agenda at the school. The Shaker Heights staff admit that they have not found any panaceas for educating at-risk students, but they are determined to help the students meet their high standards, rather than lower their standards to cope with the students. As one staff member put it: 'Some schools left the basics in 1960s, we didn't; we stuck with solid courses, final exams, and rigorous grading'.

Crater High School, Central Point, OR

This small, rural school in Oregon served over 900 students in 1983, thirty per cent of whom were from low-income families. The school was overcrowded and in poor physical condition. Attendance was poor (less than 80 per cent), student attitudes about their teachers and the school were negative, and the drop-out rate was high. Academic standards were low and few courses were offered for the college-bound. Only 20 per cent of the school's graduates went on to four-year colleges and universities.

The school leaders attribute the dramatic turn-around in the school to: higher academic standards; strong internal and external communication; strong management; improved curriculum; recruitment of high-quality staff; better services for students with special needs; community outreach; student recognition and service; and greater faculty participation in school life. The changes began with a self-study of student attitudes in 1977 and continue. Roughly in sequence, the actions taken were:

- Physical improvements such as fresh paint, lockers, new furniture, etc.;
- New academic courses;
- A teacher-advisor program to personalize the school;
- Staff increases to lower class sizes;
- Doubling of administrative staff;
- A successful bond issue to improve the facility (due to the changes already made in the social climate) and maintenance was improved;
- Stronger staff evaluation procedures and new hiring practices were adopted to select committed teachers;
- Tougher attendance and discipline policies;
- Review of the total curriculum; and
- New programs in writing, arts, community services, and peer tutoring.

The school directed special attention to at-risk students by developing a variety of new approaches:

At Crater, remediation of basic skills is provided primarily in regularly scheduled remedial classes, in a tutorial program, and through the services of a learning specialist. Remedial classes include the math 100 series (four semesters), fundamentals of communication (two semesters at each grade level), and special materials biology (two semesters). Enrollment in remedial classes is limited to 20 students or less per class per period. In the study enrichment, a tutorial program which is partially funded with Chapter 1 monies, two teachers and an aide help low-skilled students with work assigned in their required courses. Since the student to teacher ratio does not exceed six to one, students are offered intensive, personalized assistance which focuses on developing study and basic skills, a positive self-concept, and success in the school setting. The learning specialist not only teams with teachers in remedial classes, but also serves as a resource for teachers of students who have LEPs or special needs. Teachers also adapt lessons to accommodate student learning styles and skill levels. This is especially true in an extended day program where instruction is completely individualized. The extended day allows students who are short of credits for graduation the opportunity of completing required courses after regular school hours. Remediation of skills is a primary target of the extended day.

By 1983, student attendance at Crater was up to 93.5 per cent and staff attendance was up to 97 per cent. Test scores had improved. The drop-out rate had been reduced to 9 per cent and attendance at four-year colleges had doubled to 40 per cent. The principal explained the gains this way:

This drop-out rate has improved dramatically in the past five years.

We believe that improved personal attention to students, special help programs, and high standards (which tend to make students feel education is important) have all contributed to a low drop-out rate.

Crater High School went from being a mediocre school to being a healthy, vital place in less than five years, demonstrating that dramatic improvement is possible.

Pioneer High School, Whittier, CA

The student body at Pioneer High School is 72 per cent Hispanic and 27 per cent white. In 1983, over 1700 students were attending the school and one third of them were from low-income families. In 1979, the school had the classic symptoms of a school in trouble — poor attendance, severe tardiness and truancy, low staff and student morale, a high suspension rate, problems with gang intimidation, poor test results, and a negative image in the community. With 35 to 40 per cent of the students entering with scores 2 or 3 grade levels below expectancy, state achievement scores at Pioneer were at the 8th percentile state-wide and the school's college prep programs were dying. Only 28 per cent of the school's graduates were seeking post-secondary education.

By 1982, these conditions had been reversed and the school was receiving high marks from the California State Department of Education and from its staff and students. How was this miracle accomplished? The steps taken included:

- A school-within-a-school was developed for college prep students to offer more educational experiences including courses in colleges and local businesses. Shorter electives, more courses, advanced courses, personalized instruction, and teacher counseling were provided to 250 students.
- A restructured math curriculum with courses for students operated at grades 3–4, 5–6, 7–8, and college prep was developed. All below level 7 were highly individualized. The math requirement was raised to two years. A math lab was offered twice a week for students below the 30th percentile and math proficiency clinics were offered in the summer. The number of students enrolled in math courses increased from 34 per cent to 70 per cent and math scores improved dramatically.
- A Chapter 1 Clinic was provided five days a week for all students reading below 5th grade level (75 per cent of the 9th grade) and another program was developed for 10–12th graders with reading difficulties using a small group approach and non paper and pencil methods. Other initiatives included: Scramble, a program that

provides reading to all remaining students during English classes in the 2nd and 4th quarters and the Proficiency Clinic, a summer clinic, and the main remediation for those with reading and English deficits.

- A new homework policy was developed by a committee composed of staff, counselors, and administrators.
- A comprehensive and sequential career education program was introduced.
- Extensive computer instruction was introduced.
- A multicultural program, funded by local and Chapter 1 funds, provided tutoring, college counseling, field trips to colleges, and assistance with applications.
- Staff in-service was conducted over four years, planned by staff, parents, students, and focusing on curriculum and instruction.

School climate was improved by focusing on attendance, tardiness, suspensions, gangs, poor image and:

- creating Boys' and Girls' councils of gang-oriented students to meet weekly with the administration;
- development of a citizenship policy by staff and students;
- comprehensive supervision of the campus, making administration highly visible;
- clean campus campaign;
- emphasis on positive reinforcement and rewards;
- hiring of campus personnel aides and an attendance officer; and
- creation of a school radio station and student-run noon-time activities.

The results of these and related actions: attendance improved to 92.5 per cent from 88.75 per cent over three years; the number of suspensions was reduced from 306 to 134 in the same period; incidents of truancy declined from 2095 in 1979 to 590 in 1983; the school's ranking on the California Assessment Tests rose from the 7th percentile to the 25th; the drop-out rate was cut in half, and the number of students going on to higher education increased from 32 per cent to 47 per cent. Overall, a significant improvement in the climate of the school and the performance of the students.

Nyssa High School, Nyssa, OR

A small (478 students in 1985) high school in rural Oregon, Nyssa serves a diverse population. The student body is 57 per cent white, 40 per cent Hispanic, and the remainder are Asians, Native Americans, and Blacks. Sixty-nine per cent of the students are from low-income families and 21 per cent are classified as migrants. Yet few students drop out and almost two-thirds of the graduates of this small school go on to post-secondary education.

The school staff attribute their success to strong instructional leadership, clear goals, high expectations expressed in writing, graduation requirements exceeding those of the state, and the use of Madeline Hunter's ITIP training. Also critical to the school's success was the willingness of staff to try new ideas and programs such as peer tutoring, peer coaching for teachers, a community service requirement for graduation, an honors program now enrolling 51 per cent of the students, academic letters, weighted grades, study classes (30 minutes before and after school required for students having difficulty), use of in-service to improve instruction, and a high school improvement and advisory council.

Nyssa has had success with at-risk students because the principal and the staff have a positive attitude. They have searched for solutions rather than excuses.

Summary

The schools described above have attempted to overcome an important and ubiquitous social problem, the poor educational achievement of low-income students. The schools function in diverse social circumstances. Some are inner-city schools. Some are in rural poverty areas. Still others are in suburban communities. Their student bodies are equally diverse — white, black, Hispanic, and Asian. But they all face the same challenge of raising the educational aspirations and performance of students from low socio-economic backgrounds.

As a consequence of their diverse settings, and equally diverse resources, there are some differences in the strategies they have employed, but there are also some common elements. The common elements appear to be:

- a positive attitude towards the students;
- a willingness to question conventional practices and forms;
- a strong and competent leadership;
- highly committed teaching staff;
- high expectations and standards;
- an emphasis on high achievement in academics;
- intensive and personal support services for at-risk students;
- a willingness to act, to try new approaches; and
- stable leadership and public support for a period sufficient to implement new policies.

The specific policies and practices in use vary across the schools, but these elements seem to be present in some form. These schools work at being successful. They have not found 'the solution' to the problem of educating low-income students, but they are actively searching and they are making progress. The major lesson to be learned from these schools is the fundamental importance of staff and community commitment to the education of at-risk students. The stories of these schools make it clear that successes are hard won and take time, but it is also clear that once positive momentum is developed, success builds upon success.

Chapter 10

Implications:
The Challenges of Success

The secondary schools described in this book represent the current structure of American public education at its best. They demonstrate its continuing potential for success, a potential yet unrealized in some communities and neighborhoods across the country. These schools are working laboratories in which educators offer high quality, comprehensive education to student bodies drawn from diverse social and economic circumstances. While the contexts, programs, policies and practices of the schools vary, their staffs' dedication and commitment to excellence are constants. It is clear from these examples that quality is the hard won result of dedicated work by competent, committed people. This is their hallmark, and it is their primary message to both policy-makers and the general public. What factors induce the kind of dedication observed in many of these schools? Under what conditions will people make the necessary commitments of time and energy required for school success? What public policies attract talented people to seek careers in public education? These and related questions of public policy in education are the topic of this final chapter.

The data from these 571 successful secondary schools, while imperfect and incomplete, describe some of the best of current practices in public secondary education. The portraits of the schools are incomplete because information was lacking on important dimensions of policy and practice such as curriculum, assessment procedures, and instructional methods. The data presented, however, suggest that many of these schools have for years followed practices similar to those reformers are now seeking to introduce into all public secondary schools. In most cases, these practices are less radical and less sweeping than those being advocated by the leaders of the reform movement. As a consequence, they have less political appeal. Yet they offer the advantage of working models; their effectiveness has been demonstrated.

Students attending these schools have generally achieved at levels consistently higher than public school students in general. Yet their teaching staffs would readily admit that much more can and should be done. They would further concede that they have not solved the educational problems of disadvantaged students. While some of the schools have made significant progress in raising the performance of poor and minority students, few, if any, of them would claim to have overcome the pervasive relationship between achievement and social background. Without disaggregated test data, of course it is impossible to ascertain just how well the entire set of schools have served at-risk students. Obviously, some of the schools have made dramatic gains with such students. The data available from these schools belie the claims of those who argue that the failure to achieve equal educational results regardless of race or class ensues from a lack of commitment or incompetence on the part of educators. There is considerable evidence in these schools of commitment, concern and competence. The experience of these school staffs suggests that we do not yet know how to eliminate the influence of social background on student performance. Accepting this unpopular, but obvious, conclusion may be politically difficult, but it is essential to the formulation of fair and effective public policy. These schools represent the best of current educational practice. Their performance may fall short of what we as a nation aspire to, but it far exceeds the general performance of the public schools.

The experiences of these schools speak to the limits of incremental approaches to change in public institutions and, in that regard, bolster the arguments of those who desire more drastic changes in public education. After all, if the best of our institutions fall short of our social goals, should we not consider fundamental changes in the institutions? However, the relative success of these schools can also be viewed as evidence that at least some of the ends desired by reformers could be achieved incrementally through improving the schools we have through rather modest policy changes, avoiding the costly and potentially disruptive restructuring of schools currently being advocated by some. The best course may be a middle course. One approach would be to encourage incremental reforms by using schools such as those described in this book as natural laboratories while also supporting limited and carefully designed experiments with new organizational forms. The best of traditional practice should not be neglected or disturbed in a romantic flight to new, but not necessarily more effective, structures. More educators in poor-performing schools may find it easier to adapt successful and familiar policies and practices than to invent new forms of schooling.

To stimulate thinking about the nature of the reforms implied by the experience of the 571 nationally-recognized public secondary schools, each of the six themes, reviewed in detail in Chapters 4 through 9, are briefly revisited below. The conclusions drawn from this analysis are discussed in light of related conclusions and recommendations about secondary education offered in some of the most influential reform literature. This literature has defined much of the recent debate about educational reform and stimulated some of the most significant efforts at school improvement. This reform literature includes:

- *High School: A Report on Secondary Education in America* (Ernest L. Boyer, 1983)
- *A Place Called School: Prospects for the Future* (John I. Goodlad, 1983)
- *Successful Schools for Young Adolescents* (Joan Lipsitz, 1984)
- *Horace's Compromise: The Dilemma of the American High School* (Theodore R. Sizer, 1984)
- *A Nation Prepared: Teachers for the 21st Century* (Carnegie Forum on Education and the Economy, 1986)
- *Time for Results: The Governors' 1991 Report on Education* (National Governors Association, 1986)
- *Children in Need: Investment Strategies for the Educationally Disadvantaged* (Committee for Economic Development [CED] 1987).

Comparing the recommendations made in these studies and reports with the findings drawn from the analysis presented here serves to clarify the distinctions, and the similarities, between best practice in the current system and the vision of the reform movement. It also serves as a reality test for the reformers and policy-makers as the schools discussed here have often been at the forefront of actual educational reform.

Leadership in Action

The first lesson to be drawn from the data on these schools is a familiar one: strong and competent leadership is central to the creation and maintenance of quality programs and practices in successful secondary schools. While this observation may appear simplistic, even trite, the examples given in chapter 4 make it clear that leading a public secondary school is a complex and demanding task. It requires a continual and delicate balancing of freedom and constraint. Successful school leaders must establish and reinforce a consistent set of concrete rules and procedures, while providing enough flexibility and autonomy for staff and students to let creativity flourish. They must build consensus around a common belief system and provide for continuity through goals that guide the direction of the school. All of this must be accomplished in a setting in which most of the interchanges among professionals are brief, in which there is rarely enough time to give problems the time or energy that they require. The ability to take advantage of the rather weak leadership tools and symbols available in schools to create a strong and coherent community is what separates the leaders in these schools from the norm. Leadership is not limited to the top administrators or to formal management techniques. It is accomplished through many different routes and by involving a wide range of staff, for as Schlechty (1985) notes,

'. . . effective principals are those who provide *or cause others to provide* strong leadership'.

The studies and reports cited above were unanimous in their view that strong, effective leadership in schools is vital to success. While the reports took somewhat different perspectives on how to enhance leadership in schools, there was a common thread in their recommendations. The reports all mentioned the need for decentralization of authority in education to increase the decision-making power of individual school staffs. This reflects a prevailing view that the most critical decisions affecting children are, and should be, made in schools and that the most important unit for change is the individual school.

Goodlad (1983) has suggested that schools should be largely self-directive and should have more control over their budgets, staffing, time allocations, and programs; Sizer (1984) has maintained that substantial authority should be granted to each school; Lipsitz (1984) called for principals to secure the autonomy of their schools in their districts; and Boyer (1983) has argued for more control over budgets and teacher selection/rewards at the school level. The National Governors Association (1986) and CED (1987) also have endorsed school site management and collaboration, but also have suggested that parents be involved in school governance. The report issued by the Carnegie Forum (1986) offered the most radical recommendations, calling for new forms of school management that encouraged collaboration and gave new leadership responsibilities to teachers. The Carnegie Report included a scenario of a school led by teachers, with no principal.

In general, the recommendations of these studies and reports seem consistent with the data presented in chapter 4. They acknowledge that effective school leaders create compelling visions for their schools. Second, they implicitly or explicitly recognize that different schools serve very different populations and that this diversity requires a great deal of flexibility and adaptability in setting visions for schools — what works in one place may not work in another. Third, most of them call for improvements in the training required of school leaders. However, better preparatory training is not seen as suffucient. Meeting the need for leadership development on the job has also become part of the reform agenda.

Concern has also been expressed about the role of principals. Too many demands are made on principals. Moving some administrative tasks to the central office and delegating more planning and decision-making to teachers would free principals to perform other important leadership functions. As a corollary to this, it also has been recognized that leadership is seldom the responsibility of a single person. It is a mistake to place all the responsibility on one charismatic person and it is a fantasy to pursue reform that requires heroic individuals as leaders. As Lipsitz (1984) noted, one of the primary contributions of effective school leaders is to make their schools larger than one person.

The findings presented in this book appear to be consistent with the recommendations in the reform reports. Taken together, they have the following implications for policy:

- Policy-makers should examine their recruitment, selection and promotion policies and practices for school leaders. Are policy-makers getting the best people they can? How do they know? Are they recruiting leaders who can take initiative and inspire excellence? Do they provide environments that attract talent, permit entrepreneurship, risk-taking, and reward the pursuit of excellence?

- Policy-makers should encourage school administrators to involve their staffs in setting clear and appropriate goals for their schools. Follow up efforts should be fostered to ensure that staffs buy into the vision of the school and that the vision is taken seriously. Allocations of people, time, and money should be monitored to promote a tight fit with the goals of the school.

- Policy-makers should grant greater autonomy to school leaders to make decisions that respond to the needs of their students. Leadership should be focused on building supportive learning environments that benefit students, rather than on administrative matters that benefit the larger organization. With the increased latitude given to school staffs should come carefully considered and broadly defined accountabilities for actions taken in these schools.

- Policy-makers should regard reform of the preparation of school leaders as a high priority. Incentives should be provided to attract talented candidates. Potential recruits should be groomed for positions. Internships with successful principals should be encouraged. Course requirements should be redesigned to promote greater understanding of how school leaders' actions influence school cultures and the impact those cultures have on school success.

- Policy-makers must recognize that development of school leaders is an ongoing process and does not end with certification. School leaders should be encouraged to seek opportunities for professional development on a regular basis. Group process skills and organizational dynamics should be taught as well as management and administrative techniques.

- Policy-makers should persistently and critically review proposals to standardize or further centralize decision-making and ask if they are essential or if there are other alternatives that permit greater diversity and school-level decision-making.

Conditions of Teaching

The schools described in this book provide good working conditions for their teaching staffs. Examples of their policies and practices are found in

Chapter 5. Their leaders have fostered strong communal identities among their professional staffs. The goals and values of the schools are widely shared. Respect is shown for teachers and for teaching. In most cases, teachers are treated with dignity and deference and held in esteem by colleagues, students and community members. In many of the schools, teachers have been granted discretion and influence to carry out their work. As a consequence, there is a stronger sense of professionalism present in these schools and a greater willingness by staff to accept responsibility for quality than is the norm in public education. Their staffs do not seem to suffer as much from the isolation and alienation experienced by so many public school teachers. There are collegial professional cultures directed by common goals that give rise to strong feelings of personal efficacy by teachers.

Teacher recognition is more common in these schools. There are many opportunities for personal growth: in-service programs, pursuit of advanced degrees, sabbaticals, service on curriculum committees, and other professional activities are available to teachers. Even the physical conditions seem to be generally superior in these schools. While not all the schools are new, they are generally well-maintained and are attractive places to work. Teachers feel safe and secure in these schools and they have usable and comfortable work space.

Taken as a group, these schools provide a model for teacher working conditions that could be emulated in most public schools. The characteristics of this model are:

1. shared goals and high expectations of success to create a strong communal identity;
2. respectful and dignified treatment as professionals by superiors and by parents and students;
3. participation by teachers in decisions affecting their work;
4. regular opportunities for staff interaction and sharing with colleagues to promote a collective identity;
5. recognition and rewards for staff effort and achievement;
6. opportunities for professional and personal growth;
7. decent physical working conditions and access to the resources needed to do the work assigned.

These seven factors describe conditions within schools that positively affect teacher behavior and attitudes. These factors have been found to be related to teacher attendance, level of effort, commitment to the school, sense of efficacy, and job satisfaction (Rosenholtz, 1985; Firestone, 1985). They define the broad agenda for the reform of the school as a workplace.

Those who would reform the public schools have recognized that good teachers and good teaching are the essence of effective schools. For example, the Carnegie Forum (1986), the National Governors Association (1986) and the Committee for Economic Development (1987) have recommended the creation of better work environments for teachers, including more influence over decisions, more time to plan collegially, stronger incentives for good performance, and greater opportunities for professional advancement. Boyer (1983), Goodlad (1983), Lipsitz (1984) and Sizer (1984) have written elegantly about the isolation and frustration that characterize teaching in the public schools and recommended changes similar to those in the national reports. While these organizations and scholars may differ occasionally over the details of how to improve the conditions of teaching, they are agreed that it is a priority if schools are to become more effective.

None of the schools described here provides the degree of teacher autonomy and control over curriculum, instruction, or time allocation that has been recommended by the Carnegie Forum (1986). Yet they have been able to provide exceptional working conditions, and, as a consequence, attract and hold exceptional staffs, within the existing structure of public education. While experiments with new structures are being undertaken, the productivity and satisfaction of teaching staffs in other public schools could be enhanced by adopting practices similar to those described in chapter 5. To foster such improvements, the following steps might be taken:

- Policy-makers should review the school attributes described in this report and re-examine and revise their accreditation procedures to focus more attention on the conditions of teaching in schools.
- Policy-makers should demonstrate their respect for teaching and teachers by providing them with the levels of discretion and autonomy normally associated with professional status.
- Policy-makers should work with and through teacher organizations to improve schools and conditions of teaching rather than treating such organizations as adversaries.
- Policy-makers should examine the effects that local and state testing and accountability procedures have on the conditions of teaching and teacher attitudes and performance. Increased monitoring of school outcomes should be accompanied by commensurate increases in discretion over program and curriculum at the school level.
- Policy-makers should take steps to increase the amount of time that school staffs have to plan and work collaboratively and engage in advising and tutoring students.
- Policy-makers should sponsor school visits and increased dialogue among practitioners to promote the diffusion not only of effective practices and policies but of norms of professional conduct and expectations of success.
- Policy-makers should review regulations and requirements governing the construction of school facilities to ensure that optimal physical environments are provided for teaching and learning, including adequate work, meeting, and storage space for teachers.

- Policy-makers should continue their efforts to upgrade teacher preparation, to raise the standards for entry and continuation in the profession, and to recruit talented people into teaching.
- Policy-makers should consider broadly-defined competitive grant programs to foster incremental changes in the public schools and attend to issues of school culture and climate by supporting teacher participation in school curriculum development, and greater opportunities for professional development.
- Policy-makers also should use competitive grants to encourage creation and evaluation of new structures and incentives at both the local and state levels including merit pay, career ladders, school-site management, redefinitions of professional roles and responsibilities, teacher cooperatives and labor management cooperation in public education.

Learning Environments

Good working conditions for students are equally important. Chapter 6 describes how the schools try to set expectations and how they use rewards and recognition to raise the level of student performance. These schools generally provide more challenging environments for their students than is the general case. The adults associated with the schools, parents, teachers, and administrators gave many examples of their commitment to high standards. Most of them expressed the view that all students can be motivated to master essential skills and content. Site visitors to the schools often were surprised by student accounts of what was expected of them. Although student work loads varied within as well as between schools, the students clearly understood that high levels of achievement depended on their efforts. They often praised their teachers for making them work hard.

In the schools that had made significant improvements, this change in expectations stood out as a significant factor. It was expressed through higher academic standards, tougher disciplinary policies, increased work demands, and pressure to take more rigorous academic courses. This change in staff attitude seems to be an essential first step in improvement. School leaders sought to alter the attitudes of staff toward the students and develop a climate more conducive to learning.

Strong reward systems reinforce high expectations and standards. Increasing the work demands on students requires greater attention to their motivation; their accomplishments must be recognized. As described in Chapter 7, the schools used diverse and multiple means to provide this recognition.

Academic achievement in many American secondary schools, as measured by standardized tests and courses taken, declined during the 1960s and 1970s. Some of the schools were able to maintain high standards during this period, but others lowered their standards in response to student or community pressure and had to struggle to restore them later. Their stories demonstrate that expectations and standards can be raised. These school staffs decided not to accept mediocrity.

The reform literature espouses higher standards. Everyone is for raising expectations. Boyer (1983), Goodlad (1983) and Sizer (1984) have advocated elimination of tracking and the adoption of core academic curricula to ensure that the same expectations and standards are applied to all students. They also have proposed strengthening the bonds between students and their schools, through smaller schools, more flexible use of time, closer relationships with teachers, stronger incentives for performance, more personalization of learning. Lipsitz (1984) describes how successful middle schools respond to the individual differences of their students and nurture positive relationships with adults. She points to the difference that good facilities and organization make to school climate and how the students' frame of reference affects their sense of community. Similar, but less specific, recommendations about student learning environments were either offered or were implicit in the reports from the Carnegie Forum (1986), the National Governors Association (1986), and the Council for Economic Development (1987).

None of these studies adequately address how educators can motivate students to work harder and achieve more. Nor do they address how to deal with the students who can't or won't do the work demanded by the core curriculum. Lipsitz (1984) and Sizer (1984) have examined how human relationships within schools affect student motivation and performance. Proposals for elimination of tracking, more remediation, alternate programs, smaller classes, and redefining student responsibilities all have merit, but action on such proposals seems unlikely to be sufficient to overcome student apathy and alienation.

The schools studied here employ many recommended practices, such as smaller classes, strong remediation, alternate programs, and various strategies to personalize education, but they do not have well-defined core curricula, nor have most of them eliminated tracking or altered the basic responsibilities of the student. Nevertheless, much could be learned by more careful examination of the student experience in these schools. Some of the schools have followed the recommended practices for some time and it would be useful to know just how much difference they have made and for whom. While the reform literature tends to speak to the macro issues of educational policy and school organization, successful reform requires greater understanding of the conditions under which students work their hardest and reach their highest levels of performance.

To improve learning environments and further our understanding of student motivation:

● Policy-makers should support research on student working conditions and climates in public schools and determine how students view environments for teaching and learning.

- Policy-makers should seek to optimize teacher–student interaction inside and outside of the classroom. This fits with the earlier recommendation that teachers be given more time for planning and tutoring.
- Policy-makers should encourage forms of school organization that foster closer relationships among students and between students and teachers.
- Policy-makers should examine their policies and practices with regard to rewards and incentives for students. Are they effective for all, or most, students? Do they reflect the goals and values of the community. Do they reach enough people?
- Policy-makers should examine and strengthen the standards that are applied in the classroom as well as those on tests and examinations.
- Policy-makers should take the lead in encouraging public and private organizations to foster and support stronger co-curricular programs and academic competitions.
- Policy-makers should revise accreditation criteria and facilities standards to reflect concerns about students' climates and working conditions.

Public Involvement

Historically, the local community has played a central role in the American public schooling process. While educational governance has retained a strong local flavor, community involvement has declined in significance as we have progressed through the twentieth century. Professionalization of education, centralized management, collective bargaining, and the sheer size of school systems have worked against active roles by parents and community members. The school staffs studied in this book, mindful of the pitfalls in such a trend, have worked hard to involve families and communities in their activities.

It is the expressed belief of their leaders that such involvement is positively related to student performance in school. By taking advantage of the human and fiscal resources in their communities, introducing aggressive public relations campaigns, and developing programs that take students into the community as well as bring community members into the school, these educators have established clear and positive identities for their schools as integral and essential parts of their communities. These successful schools have built reputations for educational quality and strengthened and, in some cases, created public support for their programs. By working collaboratively with the public, these schools have expanded and improved their services, built political support among residents, provided their students with access to positive adult role models, and created school cultures that communicated concern about the quality of community life.

There may be more divergent points of view about the form and value of public involvement in schools than any of the other themes discussed in this book. For example, Sizer (1984) maintains there are five imperatives for better schools. The five give specific attention to students, teachers and the organizational structure of schools; but he makes no mention of the role for parents and the larger community. Similarly, the Carnegie Forum report (1986) calls for restructuring of schools, but suggests no changes in the roles or responsibilities of parents. Boyer (1983) has called for parental involvement, but with the exception of an unrelated discussion of business partnerships, he offers little insight into the role of the larger community. On the other hand, Lipsitz (1984), Goodlad (1983), the Committee for Economic Development (CED) (1987), and the National Governors Association (NGA) (1986) have pointed out the importance of the community and directed considerable attention to the roles that parents can play.

Goodlad, in particular, has argued for a tight linkage between the school and the community. He calls for the creation of community schools — places where educational services are extended beyond the normal day, reach a wider age span, and accommodate more diverse subject content. In addition, he suggests that schools need to collaborate more closely with other public and private agencies to move toward a more 'educative community'. Both the CED and NGA reports have called for parent involvement in school governance and the latter goes further to recommend choice programs that allow parents to exercise consumer power by being able to determine which public school their children attend.

Two common elements run through these discussions of public involvement in education, as conveyed by these reports. First, there is a recognition that parents and other community members can contribute. Parent-advisory councils and parent volunteer programs were cited by Lipsitz (1984) as good ways to broaden the level of participation. She suggests that these programs serve two important functions: they inform parents about school practices and they also offer an outlet for parents to communicate their concerns to the school. A third important function is the employment of an under-utilized pool of talent.

A second message from the reform literature is the need for policy-makers to appreciate the diversity of the communities being served and the need to respect and respond to that diversity. No single set of practices, guidelines, or policies can be applied successfully in all schools. What works in one community setting may not work well in another. As Sizer (1984) has suggested, good schools may resist the appeal to standardization. They recognize that how well they meet the particular needs of their different student populations should be the primary measure by which they are judged.

This discussion and that which preceded it in Chapter 7 suggest that policy-makers should adopt the following perspectives:

- School leaders should be encouraged to reach out to the public and provide opportunities for involving them meaningfully in the schools. The public should be given more access, more input into the decision-making process, and be invited to assist in a wide range of school activities. Such efforts will help build greater support for a shared vision of public education within communities.
- Indicators of school quality should be published regularly to provide the public with reliable information and to stimulate public action. The public should be involved in the process of defining these indicators of quality and the process should recognize the diverse needs of different student populations. Multiple indicators should be used as well as multiple standards of reference.
- School leaders should take advantage of the strengths of local communities in defining their visions for the schools. Talents of parents and other community members should be employed and linkages with business, social service agencies, and cultural organizations should be encouraged. Schools should capitalize on the positive images that already exist in their communities. They should not be embarrassed to let the community know of their successes.
- Policy-makers should resist the temptation to isolate students from their larger environments in pursuit of higher academic standards. Programs should be encouraged that bring students into their communities in a regular and responsible way. Students learn valuable lessons from community service. It is not fair to simply take from a community without giving something in return.

Institutional Vitality

Success does not come easily. It requires effort and it involves risk. This is particularly true for complex organizations like public secondary schools. Once you achieve a measure of success, it is not always a simple matter to maintain it. With a constantly changing population (students rarely stay in a school for more than four years), an uncertain technology (there is still no agreement about best pedagogical practices), a turbulent environment (tax-payer support is unstable and states are making increasing demands on schools), and disagreement about outcomes (society expects more of the educational system that it can deliver), it is easy to understand why so many schools are less successful than their publics desire. Yet, despite these adverse circumstances, there are public schools that have maintained their reputations for quality over decades and still others that have made great improvements in the face of serious obstacles.

Clearly efforts to improve the public schools can succeed. The successful schools described in Chapter 8 have not been immune to the problems plaguing public secondary education, but the attitudes of their staffs have been different. They are best characterized by old slogans such as 'can do' and 'what if'. They have been decisive; when faced with problems, they have acted and they often have come up with creative responses. Rather than succumbing to constraints that provide others with convenient rationalizations for mediocrity, these school staffs have faced their problems head-on and seen them as challenges to be overcome. Their positive, entrepreneurial approach has maintained the institutional vitality of their schools and is the basis for their continued success.

While none of the reform reports address institutional vitality as a separate and discrete issue, concern about this issue permeates the entire literature. One explanation may be that, with the exception of Lipsitz (1984), these reports deal with what should be rather than what is. It is more difficult to capture and explain the dynamism of a school that has struggled against unfavorable odds, yet managed to succeed than it is to draw visions of ideal states of affairs. Sizer (1984) describes this staff quest for success as an inspiration, a hunger for success; Lipsitz (1984) refers to it as an attitude: 'We can make a difference'. She points out how disquieting it can be to visit a successful secondary school because of the strong convictions on the part of staff that they have control over what happens and that they can make a difference for children.

Successful schools must be renewed; their staffs need a sense of renewal. Central to that renewal is the understanding that improvement is a continuous process rather than some achievable end result. As Goodlad (1983) indicates, successful schools need ongoing processes to identify problems, gather relevant data, discuss and debate issues, formulate solutions, and monitor actions. All of this must be accomplished in an atmosphere that encourages flexibility, rewards risk-takers, encourages innovation, and, rather than penalizing failure, seeks to learn from the experience.

Policy-makers need to identify or invent levers to encourage self-renewal and strengthen institutional vitality. To date, far too much reliance has been placed on regulations and directives. The assumption has been that uniformity is good and diversity is bad, that left to their own devices, administrators and teachers will do the wrong thing. The entire educational system suffers from a lack of trust. The result has been to squelch creativity and diversity in the public schools. In line with this reasoning, the authors suggest the following:

- Policy-makers should avoid mandating single formulas for success. The process of improvement is complex, and local differences have a profound impact on the implementation of change efforts. However, policy-makers should not shy away from recognizing educational excellence or drawing attention to unusually successful schools.

- Policy-makers should support research on successful secondary schools to better understand how various factors interact to maximize learning for students. As part of that process, an accessible data base should be established which can serve as a bridge for practitioner-to-practitioner exchange. Efforts to link practitioners through school visitations and school presentations at national and state conventions should be encouraged.

- Policy-makers should create incentives for change and experimentation which allow some flexibility in dealing with currently restrictive rules and regulations. This might include broadly defined competitive grant programs that promote changes in organizational structure, curriculum development, new co-curricular programs, new incentive programs, and attempts to better define or reinforce school cultures. It might also include offers to waive regulations when substantive educational arguments can be advanced on behalf of their removal.

- Policy-makers should consider all improvement efforts in terms of their unintended as well as intended effects on students. Will the change improve the system's ability to educate students? Will one outcome be enhanced at the expense of another?

- Policy-makers must temper their desires for immediate and total change with an understanding of the complexity of the change process. In so doing, they must be sensitive to the cultural as well as the technical aspects of change. Significant changes do not happen over-night nor can staff be expected to take on a large number of changes at one time.

Equalizing Opportunity

Raising the achievement levels of poor and minority students and reducing drop-out rates have been major objectives in the United States for over twenty years. Yet a strong relationship persists between educational achievement and the ethnic social background of students in the United States. Children from poor and minority families have lower levels of achievement, are less likely to enroll in higher level courses, and are more likely to drop out of school. Since the public schools are expected to be primary vehicles for social and economic mobility, this correlation between ethnic and social background and school success has posed a serious social problem. The problem has become more serious as the numbers of such children have increased and alternative routes to economic success have diminished.

Breaking through this educational barrier is an important goal for social reformers. The schools described in Chapter 9 have pursued this goal with at least limited success. Operating under extremely diverse conditions, they have had to face the same challenges and there have been some common elements in their strategies. Among these common elements are:

- a positive attitude towards the students
- a willingness to question conventional practices and forms
- strong and competent leadership
- highly-committed teaching staff
- high expectations and standards
- an emphasis on high achievement in academics
- intensive and personal support services for at-risk students
- a willingness to act, to try new approaches
- stable leadership and public support for a period sufficient to implement new policies.

These schools have worked at success and have searched for solutions to the problem of educating low-income students.

Improving the educational performance of at-risk youth is a major focus of the reform literature. Many of the recommendations for improving schools and learning environments discussed above are offered because they are perceived as being especially beneficial to at-risk youth. The studies by Boyer (1983), Goodlad (1983) and Sizer (1984) have pointed out the need for common curricula, higher expectations, and alternative programs. The Carnegie Forum report (1986) offers suggestions for the recruitment of more minority teachers and the strengthening of counseling and tutoring programs for minority students. The National Governors Association (1986) and the Committee for Economic Development (1987) recommend provision of early childhood programs, increased health and social services, smaller classes, more remediation, alternative programs, and other measures to assist low-achieving students. Basically, the recommendations seek new or strengthened efforts at prevention of learning problems through early intervention to provide better nutrition, healthcare, and support for parents; changes in the structure, staffing, and programs of the public schools; and new programs to aid potential or actual drop-outs.

These proposals go far beyond what the schools in this study have been able to do, but they differ more in scope than in kind. The schools that have made progress with at-risk students have incorporated similar strategies to raise their school achievement. Based on their experience, the following steps would contribute to improved performance by at-risk students:

- Policy-makers should incorporate the full range of characteristics of effective programs and schools into their school evaluation and accreditation processes.
- Policy-makers should require schools to disaggregate performance data to determine which groups of students are experiencing success. This would draw attention to problems and create pressure for efforts at improvement.

- Policy-makers should support studies of the courses and curricular paths taken by different groups of students and their actual educational experience to ensure that all students are receiving similar opportunities.
- Policy-makers should require school systems to provide all students access to the full range of high school courses, including honors and advanced placement courses, either by providing for them at each school or by arranging access at nearby schools or colleges.
- Policy-makers should develop criteria for the evaluation of schools that cover the entire curriculum to ensure that schools serving poor and minority youth do not neglect or eliminate some subjects in order to improve basic skills achievement.
- Policy-makers should provide special funding for the extra services such as health clinics, after-school tutoring and homework assistance, alternate programs, employment counseling, tracking and monitoring systems, and attendance improvement programs that have shown promise of improving the educational performance of at-risk students, but which place extra fiscal burdens on many communities.
- Policy-makers should support studies of the experience of at-risk students enrolled in 'successful' schools as compared to those attending more typical schools and inner-city schools. The value of social and academic integration needs to be re-examined.
- Policy-makers should review school evaluation systems to ensure that they are rewarding genuine progess by at-risk students rather than encouraging mediocrity by being too weak or punishing effort by being too high or too rigid.
- Policy-makers should support experimental programs that restructure the curriculum and the organization of secondary schools as long as efforts are based on promising educational strategies and guided by sound principles. They should be willing to waive laws and regulations that obstruct such experiments.
- Policy-makers should support the earlier recommendations for the improvement of leadership, teaching conditions, and learning environments as they are likely to be especially beneficial to at-risk students.

The information on successful schools presented in this book highlights what can be accomplished when communities accept their civic responsibilities for educating their youth. Much can be learned from these successes, although the lessons are not easily translated into public policy. The challenge to policy-makers is to capitalize on the experiences of these schools and develop, foster, and implement policies that encourage replication of their practices without undermining the conditions that underlay their success.

References

ADLER, M. J. (1982) *The Paideia Proposal*, New York: MacMillan Publishing Co.

ALEXANDER, K. L. and COOK, M. A. (1982) 'Curricula and coursework: A surprise ending to a familiar story', *American Sociological Review*, 47 (5), 626–640.

ANDERSON, C. S. (1982) 'The search for school climate: A review of the research', *Review of Educational Research*, 52 (3), 368–420.

ANDERSON, G. L. (1970) 'Effects of classroom social climate on individual learning', *American Educational Research Journal*, 7 (2), 135–152.

ARIZONA DEPARTMENT OF EDUCATION (1983) *Effective Schools are Arizona's Best Bet*, Phoenix: Author.

BACHARACH, S. B., BAUER, S. C., and SHEDD, J. B. (1986) *The Learning Workplace: The Conditions and Resources of Teaching*, Ithaca, NY: Organizational Analysis & Practice.

BARKER, R. G., and GUMP, P. (1964) *Big School, Small School: High School Size and Student Behavior*, Stanford, CA: Stanford University Press.

BARTH, R. S. (1980) *Run School Run*, Cambridge, MA: Harvard University Press.

BARTH, R. S. (1984) 'Sandbags and honeybees', *Education Week*, (May 9, 1984) 24.

BASSIN, M., GROSS, T., and JORDAN, P. (1979) 'Developing renewal processes in urban high schools', *Theory into Practice*, 18, (2), 73–81.

BECHER, R. M. (1984) 'Parent involvement: A review of research and principles of successful practice', in KATZ, L. G. (Ed), *Current Topics in Early Childhood Education, Volume VI*, Norwood, NJ: Ablex.

BERMAN, P. W. (1981) 'Educational change: An implementation paradigm', in Lehming, R. and KANE, M. (Eds), *Improving Schools: Using What We Know*, Beverly Hills, CA: Sage.

BERMAN, P. and MCLAUGHLIN, M. W. (1977) *Federal Programs Supporting Change, Vol VII: Factors Affecting Implementation and Continuation*, Santa Monica, CA: Rand.

BIDWELL, C. E. (1965) 'The school as a formal organization', in MARCH J. G. (Ed), *Handbook of Organizations*, Skokie, IL: Rand-McNally.

BIRD, T. and LITTLE, J. W. (1986) 'How schools organize the teaching occupation', *Elementary School Journal*, 86 (4): 493–511.

BOYER, E. (1983) *High School: A Report on Secondary Education in America*, New York: Harper & Row.

BROOKOVER, W. B. (1981) *Effective Secondary Schools*, Philadelphia, PA: Research for Better Schools.

BROOKOVER, W. B., BEADY, C., FLOOD, P., SCHWEITZER, J. and WISENBAKER, J. (1979) *School Social Systems and Student Achievement: Schools Can Make a Difference*, New York: Praeger.

CALIFORNIA ASSEMBLY OFFICE OF RESEARCH (1984) *Overcoming the Odds: Making High Schools Work*, Sacramento, CA: Author.

CARNEGIE FORUM ON EDUCATION AND THE ECONOMY (1986) *A Nation Prepared: Teachers for the 21st Century*, Hyattsville, MD: Author.

CENTER FOR PUBLIC INTEREST POLLING (1986) *The New Jersey Public School Teacher: A View of the Profession*, New Brunswick, NJ: The Eagleton Institute.

CHAPMAN, D. M. (1984) 'Teacher retention: A test of a model', *American Educational Research Journal*, 21 (3), 645–658.

CHUBB, J. E. and MOE, T. E. (1986) 'No school is an island: Politics, markets, and education', *The Brookings Review*, Fall, 21–28.

CLARK, D. L., LOTTO, L. S. and ASTUTO, T. A. (1984) 'Effective schools and school improvement: A comparative analysis of two lines of inquiry', *Educational Administration Quarterly*, 20 (3), 41–68.

COHEN, M. (1983) 'Instructional, management and social conditions in effective schools', in ODDEN, A. and WEBB, L. D. (Eds), *School Finance and School Improvement: Linkages in the 1980s*, New York: American Educational Finance Association.

COLEMAN, J., HOFFER, T. and KILGORE, S. (1982) 'Cognitive outcomes in public and private schools', *Sociology of Education*, 55 (2/3), 65–76.

THE COLLEGE BOARD (1983) *Academic Preparation for College: What Students Need to Know and be Able to do*, New York: College Entrance Examination Board.

COMER, J. P. (1980) *School Power: Implications of an Intervention Project*, New York: Free Press.

COMMITTEE FOR ECONOMIC DEVELOPMENT (1987) *Children in Need: Investment Strategies for the Educationally Disadvantaged*, New York: Author.

CORBETT, H. D., DAWSON, J. A. and FIRESTONE, W. A. (1984) *School Context and School Change: Implications for Effective Planning*, New York: Teachers College Press.

CORCORAN, T. B. (1985) 'Effective secondary schools', in KYLE, R. M. J. (Ed.), *Reaching for Excellence: An Effective School Sourcebook*, Washington, DC: Government Printing Office.

CORCORAN, T. B. (1986a) *The Relationship between Educational Expenditures and National Recognition of Public Schools*, Paper prepared for the Education Law Center, Newark, NJ.

CORCORAN, T. B. (1986b) *An Assessment of Common Models of Teacher Participation in Public School Decision Making*, Paper prepared for the Work in America Institute.

CORCORAN, T. B. (1987) 'The district role in school effectiveness', in US House Committee on Education and Labor, *Increasing Educational Success: The Effective Schools Model*, 100th Congress, 1st session, 1987. Committee print no. 100–K.

CORCORAN, T. B. and HANSEN, B. J. (1983) *The Quest for Excellence: Making Public Schools more Effective*, Trenton, NJ: The New Jersey School Boards Association.

CORCORAN, T. B. and WILSON, B. L. (1986) *The Search for Successful Secondary Schools: The First Three Years of the Secondary School Recognition Program*, Washington, DC: US Department of Education.

CRANDALL, D. et al. (1982) *Helping Schools Get Better: Strategies for School Development in the 1980s— Final Report*, Andover, MA: The Network.

CRANDALL, D. P. and LOUCKS, S. F. (1983) *A Roadmap for School Improvement, Vol. X of People, Policies and Practices: Examining the Chain of School Improvement*, Andover, MA: The Network.

CUBAN, L. (1984) 'Transforming the frog into a prince: Effective schools research, policy, and practice at the district level', *Harvard Educational Review*, 54 (2), 129–151.

CUSICK, P. (1981) 'An Rx for our high schools', *Character*, 2 (7), 1–6.

CUSICK, P. (1983) *The Egalitarian Ideal and the American High School*, New York: Longman.

DAVIES, D. (1985) *Parent Involvement in the Public Schools in the 1980s: Proposals, Issues, Opportunities*, Philadelphia: Research for Better Schools.

DEAL, T. E. (1985) 'The symbolism of effective schools', *Elementary School Journal*, 85, 601–620.

DEAL, T. E. and KENNEDY, A. A. (1982) *Corporate Cultures: The Rites and Rituals of Corporate Life*, Reading, MA: Addison-Wesley Publishing Co.

DORNBUSCH, S. (1986) 'Helping your kid make the grade', *Stanford Magazine*, 14 (2), 47–51.

EDMONDS, R. (1979) 'Effective schools for the urban poor', *Educational Leadership*, 37 (1), 15–23.

EDUCATION COMMISSION OF THE STATES (1983) *Action for Excellence: A Comprehensive Plan to Improve our Nation's Schools*, Denver, CO: Author.

EDUCATION COMMISSION OF THE STATES (1985) *Reconnecting Youth: The Next Stage of Reform*, Denver, CO: Author.

EFFECTIVE SCHOOLS COUNCIL (1984) *Next Steps to Instructionally Effective Schooling*, Unpublished manuscript.

EPPS E. (1983) In foreword to CLARK, R. *Family Life and School Achievement*, Chicago: University of Chicago Press.

ETZIONI, A. (1982) 'Schools: Educational experience first', *American Education*, 18 (9), 6–10.

FARRAR, E., NEUFELD, B. and MILES, M. B. (1984) 'Effective schools programs in high schools: Social promotion or movement by merit', *Phi Delta Kappan*, 65 (10), 701–706.

FINN, C. E. (1984) 'Towards strategic independence: Nine commandments for enhancing school effectiveness', *Phi Delta Kappan*, 65 (8), 518–524.

FIRESTONE, W. A. (1983) *On Saving the Baby while Testing the Bathwater: Effective Schools Programs and Planned Change*, Philadelphia: Research for Better Schools.

FIRESTONE, W. A. (1985) *The Commitments of Teachers: Implications for Research, Policy and Administration*, Philadelphia: Research for Better Schools.

FIRESTONE, W. A. and HERRIOTT, R. E. (1982) 'Prescriptions for effective elementary schools don't fit secondary schools', *Educational Leadership*, 40 (3), 51–53.

FIRESTONE, W. A., HERRIOTT, R. E. and WILSON, B. L. (1984) *Explaining Differences between Elementary and Secondary Schools: Individual, Organizational and Institutional Perspectives*, Philadelphia: Research for Better Schools.

FIRESTONE, W. A. and WILSON, B. L. (1985) 'Using bureaucratic and cultural linkages to improve instruction: The principal's contribution', *Educational Administration Quarterly*, 21 (2), 7–30.

THE FORD FOUNDATION (1984) *City High Schools: A Recognition of Progress*, New York: The Ford Foundation.

FRUCHTER, N. (1982) 'School improvement programs: A brief review'. A discussion paper written for MEDARP, Office of Educational Evaluation, New York City Public Schools.

GALLUP, A. M. (1985) 'The 17th annual Gallup poll of the public's attitudes toward the public schools', *Phi Delta Kappan*, 67 (1), 35–47.

GOETZELS, J. W. (1978) 'The communities of education', *Teachers College Record*, 79 (4), 659–682.

GOLD, N. and MANN, D. W. (1984) *Expelled to a Friendlier Place: A Study of Effective Alternative Schools*, Ann Arbor, MI: University of Michigan Press.

GOOD, T. L. (1982) 'How teachers' expectations affect results', *American Education*, 18 (10), 25–32.

GOODLAD, J. I. (1983) *A Place Called School: Prospects for the Future*, New York: McGraw-Hill Book Co.

GOTTFREDSON, G. D., GOTTFREDSON, D. C. and COOK, M. S. (Eds), (1983) *The School Action Effectiveness Study: Second Interim Report (Report No. 342)*, Baltimore: The Johns Hopkins University, Center for Social Organization of Schools.

GRANT, G. (1982) 'The elements of a strong positive ethos', *NASSP Bulletin*, 66 (452), 84–90.

GREENFIELD, W. (Ed.) (1987) *Instructional Leadership: Concepts, Issues, and Controversies*, Boston: Allyn & Bacon.

GREISEMER, J. L. and BUTLER, C. (1983) *Education under Study: An Analysis of Recent Reports*, Chelmsford, MA: Northeast Regional Exchange.

GRIFFIN, G. A. (1982) *Staff Development*, paper presented at the National Institute of Education Conference on Research on Teaching: Implications for Practice, Airlie House, VA, February 25–27.

HALL, G. E. and GUZMAN, F. M. (1984) *Sources of Leadership for Change in High Schools*, (R & D Report No. 3185), Austin, TX: Research and Development Center for Teacher Education.

HALLINGER, P. and MURPHY, J. F. (1986) 'The social context of effective schools', *American Journal of Education*, 94 (3), 328–355.

HENDERSON, A. (1981) *Parent Participation — Student Achievement: The Evidence Grows*, Columbia, MD: National Committee for Citizens in Education.

HERRIOTT, R. E. and FIRESTONE, W. A. (1984) 'Two images of schools as organizations: A refinement and elaboration', *Educational Administration Quarterly*, 20 (4), 41–57.

HOBBS, N. (1978) 'Families, schools, and communities: An ecosystem for children', *Teachers College Record*, 79 (4), 756–787.

HODGKINSON, H. L. (1985) *All One System: Demographics of Education — Kindergarten through Graduate School*, Washington, DC: Institute for Educational Leadership.

HORD, S. M. (1984) *Facilitating Change in High Schools: Myths and Management*, (R & D Report No. 3187), Austin, TX: Research and Development Center for Teacher Education.

HOY, W. K. and FERGUSON, J. (1985) 'A theoretical framework and exploration of organizational effectiveness of schools', *Educational Administration Quarterly*, 21 (2), 117–134.

INSTITUTE FOR EDUCATIONAL LEADERSHIP (1985) *Dropouts: Everybody's Problem*, Washington, DC: Author.

JONES, B. L. and MALOY, R. W. (1986) 'Collaborations and ill-structured problems of school improvement', *Planning and Changing*, 17, (1), 3–8.

KIRST, M. W. (1983a) *The Turbulent Nature of the US Secondary School Curriculum*, (Policy Paper No. 83–C6), Palo Alto. CA: Stanford University, Institute for Research on Educational Finance and Governance.

KIRST, M. W. (1983b) 'Effective schools: Political environment and education policy', *Planning and Changing*, 14 (4), 234–244.

LIGHTFOOT, S. L. (1983) *The Good High School: Portraits of Character and Culture*, New York: Basic Books.

LINDBLOM, C. E. and COHEN, D. K. (1979) *Usable Knowledge: Social Science and Social Problem Solving*, New Haven: Yale University Press.

LINDSAY, P. (1982) 'The effect of high school size on student participation, satisfaction and attendance', *Educational Evaluation and Policy Analysis*, 4 (1), 57–66.

LINDSAY, P. (1984) 'High school size, participation in activities, and young adult social participation: Some enduring effects of schooling', *Educational Evaluation and Policy Analysis*, 6 (1), 73–84.

LIPSITZ, J. (1984) *Successful Schools for Young Adolescents*, New Brunswick, NJ: Transaction Books.

LITTLE, J. W. (1983) 'Norms of collegiality and experimentation: Workplace conditions in schools', *American Educational Research Journal*, 19 (3), 325–340.

LOMBANA, J. H. (1983), *Home-School Partnerships*, New York: Grune & Stratton.

LORTIE, D. (1975) *Schoolteacher*, Chicago: University of Chicago Press.

LOUIS, K. S., ROSENBLUM, S. and MOLITOR, J. (1981) *Strategies for Knowledge Use and School Improvement*, Cambridge, MA: Abt Associates.

MACKENZIE, D. (1983) 'Research for school improvement: An appraisal of some recent trends', *Educational Researcher*, 12 (4), 5–16.

MADAUS, G. F., AIRASIAN, P. W. and KELLAGHAN, T. (1980) *School Effectiveness: A Reassessment of the Evidence*, New York: McGraw-Hill.

MARCH, J. G. (1978) 'American Public School administration: A short analysis', *American Journal of Education*, 86, 217–250.

MCDILL, E. L., MEYERS, E. D. and RIGSBY, L. C. (1967) 'Institutional effects of the academic behavior of high school students', *Sociology of Education*, 40 (1), 181–189.

METROPOLITAN EDUCATIONAL DEVELOPMENT AND RESEARCH PROJECT DOCUMENTATION UNIT (1983) *The High School Improvement Project, 1982–83 (OEE Evaluation Report)*, New York: New York City Public Schools, Office of Educational Evaluation.

METZ, M. H. (1978) *Classrooms and Corridors: The Crisis of Authority in Desegregated Schools*, Berkeley, CA: University of California Press.

MEYER, J. W. and ROWAN, B. (1977) 'Institutionalized organizations: Formalized structure as myth and ceremony', *American Journal of Sociology*, 83 (2), 340–363.

MEYER, J. W. and ROWAN, B. (1978) 'The structure of educational organizations', in MEYER, M. and associates (Eds), *Environments and Organizations: Theoretical and Empirical Perspectives*, San Francisco: Jossey-Bass.

MICHIGAN ASSOCIATION OF SCHOOL BOARDS (1983) *School Boards Planning for Excellence: A Guidebook for the Study of Selected Excellence Reports*, Lansing, MI: Author.

MILES, M. (1981) 'Mapping the common properties of schools', in LEMING, R. and KANE, M. (Eds) *Improving Schools: Using what we Know*, Beverly Hills, CA: Sage.

MILES, M. B., FARRAR, E. and NEUFELD, B. (1983) *The Extent of Adoption of Effective Schools Programs, Vol. II of Review of Effective Schools Programs prepared for the National Commission on Excellence in Education*, Cambridge, MA: The Huron Institute.

MITROFF, I. I. (1983) 'Beyond experimenatation: New methods for a new age', in SEIDMAN, E. (Ed.) *Handbook of Social Intervention*, Beverly Hills, CA: Sage.

MORRIS, V., CROWSON, R. L., PORTER-GEHRIE, C. and HURWITZ, E. (1984) *Principals in Action: The Reality of Managing Schools*, Westerville, OH: Charles Merrill.

NATIONAL ACADEMY OF SCIENCES (1984) *High Schools and the Changing Workplace*, Washington, DC: National Academy Press.

NATIONAL COALITION OF ADVOCATES FOR STUDENTS (1984) *Barriers to Excellence: Our Children at Risk*, Boston, MA: Author.

NATIONAL COMMISSION ON EXCELLENCE IN EDUCATION (1983) *A Nation at Risk: The Imperative for Educational Reform*, Washington, DC: US Department of Education.

NATIONAL GOVERNORS ASSOCIATION (1986) *Time for Results: The Governors' 1991 Report on Education*, Washington, DC: Author.

NATIONAL SCIENCE BOARD COMMISSION (1983) *Educating Americans for the 21st Century*, Washington, DC: National Science Foundation.

NEWBERG, N. A. and GLATTHORN, A. G. (1983) *Instructional Leadership: Four Ethnographic Studies on Junior High School Principals*, Philadelphia: University of Pennsylvania.

NEWMAN, F., SMITH, M. S. and WEHLAGE, G. (1983) *The Effects of Comprehensive High Schools on Students: A Feasibility Study*, unpublished manuscript, Madison, WI: University of Wisconsin, Wisconsin Center for Education Research.

NEWMAN, F. M. and BEHAR, S. L. (1982) *The Study and Improvement of American High Schools: A Portrait of Work in Progress*, paper prepared for the Wingspread Conference on Improving the American High School, Racine, Wisconsin.

NORTHWEST REGIONAL EDUCATIONAL LABORATORY (1981) *Instructional Grouping: Ability Grouping. Research on School Effectiveness Project*, prepared for the Alaskan Department of Education, Portland: Author.

OAKES, J. (1985) *Keeping Track: How Schools Structure Inequality*, New Haven: Yale University Press.

OGBU, J. U. (1978) *Minority Education and Caste: The American System in Cross-cultural Perspective*, New York: Academic Press.

PASSOW, A. H. (1977) 'The future of the high school', *Teachers College Record*, 79 (1), 15–31.

PASSOW, A. H. (1984) 'Takling the reform reports of the 1980s', *Phi Delta Kappan*, 65 (10), 675–683.

PENNSYLVANIA DEPARTMENT OF EDUCATION (1986) *Being More Successful with More Students: Addressing the Problem of Students at Risk, K–12*, Harrisburg, PA: Author.

PETERS, T. J. and WATERMAN, R. H. (1982) *In Search of Excellence*, New York: Harper & Row.

PETTIGREW, A. M. (1979) 'On studies in organizational cultures', *Administrative Science Quarterly*, 24, 570–581.

PINCUS, J. and WILLIAMS, R. C. (1979) 'Planned change in urban school districts', *Phi Delta Kappan*, 60 (10), 729–732.

POWELL, A. G., FARRAR, E. and COHEN, D. K. (1985) *The Shopping Mall High School: Winners and Losers in the Educational Marketplace*, Boston: Houghton-Mifflin.

PRATZNER, F. C. (1984) 'Quality of school life: Foundation for improvement', *Educational Researcher*, 13 (3), 20–25.

PRESSEISEN, B. Z. (1985) *Unlearned Lessons: Current and Past Reforms for School Improvement*, Philadelphia: Falmer Press.

PURKEY, S. C. (1984) *School Improvement: An Analysis of an Urban School District Effective Schools Project*, unpublished doctoral dissertation, University of Wisconsin, Madison.

PURKEY, S. C. and DEGAN, S. (1985) 'Beyond effective schools to good schools: Some first steps', *R & D Perspectives*, Center for Educational Policy and Management, University of Oregon.

PURKEY, S. C. and SMITH, M. S. (1983) 'Effective schools: A review', *The Elementary School Journal*, 83 (4), 427–452.

PURKEY, S. C. and SMITH, M. S. (1985) 'School reform: The district policy implications of the effective schools literature', *The Elementary School Journal*, 85 (3), 353–388.

RANSON, S., HININGS, B. and GREENWOOD, R. (1980) 'The structuring of organizational structures', *Administrative Science Quarterly*, 25, 1–17.

RESEARCH FOR BETTER SCHOOLS (1982) *An Overview of Four Developing Statewide Improvement Programs*, Philadelphia: Author.

ROSENBLUM, S. and LOUIS, K. S. (1981) *Stability and Change: Innovation in an Educational Context*, New York: Plenum.

ROSENHOLTZ, S. J. (1985) 'Effective schools: Interpreting the evidence', *American Journal of Education*, 93 (3), 352–388.

ROSSMAN, G. B., CORBETT, H. D. and FIRESTONE, W. A. (1988) *Culture, Change, and Effectiveness*, Albany, NY: State University of New York Press.

ROWAN, B., BOSSERT, S. T. and DWYER, D. C. (1983) 'Research on effective schools: A cautionary note', *Educational Researcher*, 12 (4), 24–31.

RUTHERFORD, W. L. and HULING-AUSTIN, L. (1984) *Changes in High Schools: What is Happening — What is Wanted*, (R & D Report No. 3184), Austin, TX: Research and Development Center for Teacher Education.

RUTTER, M. (1983) 'School effects on pupil progress: Research findings and policy implications', in SHULMAN, L. S. and SYKES, G. (Eds), *Handbook of Teaching and Policy*, New York: Longmans.

RUTTER, M., MAUGHAN, B., MORTIMORE, P., OUSTON, J. and SMITH, A. (1979) *Fifteen Thousand Hours: Secondary Schools and Their Effects on Children*, Cambridge, MA: Harvard University Press.

SALGANIK, L. H. and KARWEIT, N. (1982) 'Voluntarism and governance in education', *Sociology of Education*, 55 (2/3), 152–161.

SCHLECHTY, P. C. (1985) 'District level policies and practices supporting effective school management and classroom instruction', in KYLE, R. M. J. (Ed,) *Reaching for Excellence: An Effective Schools Sourcebook*, Washington, DC: Government Printing Office.

SCHLECHTY, P. C. and VANCE, V. S. (1983) 'Recruitment, selection and retention: The shape of the teaching force', *Elementary School Journal*, 83, 469–487.

SCHUTZ, A. (1967) *The Phenomenology of the Social World*, Evanston, IL: Northwestern University Press.

SEDLAK, M. W., WHEELER, C. W., PULLIN, D. C. and CUSICK, P. A. (1986) *Selling Students Short: Classroom Bargains and Academic Reform in the American High School*, New York: Teachers College Press.

SEELEY, D. S. (1981) *Education Through Partnership: Mediating Structures and Education*, Cambridge, MA: Ballinger.

SHEIVE, L. T. and SCHOENHEIT, M. B. (Eds) (1987) *Leadership: Examining the Elusive*, Alexandria, VA: ASCD.

SIROTNIK, K. A. (1985) 'School effectiveness: A bandwagon in search of a tune', *Educational Administration Quarterly*, 21, 135–140.

SIZER, T. (1984) *Horace's Compromise: The Dilemma of the American High School*, Boston: Houghton-Mifflin.

SPADY, W. G. and MARX, G. (1984) *Excellence in our Schools: Making it Happen*, Washington, DC: American Association of School Administrators and the Far West Laboratory for Educational Research and Development.

STALLINGS, J. (1984) *Madeline Hunter's Model: A Study of Implementation and Student Effects*, paper presented at the annual meeting of the American Educational Research Association, New Orleans, LA.

STEDMAN, L. C. (1985) 'A new look at the effective schools movement', *Urban Education*, 20 (3), 295–326.

SYKES, G. (1983) 'Public policy and the problem of teacher quality: The need for screens and magnets', in SHULMAN, L. S. and SYKES, G. (Eds) *Handbook of Teaching and Policy*, New York: Longman.

TASK FORCE ON FEDERAL ELEMENTARY AND SECONDARY EDUCATION POLICY (1983) *Making the Grade: Report of the Task Force*, New York: The Twentieth Century Fund, Inc.

TIMPANE, M., ABRAMOWITZ, S., BOBROW, S. B. and PASCAL, A. (1976) *Youth Policy in Transition*, Santa Monica, CA: Rand Corp.

TOMLINSON, T. M. (1980) *Student Ability, Student Background and Student Achievement: Another Look at Life in Effective Schools*, paper presented at Educational Testing Service Conference on Effective Schools, New York.

TYACK, D. B., KIRST, M. W. and HANSOT, E. (1984) 'Educational reform: Retrospect and prospect', *Teachers College Record*, 81 (3), 253–269.

US DEPARTMENT OF EDUCATION (1986) *What Works: Research about Teaching and Learning*, Washington, DC: Author.

US DEPARTMENT OF EDUCATION (1987) *Schools that Work: Educating Disadvantaged Children*, Washington, DC: Author.

US GENERAL ACCOUNTING OFFICE (1982) *Labor Market Problems of Teenagers Result Largely from Doing Poorly in School*, Gaithersburg, MD: Author.

WEICK, K. E. (1976) 'Educational organizations as loosely coupled systems', *Administrative Science Quarterly*, 21, 1–19.

WEHLAGE, G. G. and RUTTER, R. A. (1986) 'Dropping out: How much do schools contribute to the problem?', *Teachers College Record*, 87 (3), 374–392.
WILSON, B. L. and FIRESTONE, W. A. (1987) 'The principal and instruction: Combining bureaucratic and cultural linkages', *Educational Leadership*, 45 (1), 18–23.
WILSON, B. L. and ROSSMAN, G. B. (1986) 'Collaborative links with the community: Lessons from exemplary secondary schools', *Phi Delta Kappan*, 67 (10), 708–711.

Appendix
List of Recognized Schools

School	Town	Year of recognition
Alabama		
Bush Middle School	Birmingham	1983–84
C. F. Vigor High School	Prichard	1983–84
East Highland Middle School	Sylacauga	1984–85
Enterprise High School	Enterprise	1983–84
Homewood High School	Homewood	1983–84
Homewood Middle School	Homewood	1983–84
Ira F. Simmons Junior High School	Birmingham	1984–85
Mountain Brook High School	Mountain Brook	1983–84
Riverchase Middle School	Birmingham	1984–85
Sylacauga High School	Sylacauga	1984–85
Alaska		
Gruening Junior High School	Eagle River	1984–85
Kenai Junior High School	Kenai	1983–84
Romig Junior High School	Anchorage	1984–85
Soldotna High School	Soldotna	1982–83
Soldotna Junior High School	Soldotna	1982–83
Valdez High School	Valdez	1982–83
Arizona		
Agua Fria Union High School	Avondale	1982–83
Amphitheater High School	Tucson	1983–84
Chandler High School	Chandler	1982–83
Flowing Wells Junior High School	Tucson	1984–85
Harvey L. Taylor Junior High School	Mesa	1984–85
John J. Rhodes Junior High School	Mesa	1982–83
Kino Junior High School	Mesa	1984–85
Mesa High School	Mesa	1983–84

Mountain View High School	Mesa	1984–85
Poston Junior High School	Mesa	1983–84
Santa Rita High School	Tucson	1984–85
Shea Middle School	Phoenix	1983–84
Utterback Junior High School	Tucson	1983–84
Westwood High School	Mesa	1983–84
Willis Junior High School	Chandler	1982–83

Arkansas

Annie Camp Middle School	Jonesboro	1982–83
Conway High School	Conway	1984–85
Douglas MacArthur Middle School	Jonesboro	1982–83
Jonesboro High School	Jonesboro	1982–83
Southside High School	Fort Smith	1982–83
White Hall High School	Pine Bluff	1983–84

California

Alvarado Middle School	Union City	1983–84
Artesia High School	Lakewood	1983–84
Borel Middle School	San Mateo	1983–84
Borrego Springs Middle School	Borrego Springs	1984–85
Castro Valley High School	Castro Valley	1984–85
Chula Vista High School	Chula Vista	1983–84
Corona del Mar High School	Newport Beach	1984–85
Davidson Middle School	San Rafael	1982–83
Fallbrook Union High School	Fallbrook	1983–84
George Leyva Junior High School	San Jose	1982–83
George W. Kastner Intermediate School	Fresno	1984–85
James Logan High School	Union City	1982–83
Lindero Canyon Middle School	Agoura Hills	1984–85
Lowell High School	San Francisco	1982–83
Marina High School	Huntington Beach	1984–85
Meadowbrook Middle School	Poway	1984–85
Mission Junior High School	Riverside	1983–84
Montebello Intermediate School	Montebello	1983–84
North Monterey County High School	Castroville	1984–85
Piedmont High School	Piedmont	1984–85
Pioneer High School	Whittier	1982–83
Rosemont Junior High School	La Crescenta	1984–85
Santana High School	Santee	1983–84
Terrace Hills Junior High School	Grand Terrace	1982–83
Twin Peaks Middle School	Poway	1983–84
Venado Middle School	Irvine	1982–83
Williams H. Crocker Middle School	Hillsborough	1982–83

Colorado

Alameda Junior High School	Lakewood	1984–85
Carmody Junior High School	Lakewood	1982–83
Cheyenne Mountain High School	Colorado Springs	1982–83
Holmes Junior High School	Colorado Springs	1983–84
Mrachek Middle School	Aurora	1982–83
Wheat Ridge High School	Wheatridge	1983–84

Connecticut

Amity Regional Junior High School	Bethany	1983–84
Amity Regional Junior High School	Orange	1982–83
Amity Regional High School	Woodbridge	1982–83
Avon Middle School	Avon	1984–85
Conard High School	West Hartford	1984–85
Conte Arts Magnet School	New Haven	1983–84
East Ridge Junior High School	Ridgefield	1983–84
Flood Intermediate School	Stratford	1983–84
Gideon Welles Junior High School	Glastonbury	1984–85
Illing Junior High School	Manchester	1982–83
Middlebrook School	Wilton	1982–83
Middlesex Middle School	Darien	1984–85
New Fairfield High School	New Fairfield	1984–85
William H. Hall High School	West Hartford	1984–85
Wooster Intermediate School	Stratford	1982–83

Delaware

Brandywine High School	Wilmington	1982–83
Caesar Rodney Senior High School	Camden	1983–84
Christiana High School	Newark	1983–84
Shue Middle School	Newark	1982–83
Skyline Middle School	Wilmington	1984–85

District of Columbia

Alice Deal Junior High School	Washington	1983–84
Brookland Junior High School	Washington	1982–83
Browne Junior High School	Washington	1984–85
Jefferson Junior High School	Washington	1982–83
Julius W. Hobson Senior Middle School	Washington	1983–84

Florida

American High School	Hialeah	1983–84
Brandon High School	Brandon	1982–83
Dixie Hollins High School	St Petersburg	1983–84
Fort Myers High School	Fort Myers	1984–85
Horace O'Bryant Middle School	Key West	1984–85

Jefferson Davis Junior High School	Jacksonville	1982–83
John Gorrie Junior High School	Jacksonville	1983–84
Largo Middle School	Largo	1983–84
Lyman High School	Longwood	1984–85
Mainland Senior High School	Daytona Beach	1983–84
North Miami Beach Senior High School	North Miami Beach	1984–85
Ribault High School	Jacksonville	1982–83
Sandalwood Junior-Senior High School	Jacksonville	1984–85
South Plantation High School	Plantation	1982–83
Southwood Junior High School	Miami	1984–85
St Petersburg High School	St Petersburg	1983–84
Terry Parker High School	Jacksonville	1983–84
Thomas Jefferson Junior High School	Merritt Island	1983–84

Georgia

Conyers Middle School	Conyers	1984–85
Dalton High School	Dalton	1983–84
Frederick Douglass High School	Atlanta	1983–84
Glynn Middle School	Brunswick	1983–84
Hardaway High School	Columbus	1984–85
Lakeside High School	Atlanta	1984–85
Luke Gareett Middle School	Austell	1983–84
North Fulton High School	Atlanta	1984–85
North Whitfield Middle School	Dalton	1984–85
Parkview High School	Lilburn	1984–85
Walton Comprehensive High School	Marietta	1983–84

Idaho

Jefferson Junior High School	Caldwell	1984–85
Mullan Junior/Senior High School	Mullan	1983–84
Silver Hills Junior High School	Osburn	1984–85

Illionis

Alan B. Shepard Junior High School	Deerfield	1984–85
Carl Sandburg High School	Orland Park	1984–85
Community High School North	Downers Grove	1983–84
Elm Place Middle School	Highland Park	1982–83
Glenbrook North High School	Northbrook	1983–84
Glenbrook South High School	Glenview	1983–84
Hoffman Estates High School	Hoffman Estates	1984–85
Homewood-Flossmoor High School	Flossmoor	1982–83
Leyden East Campus	Franklin Park	1984–85
Leyden West Campus	Northlake	1984–85
Maine Township High School	East Park Ridge	1984–85

Medinah Elementary School	Roselle	1983–84
Old Orchard Junior High School	Skokie	1983–84
Rich South High School	Richton Park	1983–84
Springman Junior High School	Glenview	1984–85
Thomas Junior High School	Arlington Heights	1983–84
Wilmot Junior High School	Deerfield	1983–84
York Community High School	Elmhurst	1982–83

Indiana

Ben Davis High School	Indianapolis	1983–84
Carmel High School	Carmel	1982–83
Carmel Junior High School	Carmel	1984–85
Chesterton High School	Chesterton	1984–85
Clay Junior High School	Carmel	1982–83
Eastwood Middle School	Indianapolis	1984–85
Fegely Middle School	Portage	1984–85
Jefferson High School	Lafayette	1984–85
John Marshall High School	Indianapolis	1984–85
Lawrence Central High School	Indianapolis	1984–85
Lawrence North High School	Indianapolis	1983–84
North Central High School	Indianapolis	1982–83
Valparaiso High School	Valparaiso	1982–83
Warren Central High School	Indianapolis	1982–83
Westchester Middle School	Chesterton	1982–83
Westland Middle School	Indianapolis	1983–84

Iowa

Ames Junior High School	Ames	1982–83
Ames Senior High School	Ames	1982–83
Franklin Junior High School	Cedar Rapids	1983–84
Indian Hills Junior High School	Des Moines	1982–83
Keokuk Middle School	Keokuk	1982–83
Kirn Junior High School	Council Bluffs	1983–84
Linn-Mar High School	Marion	1984–85
Linn-Mar Junior High School	Marion	1983–84
Metro Secondary School	Cedar Rapids	1984–85
Northwest Junior High School	Coralville	1984–85
Pleasant Valley Community High School	Pleasant Valley	1983–84
South East Junior High School	Iowa City	1982–83
Valley High School	West Des Moines	1983–84
Washington High School	Cedar Rapids	1983–84

Kansas

Horace Mann Alternative Middle School	Wichita	1983–84

Meadowbrook Junior High School	Shawnee Mission	1984–85
Oregon Trail Junior High School	Olathe	1983–84
Robinson Middle School	Topeka	1984–85
Roosevelt-Lincoln Junior High School	Salina	1983–84
Salina High School	Salina	1984–85
Santa Fe Trail Junior High School	Olathe	1984–85
Seaman High School	Topeka	1984–85
Shawnee Mission South High School	Shawnee Mission	1983–84
Shawnee Mission West High School	Sahwnee Mission	1983–84
Topeka West High School	Topeka	1983–84

Kentucky

Highlands High School	Fort Thomas	1984–85
Holmes High School	Covington	1984–85
Murray High School	Murray	1983–84
Oldham County Middle School	Buckner	1984–85
Thomas Jefferson Middle School	Louisville	1984–85

Louisiana

Baton Rouge High School	Baton Rouge	1982–83
Caddo Middle Magnet School	Shreveport	1984–85
Captain Shreve High School	Shreveport	1982–83
Grace King High School	Metairie	1982–83
Lafayette Elementary School	Lafayette	1983–84
Lakewood Junior High School	Luling	1982–83
Leesville High School	Leesville	1982–83
Lockport Junior High School	Lockport	1984–85
McKinley Middle Magnet School	Baton Rouge	1983–84
Parkway High School	Bossier City	1984–85
Raceland Junior High School	Raceland	1982–83
Ruston High School	Ruston	1983–84
Scott Middle School	Scott	1984–85
Youree Drive Middle School	Shreveport	1983–84

Maine

Auburn Middle School	Auburn	1983–84
Camden-Rockport High School	Camden	1984–85
Derring High School	Portland	1982–83
Gray-New Gloucester Junior High School	Gray	1984–85
Greely Junior High School	Cumberland Center	1984–85
Junior High School of the Kennebunks	Kennebunks	1983–84
Katahdin High School	Sherman Station	1982–83
Kennebunk High	Kennebunk	1982–83
King Middle School	Portland	1982–83

Mount Desert Island High School	Northeast Harbor	1983–84
Mt. Ararat School	Topsham	1982–83
Portland High School	Portland	1983–84

Maryland

Centennial High School	Ellicott City	1984–85
Glenelg High School	Glenelg	1984–85
Milton M. Somers Middle School	La Plata	1984–85
Parkland Junior High School	Rockville	1984–85
Redland Middle School	Rockville	1984–85
Thomas S. Wootton High School	Rockville	1984–85
Wilde Lake Middle School	Columbia	1984–85

Massachusetts

Acton-Boxborough Regional High School	Acton	1983–84
Charles Sumner Pierce Middle School	Milton	1984–85
Dartmouth High School	North Dartmouth	1984–85
Glenbrook Middle School	Longmeadow	1984–85
Nessacus Middle School	Dalton	1984–85
New Bedford High School	New Bedford	1983–84
Oliver Ames High School	North Easton	1984–85
Rockland Junior High School	Rockland	1983–84
W. S. Parker Middle School	Reading	1984–85
Wilson Junior High School	Natick	1984–85

Michigan

Abbott Middle School	Orchard Lake	1984–85
Ann Arbor Huron High School	Ann Arbor	1983–84
Berkshire Middle School	Birmingham	1984–85
Bloomfield Hills Andover High School	Bloomfield Hills	1983–84
Bloomfield Hills Lahser High School	Bloomfield Hills	1982–83
Bridgman High School	Bridgman	1983–84
Brooks Middle School	Detroit	1984–85
Cass Technical High School	Detroit	1983–84
Gaylord High School	Gaylord	1983–84
Gaylord Middle School	Gaylord	1984–85
Grosse Pointe South High School	Grosse Pointe	1982–83
Grosse Pointe North High School	Grosse Pointe Woods	1984–85
John Page Middle School	Madison Heights	1983–84
Northview High School	Grand Rapids	1983–84
Okemos High School	Okemos	1983–84
Roscommon High School	Roscommon	1982–83

Seaholm High School	Birmingham	1984–85
Slauson Intermediate	Ann Arbor	1983–84
Southfield Senior High School	Southfield	1983–84
Sturgis Public High School	Sturgis	1982–83
Traverse City Area Junior High School	Traverse City	1983–84
West Ottawa Middle School	Holland	1982–83

Minnesota

Cambridge Middle School	Cambridge	1984–85
Edina High School	Edina	1983–84
Hastings Junior High School	Hastings	1984–85
Hopkins High School	Minnetonka	1982–83
Hopkins North Junior High School	Minnetonka	1983–84
Hopkins West Junior High School	Minnetonka	1983–84
John Adams Junior High School	Rochester	1982–83
John F. Kennedy Senior High School	Bloomington	1984–85
Oak-Land Junior High School	Lake Elmo	1983–84
Richfield Senior High School	Richfield	1983–84
South St. Paul High School	South St. Paul	1984–85
Stillwater Senior High School	Stillwater	1984–85
Valley Middle School	Rosemount	1984–85

Mississippi

Brookhaven High School	Brookhaven	1983–84
Clinton High School	Clinton	1982–83
McComb High School	McComb	1982–83
Meridian Senior High School	Meridian	1984–85
Tupelo High School	Tupelo	1983–84

Missouri

Blue Springs High School	Blue Springs	1982–83
Brentwood Junior High School	Brentwood	1983–84
Clayton High School	Clayton	1984–85
David H. Hickman High School	Columbia	1984–85
Holman Middle School	St. Ann	1984–85
Horton Watkins High School	St. Louis	1982–83
Jennings Junior High School	Jennings	1984–85
Kickappoo High School	Springfield	1982–83
Ladue Junior High School	St. Louis	1983–84
Lewis Middle School	Excelsior Springs	1983–84
McCluer North High School	Florissant	1983–84
Parkway North High School	Creve Coeur	1984–85
Parkway West Senior High School	Ballwin	1982–83
Pattonville Heights Middle School	Maryland Heights	1983–84

Wydown Junior High School   Warson Woods   1984–85

Montana
Will James Junior High School   Billings   1984–85

Nebraska
Arbor Heights Junior High School   Omaha   1983–84
Beatrice Senior High School   Beatrice   1982–83
Bellevue East High School   Bellevue   1984–85
Harry A. Burke High School   Omaha   1983–84
Hastings Junior High School   Hastings   1984–85
Kearney Junior High School   Kearney   1982–83
Kearney Senior High School   Kearney   1983–84
Lincoln East Junior/Senior High School   Lincoln   1983–84
Lincoln High School   Lincoln   1983–84
McMillan Junior High School   Omaha   1984–85
Millard North High School   Omaha   1983–84
Millard South High School   Omaha   1982–83
Norfolk Public Senior High School   Norfolk   1984–85
Norris Middle School   Firth   1984–85
Tri County Senior High School   DeWitt   1984–85
Valley View Junior High School   Omaha   1984–85
Westbrook Junior High School   Omaha   1984–85
Westside High School   Omaha   1983–84

Nevada
Darrel C. Swope Middle School   Reno   1982–83
Edward C. Reed High School   Sparks   1984–85
Elko High School   Elko   1982–83
Helen C. Cannon Junior High School   Las Vegas   1983–84
Kenny C. Guinn Junior High School   Las Vegas   1982–83
Las Vegas High School   Las Vegas   1984–85
Reno High School   Reno   1983–84

New Hampshire
Exeter Area Junior High School   Exeter   1983–84
Hanover High School   Hanover   1982–83
Kearsarge Regional High School   North Sutton   1983–84
Lebanon Junior High School   Lebanon   1982–83
Londonderry Junior High School   Londonderry   1984–85

New Mexico
Albuquerque High School   Albuquerque   1982–83
Carrizozo High School   Carrizozo   1983–84
Eisenhower Middle School   Albuquerque   1984–85

Highland High School	Albuquerque	1984–85
Hoover Middle School	Albuquerque	1982–83
Jefferson Middle School	Albuquerque	1983–84
Las Cruces High School	Las Cruces	1984–85
Manzano High School	Albuquerque	1982–83
Taft Middle School	Albuquerque	1982–83
Van Buren Middle School	Albuquerque	1984–85
West Mesa High School	Albuquerque	1983–84

New York

Benjamin N. Cardozo High School	Bayside	1983–84
Blue Mountain Middle School	Peekskill	1982–83
Bronx High School of Science	Bronx	1982–83
Brooklyn Technical High School	Brooklyn	1982–83
Edgemont Junior/Senior High School	Scarsdale	1983–84
Garden City Junior High School	Garden City	1984–85
Greece Athena Senior High School	Rochester	1983–84
Jamaica High School	Jamaica	1984–85
Liverpool High School	Liverpool	1984–85
Louis Armstrong Middle School	East Elmhurst	1982–83
Miller Place High School	Miller Place	1983–84
New Rochelle High School	New Rochelle	1983–84
Niskayuna High School	Schenectady	1982–83
Northport High School	Northport	1983–84
Paul D. Screiber High School	Port Washington	1984–85
Pierre Van Cortland Middle School	Croton-on-Hudson	1984–85
Robert Cushman Murphy Junior High School	Stony Brook	1983–84
Scarsdale High School	Scarsdale	1982–83
School #59-Science Magnet	Buffalo	1984–85
Shaker High School	Latham	1984–85
Shoreham-Wading River Middle School	Shoreham	1982–83
Stuyvesant High School	New York	1982–83
The Fox Lane Middle School	Bedford	1983–84
Vestal Senior High School	Vestal	1984–85

North Carolina

Carmel Junior High School	Charlotte	1983–84
John A. Holmes High School	Edenton	1984–85
Lee County Senior High School	Sanford	1982–83
Manteo High School	Manteo	1983–84
McDowell High School	Marion	1984–85
Needham Broughton High	Raleigh	1983–84
North Davie Junior High School	Mocksville	1984–85

Successful Secondary Schools

William G. Enloe High School	Raleigh	1982–83

North Dakota

Benjamin Franklin Junior High School	Fargo	1982–83
Divide County High School	Crosby	1983–84
Hazen Public High School	Hazen	1982–83
Hughes Junior High School	Bismarck	1984–85

Ohio

Arbor Hills Junior High School	Sylvania	1983–84
Berea High School	Berea	1984–85
Brunswick Middle School	Brunswick	1984–85
Centerville High School	Centerville	1983–84
Columbus Alternative High School	Columbus	1984–85
East Muskingum Middle School	New Concord	1983–84
Eastview Middle School	Bath	1982–83
Hastings Middle School	Upper Arlington	1984–85
Herman K. Ankeney Junior High School	Beavercreek	1983–84
Hudson High School	Hudson	1983–84
Hudson Junior High School	Hudson	1983–84
Indian Hill High School	Cincinnati	1983–84
Jennings Middle School	Akron	1984–85
Jones Middle School	Columbus	1983–84
Madeira High School	Cincinnati	1984–85
Mariemont High School	Cincinnati	1984–85
Ottawa Middle School	Cincinnati	1984–85
Perkins Junior High School	Akron	1982–83
Perry Middle School	Worthington	1984–85
Princeton Junior High School	Cincinnati	1982–83
Princeton High School	Cincinnati	1983–84
School for Creative & Performing Arts	Cincinnati	1984–85
Shaker Heights High School	Shaker Heights	1982–83
Theodore Roosevelt High School	Kent	1984–85
Upper Arlington High School	Upper Arlington	1984–85
Walnut Hills High School	Cincinnati	1984–85
William Henry Harrison Junior High School	Harrison	1983–84
Woodbury Junior High School	Shaker Heights	1983–84
Wyoming High School	Wyoming	1982–83

Oklahoma

Ardmore High School	Ardmore	1982–83
Booker T. Washington High School	Tulsa	1982–83
Byng High School	Ada	1983–84
Gans Junior-Senior High School	Muldrow	1983–84

John Marshall High School	Oklahoma City	1982–83
Millwood High School	Oklahoma City	1983–84
Northeast High School	Oklahoma City	1983–84
Seiling High School	Seiling	1984–85

Oregon

Beaumont Middle School	Portland	1984–85
Beaverton High School	Beaverton	1984–85
Calapooia Middle School	Albany	1982–83
Cedar Park Intermediate School	Beaverton	1982–83
Clackamas High School	Milwaukie	1983–84
Crater High School	Central Point	1982–83
Floyd Light Middle Sehool	Portland	1983–84
Lake Oswego High School	Lake Oswego	1982–83
Lake Oswego Junior High School	Lake Oswego	1984–85
McLoughlin Junior High School	Milwaukie	1983–84
Monroe Middle School	Eugene	1983–84
Nyssa High School	Nyssa	1984–85
Oaklea Middle School	Junction City	1982–83
Obsidian Junior High School	Redmond	1984–85
Oregon City High School	Oregon City	1984–85
Pleasant Hill High School	Pleasant Hill	1983–84
Renne Intermediate School	Newburg	1982–83
Rex Putman High School	Milwaukie	1984–85
South Eugene High School	Eugene	1982–83
Sunset High School	Beaverton	1982–83
West Linn High School	West Linn	1983–84

Pennsylvania

Bala Cynwyd Middle School	Bala Cynwyd	1983–84
Conestoga Senior High School	Berwyn	1983–84
Delaware Valley Middle School	Milford	1984–85
Downingtown Area Middle School	Downingtown	1984–85
E. T. Richardson Middle School	Springfield	1984–85
East Junior High School	Waynesboro	1984–85
General Wayne Middle School	Malvern	1984–85
Harriton High School	Rosemont	1983–84
Louis E. Dieruff High School	Allentown	1984–85
Mount Lebanon High School	Pittsburgh	1983–84
Pennsbury High School	Fairless Hills	1984–85
Radnor High School	Radnor	1983–84
Sandy Run Middle School	Dresher	1983–84
Strath Haven High School	Wallingford	1984–85
Upper St. Clair High School	Pittsburgh	1983–84
Welsh Valley Middle School	Narberth	1983–84

| Wissahickon Middle School | Ambler | 1984–85 |

Rhode Island

East Greenwich High School	East Greenwich	1983–84
Hugh Bain Junior High School	Cranston	1982–83
Lincoln High School	Lincoln	1982–83
South Kingston Junior High School	Peace Dale	1984–85
Western Hills Junior High School	Cranston	1983–84

South Carolina

Camden High School	Camden	1982–83
Conway High School	Conway	1984–85
Dent Middle School	Columbia	1984–85
E. L. Wright Middle School	Columbia	1983–84
Hillcrest Middle School	Simpsonville	1984–85
Irmo High School	Columbia	1982–83
League Middle School	Greenville	1982–83
Maudlin High School	Maudlin	1984–85
Richland Northeast High School	Columbia	1984–85
Rock Hill High School	Rock Hill	1983–84
Spartanburg Senior High School	Spartanburg	1982–83
Spring Valley High School	Columbia	1982–83

Tennessee

Cleveland High School	Cleveland	1982–83
Collierville Middle School	Collierville	1982–83
Hillsboro High School	Nashville	1984–85
Hixson High School	Hixson	1984–85
Snowden School	Memphis	1982–83

Texas

Bellaire Senior High School	Bellaire	1983–84
Desert View Middle School	El Paso	1983–84
Dr. Karl Bleyl Junior High School	Houston	1983–84
Highland Park High School	Dallas	1984–85
John Foster Dulles High School	Sugar Land	1984–85
Kingwood High School	Kingwood	1984–85
Plano Senior High School	Plano	1984–85
Richardson High School	Richardson	1983–84
Rockdale High School	Rockdale	1984–85
Stephen F. Austin High School	Austin	1982–83
Stratford High School	Houston	1983–84
Travis Middle School	Port Lavaca	1983–84
Winston Churchill High School	San Antonio	1982–83

Utah

Bountiful High School	Bountiful	1982–83
Brighton High School	Salt Lake City	1982–83
Butler Middle School	Salt Lake City	1982–83
Eastmont Middle School	Sandy	1983–84
Highland High School	Salt Lake City	1982–83
Logan Junior High School	Logan	1983–84
Logan Senior High School	Logan	1982–83
Mound Fort Middle School	Ogden	1984–85
Olympus High School	Salt Lake City	1984–85
South High School	Salt Lake City	1983–84
Timpview High School	Provo	1983–84
Wasatch Middle School	Heber City	1982–83

Vermont

Hazen Union School	Hardwick	1983–84
South Burlington High School	South Burlington	1984–85

Virginia

Breckinridge Junior High School	Roanoke	1983–84
Brookland Middle School	Richmond	1984–85
Cave Spring High School	Roanoke	1982–83
Dunbar-Erwin Middle School	Newport News	1983–84
E. C. Glass High School	Lynchburg	1982–83
George Mason Junior-Senior High School	Falls Church	1982–83
Hampton High School	Hampton	1984–85
Hermitage High School	Richmond	1983–84
Hidden Valley Junior High School	Roanoke	1983–84
Huntington Middle School	Newport News	1984–85
Menchville High School	Newport News	1983–84
Prospect Heights Middle School	Orange	1982–83
T. C. Williams High School	Alexandria	1982–83
Washington-Lee High School	Arlington	1984–85

Washington

Blaine High School	Blaine	1984–85
Battle Ground High School	Battle Ground	1983–84
Cashmere Middle School	Cashmere	1982–83
Charles A. Lindbergh High School	Renton	1983–84
Colville High School	Colville	1983–84
Curtis High School	Tacoma	1982–83
Curtis Junior High School	Tacoma	1983–84
Hanford Secondary School	Richland	1982–83
Jefferson Middle School	Olympia	1983–84
John H. McKnight Middle School	Renton	1984–85

Successful Secondary Schools

Kentridge High School	Kent	1984–85
Lake Washington High School	Kirkland	1984–85
Mead Junior High School	Mead	1982–83
Meridian Junior High School	Kent	1984–85
Mount Rainier High School	Des Moines	1984–85
Omak Middle School	Omak	1983–84
Pasco Senior High School	Pasco	1982–83
Pleasant Valley Intermediate School	Vancouver	1984–85
Redmond High School	Redmond	1983–84
Ringdall Middle School	Bellevue	1984–85
Sacajawea Junior High School	Spokane	1982–83
Shorewood High School	Seattle	1982–83
Stevens Middle School	Port Angeles	1984–85
West Valley Junior High School	Yakima	1984–85
Wilbur High School	Wilbur	1983–84

West Virginia

Bridge Street Junior High School	Wheeling	1982–83
George Washington High School	Charleston	1983–84
St. Mary's High School	St. Mary's	1984–85
Tridelphia Junior High School	Wheeling	1982–83
Wheeling Junior High School	Wheeling	1982–83
Wheeling Park High School	Wheeling	1983–84

Wisconsin

Brown Deer High School	Brown Deer	1983–84
Columbus High School	Columbus	1984–85
John Burroughs Middle School	Milwaukee	1983–84
Lafollette High School	Madison	1983–84
Memorial High School	Eau Claire	1982–83
Merrill Senior High School	Merrill	1984–85
Morse Middle School	Milwaukee	1984–85
Neenah High School	Neenah	1984–85
Owen-Withee High School	Owen	1983–84
Phoenix Middle School	Delavan	1984–85
Rufus King High School	Milwaukee	1982–83
Stevens Point Area Senior High School	Stevens Point	1984–85
Stoughton Middle School	Stoughton	1984–85
Webster Transitional School	Cedarburg	1982–83
West Senior High School	Madison	1984–85
Whitman Middle School	Wauwatosa	1984–85

Wyoming

Douglas Middle School	Douglas	1982–83
Kelly Walsh High School	Casper	1983–84

Pine Bluffs High School	Pine Bluffs	1982–83

Department of Defence Overseas Dependent Schools

Bahrain Elementary School/High School	Bahrain	1984–85
Frankfurt American High School	Frankfurt	1983–84
Heidelberg High School	Heidelberg	1983–84
Heidelberg Middle School	Heidelberg	1984–85
Rhein Main Junior High School	Rhein Main	1983–84
Seoul American High School	Seoul	1984–85

Author Index

Abramowitz, S. 22, 23
Adler, M. J. 23
Airasian, P. W. 27
Alexander, K. L. 8
Anderson, C. S. 21, 82
Anderson, G. L. 10
Arizona Department of Education 2
Astuto, T. A. 2, 27, 121

Bacharach, S. B. 85
Barker, R. G. 8
Barth, R. S. 109
Bassin, M. 121
Bauer, S. C. 85
Beady, W. B. 15, 70, 99
Becher, R. M. 117
Behar, S. L. 9
Berman, P. W. 5, 16, 17, 120, 121, 122
Bidwell, C. E. 69
Bird, T. 85
Bobrow, S. B. 22, 23
Bossert, S. T. 4
Boyer, E. 10, 23, 148, 149, 152, 154,
    156, 160
Brookover, W. B. 15, 27, 70, 99, 100
Butler, C. 24

California Assembly Office of Research
    9, 10, 12, 14, 16, 18, 20
Carnegie Forum on Education and the
    Economy 84, 148, 149, 151, 152,
    154, 156, 160
Centre for Public Interest Polling 85
Chapman, D. M. 85
Chubb, J. E. 7
Clark, D. L. 2, 119, 121
Cohen, D. K. 5, 6, 10, 23

Cohen, M. 2, 6, 21, 27
Coleman, J. 9, 10, 15, 16, 19, 20, 27
College Board, The 23
Comer, J. P. 109
Committee for Economic Development
    132, 148, 149, 151, 154, 156, 160
Cook, M. 8, 132
Corbett, H. D. 21, 71, 74, 120
Corcoran, T. B. 1, 12, 15, 16, 46, 85,
    102, 119
Crandall, D. P. 16, 121
Crowson, R. L. 71, 110, 118
Cuban, L. 4, 12, 16, 97
Cusick, P. A. 6, 10, 23, 71, 105, 123

Davies, D. 117
Dawson, J. A. 120
Deal, T. E. 21, 70, 71, 106, 117
Department of Education, US 16, 133
Dornbusch, S. 110
Dwyer, D. C. 4

Edmonds, R. 2, 12, 99
Education Commission of the States 23,
    131
Effective Schools Council 27
Epps, E. 110
Etzioni, A. 19, 27

Farrar, E. 6, 10, 23, 123, 124
Ferguson, J. 28
Finn, C. E. 5, 17
Firestone W. A. 6, 7, 13, 21, 69, 71, 74,
    86, 120, 151
Flood, P. 15, 70, 99
Ford Foundation, The 28, 29
Fruchter, N. 124

Author Index

Gallup, A. M. 117
General Accounting Office, US 8
Glatthorn, A. G. 71
Goetzels, J. W. 111
Gold, N. 132
Good, T. L. 100
Goodlad, J. I. 8, 10, 23, 148, 149, 152, 154, 156, 158, 160
Gottfredson, D. 132
Gottfredson, G. 132
Grant, G. 27
Greenfield, W. 69
Greenwood, R. 70
Greisemer, J. L. 24
Griffin, G. A. 14
Gross, T. 121
Gump, P. 8
Guzman, F. M. 13, 123

Hall, G. E. 13, 123
Hallinger, P. 5
Hansen, B. J. 15, 102, 119
Hansot, E. 123
Henderson, A. 15, 109
Herriott, R. E. 6, 7, 13
Hinings, B. 70
Hobbs, N. 110
Hoffer, T. 9, 10
Hord, S. M. 123
Hodgkinson, H. L. 85, 131
Hoy, W. K. 28
Huling-Austin, L. 123
Hurwitz, E. 71, 110, 118

Institute for Educational Leadership 131–2

Jones, B. L. 111
Jordan, P. 121

Karweit, N. 15
Kellaghan, T. 27
Kennedy, A. A. 21, 70, 71
Kilgore, S. 9, 10
Kirst, M. W. 5, 14, 123

Lightfoot, S. L. 9–13, 17–20, 22, 71, 78
Lindblom, C. E. 5
Lindsay, P. 8, 16
Lipsitz, J. 9–13, 17–20, 28, 102, 148, 149, 152, 154, 156, 158
Little, J. W. 14, 17, 73, 85
Lombana, J. H. 109
Lortie, D. 91

Lotto, L. S. 2, 27, 121
Loucks, S. F. 16, 121
Louis, K. S. 17, 121, 122

McDill, E. L. 10
MacKenzie, S. 2, 6, 18,
McLaughlin, M. W. 122
Madaus, G. F. 27
Maloy, R. W. 111
Mann, D. W. 132
March, J. G. 69
Marx, G. 24
Maughan, B. 4, 10, 14–21, 100, 102
Metropolitan Educational Development and Research Project Documentation Unit 124
Metz, M. H. 77
Meyer, J. W. 70, 117
Meyers, E. D. 10
Michigan Association of School Boards 24
Miles, M. 70, 121, 123, 124
Mitroff, I. I. 111
Moe, T. W. 7
Molitor, J. 17, 121
Morris, V. 71, 110, 118
Mortimore, P. 4, 14–21, 100, 102
Murphy, J. F. 5

National Academy of Sciences 23
National Coalition of Advocates for Students 132
National Commission on Excellence in Education 23, 84
National Governors Association 84, 132, 148–9, 151, 154, 156, 160
National Science Board Commission 23
Neufeld, B. 123, 124
Newberg, N. A. 71
Newman, F. 9, 27–8
Northwest Regional Educational Laboratory 8

Oakes, J. 8
Ogbu, J. U. 100
Ouston, J. 4, 10, 14–21, 100, 102

Pascal, A. 22, 23
Passow, A. H. 22, 24
Peters, T. J. 21, 71, 106, 122
Pettigrew, A. M. 70
Pincus, J. 121
Porter-Gehrie, C. 71, 110, 118
Powell, A. G. 6, 10, 23
Pratzner, F. C. 22

Presseisen, B. Z. viii, 85
Pullin, D. C. 10, 23
Purkey, S. C. 2–4, 11, 16, 19, 21, 43, 57, 66, 85, 99, 116, 124

Ranson, S. 70
Research for Better Schools 124
Rigsby, L. C. 10
Rosenblum, S. 17, 121, 122
Rosenholtz, S. J. 85, 86, 151
Rossman, G. B, 21, 71, 74, 109
Rowan, B. 4, 70, 117
Rutherford, W. L. 123
Rutter, M. 4, 6, 10, 14–21, 27, 99, 100, 102
Rutter, R. A. 132

Salganik, L. H. 15
Sawson, J. A. 120
Schlechty, P. C. 12, 85, 148
Schoenheit, M. B. 69
Schutz, A. 111
Schweitzer, J. 15, 70, 99
Sedlak, M. W. 10, 23
Seeley, D. S. 109
Shedd, J. B. 85
Sheive, L. T. 69
Sirotnik, K. A. 4, 5

Sizer, T. 6, 10, 23, 105, 148–9, 154, 156, 158, 160
Smith, A. 4, 10, 14–21, 100, 102
Smith, M. S. 2–4, 9, 11, 16, 19, 21, 27–8, 43, 57, 66, 85, 99, 116
Spady, W. G. 24
Stallings, J. 14
Stedman, L. C. 4
Sykes, G. 85

Task Force on Federal Elementary and Secondary Education Policy 23
Timpane, M. 22, 23
Tomlinson, T. M. 2
Tyack, D. B. 123

US Department of Education 16, 133
US General Accounting Office 8

Vance, V. S. 85

Waterman, R. H. 21, 71, 106, 122
Wehlage, G. 9, 27–8, 132
Weick, K. E. 69
Wheeler, C. W. 10, 23
Williams, R. C. 121
Wilson, B. L. 7, 13, 69, 74, 109
Wisenbaker, J. 15, 70, 99

Subject Index